The Professional Stranger

An Informal Introduction to Ethnography

This is a volume in

STUDIES IN ANTHROPOLOGY

Under the consulting editorship of
E. A. Hammel, University of California, Berkeley

The complete listing of books in this series is available from the Publisher
upon request.

The Professional Stranger

An Informal Introduction to Ethnography

Michael H. Agar

Department of Anthropology
University of Houston
Houston, Texas

ACADEMIC PRESS

A Subsidiary of Harcourt Brace Jovanovich, Publishers

New York   London   Toronto   Sydney   San Francisco

ACADEMIC PRESS, INC.
111 Fifth Avenue, New York, New York 10003

United Kingdom Edition published by
ACADEMIC PRESS, INC. (LONDON) LTD.
24/28 Oval Road, London NW1 7DX

Library of Congress Cataloging in Publication Data

Agar, Michael.
    The professional stranger.

    (Studies in anthropology)
    Includes index.
    Bibliography: p.
    1. Ethnology––Field work. 2. Ethnology––Methodol–
ogy. I. Title.
GN346.A42   301'.01'8   79–8870
ISBN 0–12–043850–X

PRINTED IN THE UNITED STATES OF AMERICA

82 83   9 8 7 6 5 4 3 2

Contents

4

Ethnography 63

5

Beginning Fieldwork 83

6

Narrowing the Focus 119

7

Informal to Formal: Some Examples 137

8

The Ethnographic Research Proposal 175

9

Ethnography in Context   189

References   205

Index   215

Preface

Since 1968, when I took my first job as a professional ethnographer, I have often been in situations in which administrators, clinicians, and other social scientists have raised questions about the nature of ethnographic research. Such questions arise with increasing frequency as time goes on, both within other academic disciplines and among agency persons who see in ethnography a possible way to achieve a better understanding of themselves and the groups they serve. Yet at the same time there is a shortage of attempts to articulate clearly what it is that constitutes ethnographic research.

I hope this book serves as something someone—anthropologist or especially nonanthropologist—can pick up and read for a sense of what an ethnographic view of research is all about. I also hope it sets up some issues clearly enough so that other ethnographers can agree or argue. My feeling is that underneath the growth and decline of various anthropological issues lies a continuing way of seeing and understanding the human situation, and that this way of seeing is what we have to offer the world. But without methodological development most of us are doomed to a future as mediocre poets or amateur experimentalists.

During the editing process, questions came up about my use of "he" and "she" in the text. Traditionally, the third person singular indefinite pronoun in English is represented by "he." Many women now find this objectionable. A social psychologist friend of mine even pointed out that comprehension among female readers declines with the exclusive use of "he." On the other hand, I don't care for "he and/or she" or "s/he," though sometimes the editors convinced me that such usage was appropriate. My solution, as you will see in the text, was to use the masculine form sometimes, and the feminine other times. I can only hope that the reader finds this strategy more appropriate than awkward.

Acknowledgments

I have benefited from the comments of several people. Richard Stephens, whose work is discussed at length in the book, has been a close friend for many years. His careful reading and comments were invaluable. Theresa Mason and Andrea Meditch, graduate students in anthropology at the University of Texas, both read over the text carefully and made helpful suggestions that also guided the revisions. Reviewers provided by Academic Press offered helpful comments in the earlier and second versions. Kathy Williams at the University of Houston performed a remarkable deadline-meeting sprint on the typewriter to finish the draft of the book on time. Bambi Schiefflin suggested the cover, and Paul Spragueus did a remarkable job on the index.

My association as reviewer and consultant with the National Institute on Drug Abuse has been a source of much of the material in the book. The late Eleanor Carroll, advocate for ethnography in the drug field, made possible my association with the agency. I owe to NIDA a chain of experiences that have been at the same time stimulating and frustrating, exhilarating and depressing. The "real world" that anthropologists talk of invading is a complicated niche. Comparing it to my current academic slot is a little like comparing an animal in its zoo cage to another one surviving on the savannah. Anthropology as a discipline has, I think, much to learn about the difference.

I would like to note the support of a Research Career Development Award (KO2DA00055) from NIDA which gave me the time to complete this book.

I would also like to acknowledge the influence of two of my teachers. I have had many good ones; some only became teachers after I left school. But two in particular were key figures in my anthropological education. In chronological order, they are Alan Beals and Paul Kay. Alan is discussed much in the book. It was he who took the time to respond to the interest of a naive undergraduate who wanted to accompany him to India.

Paul was my graduate and dissertation adviser. His openness allowed me to range across several topics that were then "deviant" in anthropology, including developing a dissertation out of my experience at Lexington before the normal period of fieldwork in graduate training. With some recent letters to the *Anthropology Newsletter*, Paul has acquired a reputation as being "anti-applied." The irony is that many of his students currently do applied work with his encouragement and continued support. He doesn't much care what you work on; he does care greatly that you do it well, and gives generously of his time to help.

As a way of publicly saying "thanks," I would like to dedicate the book to my two main teachers. I hope they see in it some positive results of the energy they invested in showing me the ways of ethnography.

1

The Concept of Fieldwork

Somewhere underneath the prose of social science lies some human contact. Before the clatter of the typewriter begins, some person (a social science researcher) collaborates with another person (variously called *subject, respondent,* or *informant*) to create a social relationship within which an exchange of information occurs. This book is about those relationships. More specifically, it is about those relationships—fortuitously encountered or consciously constructed—that constitute the core of ethnographic fieldwork.

Ethnography is an ambiguous term, representing both a process and a product. As a product, an ethnography is usually a book. The book almost always focuses on some social group, though it may be guided by any number of theories and methods. While the book usually has some central point, the discussion of the social group often covers a lot of territory. There will be a dash of history, something about the various environments—physical, biological, and social—and some detail on the things the group does and the beliefs they hold.

Ethnographies differ, of course, and they are not just books. In fact, a teacher of mine once described a vision of the future where ethnographies would not be distributed. With the growth of narrative and visual documentation, he reasoned, and the increase in specimens of things like material culture and plant samples, there would simply be too much information to transmit. Instead, the material would be gathered in one place, and people interested in the ethnography of such-and-such a group would travel there to study it.

At any rate, my concern here is with ethnography as a process. How is it that an ethnographer attempts a comprehensive understanding of

1

some human group? The name for "doing ethnography" is "fieldwork." There is a tradition in cultural anthropology that one cannot be told how to do fieldwork.[1] A bit of graduate student folklore that I learned at Berkeley goes like this: A graduate student, at the end of her first year, was given a few hundred dollars by the department and told to go and study an Indian group during the summer. Not only had no one told her how to do ethnography; neither had anyone bothered to describe the location of the tribe.

With trembling heart and sweaty palms, she approached the door of Kroeber[2] himself for some advice. After several passes by the open door, she entered and nervously cleared her throat. Kroeber was typing (naturally) and did not look up for a minute or so. When he did, the student explained her dilemma and asked for advice. "Well," said Kroeber, returning to his typing, "I suggest you buy a notebook and a pencil."

It does not matter whether the story is true or false. As folklore always does, it tells us something important about the group that generated it. Fieldwork was not something you could train people for. You just had to do it, and then exchange knowing glances with others who had been initiated. There was a mystique about fieldwork, the emotional aura of a rite of passage into professional adulthood.

In some ways I am sympathetic to this view, and I will write about it more later. I have met few ethnographers who were not personally affected in some profound way by their fieldwork. Besides, there are some areas in which experience is the best teacher—not just classroom assignments, but the whole experience.[3] But, it is madness to conclude from this that field training must be limited to a few concepts and a couple of unstructured ways of recording information.

I do not think many ethnographers would make this argument as a matter

---

[1] There are numerous references to a lack of fieldwork training in the literature. For example, see the opening comments in Berreman (1962) and Wax (1971). As another example, Adams and Preiss (1960), in their introduction to a collection of methods articles, note that roughly two-thirds of the articles are by sociologists. They then speculate on some reasons why anthropologists are not more methodologically reflective. Freilich (1970a), in his introduction to a collection of personal accounts by anthropologists, discusses the development of a "culture of fieldwork" to account for the lack of a methodological tradition in anthropology. This neglect is made more confusing when you consider that field methods discussions are scattered throughout the literature. There are some classic early positions, such as Boas (1920), Radin (1933), Mead (1933), and Malinowski (1961, originally published in the 1920s). In their histories of fieldwork, Wax (1971) and Pelto and Pelto (1973) show how the tradition of ethnography goes back even further. I can only agree with Gutkind and Sankoff (1967), who, in the introduction to their annotated bibliography on field methods, note the abundance of fieldwork literature and the lack of attempts to systematically discuss it.

[2] A. L. Kroeber is one of the founding fathers of American anthropology.

[3] There is a good manual by Crane and Angrosino (1974) that leads students step-by-step through some field projects to train them in important ethnographic tasks.

of intent, but the argument does represent the consequence of the tradition, or lack of a tradition, of fieldwork training. Though I have not done the study, I bet if you plotted a graph of the proportion of anthropology departments offering a "field methods" course over time, there would in fact be an upward turn in the curve, although quite recently.

Even where such courses are offered, they sometimes deal mainly with research designs of the classic hypothesis-testing sort—statistics, or perhaps survey research or experimental design. There is nothing wrong with learning these things; in fact, they are essential. But they are not the same as ethnography. Good ethnographers draw on such knowledge, but they draw on it as one or two items within a process that includes numerous other activities as well. Many of these "other activities" are part of the mystique of fieldwork. In this book, I hope to contribute to the demystification of at least some of them.

Reasons for Becoming an Ethnographer

People may be attracted to cultural anthropology for a variety of reasons. They might be intellectually stimulated by ecological systems, or they might like the esthetic of structural analysis, or they might enjoy the relevance of alternative technologies. Then again, they might be personally curious about the variety of lifeways practiced on the planet in general. But these same people may or may not like doing ethnography. In fact, for some, the process of acquiring the information that is the bedrock of anthropological theory is downright painful.

So what kind of people enjoy doing ethnography? Probably many different kinds. Around a dinner table not too long ago I sat with a group of ethnographers who were hosted by a clinical psychologist. He asked that question, and since it was his treat, we explored childhood and adolescence as possible sources of our initial interest. From our sample of four, we came up with two theories of origin.

The first theory held that ethnographers grew up in communities where they felt no personal involvement. While they, of necessity, participated in the flow of social life, they felt detached from activities to which others attached high emotional significance. This corresponds to another item of professional folklore; namely, that anthropologists are people who are alienated from their own culture. As a result, the story goes, they do not share any attachments that prevent an appreciation of other cultures. In fact, they may seek the experience of other cultures as a quest for an identity that makes sense to them. It may not be an accident that during a period of recent American history that saw an increasing alienation among students there were also dramatic increases in enrollments in anthropology courses. In the late 1970s, this trend is reversing, to the chagrin of university faculty, for whom enroll-ments are the currency in the academic Kula ring.[4]

The second theory held that ethnographers are products of multicultural environments. They grow up in, and become accustomed to, cultural diver-sity. Rather than feeling threatened by the different lifeways they encoun-tered, they became fascinated by the differences. As an ethnographer, they find a professional role to justify their move from one way of life to another. Once again, another piece of professional folklore becomes relevant. I have at times heard a belief that anthropologists' children copy their parent's profes-sion more often than is normal in the U.S. population. I have never seen any data on this, but I do know three anthropologists, all excellent ethnographers and all siblings, who are the children of an anthropologist who also relishes fieldwork. When you talk with them, they do say that the experience of "growing up in the field" addicted them to cultural diversity. Short of being independently wealthy, what better role for a "culture-hopper" than a profes-sional ethnographer?

So, some people like ethnography because it justifies their detachment from what others consider important. Others like ethnography because it justifies an interest in exploring different lifeways. I am sure there are many other possible explanations as well, and, like all explanations, the two that fell out of the dinner party were constructed for a host and an occasion. But it raises a question that, to my knowledge, has not been treated much in the literature on ethnography.[5] You, dear reader, might wonder about yourself, as a person who is interested in doing ethnography. Are we all sociopaths and gadflys? If not, then what, in fact, are we doing here?

Mystique as a Communication Problem

If you read through discussions of field methods, you will find a variety of reasons offered for the mystique of fieldwork—the "culture" of fieldwork,

---

[4] The Kula ring is described by Malinowski (1961). Briefly, it is a series of trading relationships among Pacific Islanders where certain goods flow in one direction while other goods flow in the opposite direction. In academic situations, enrollment figures go to the administration and departmental resources come back.

[5] The issue of the ethnographer's personality will be discussed in more detail in Chapter 3. Wintrob (1969), comparing a group of seven graduate students with eight anthropologists analyzed by Roe (1952a, 1952b), notes some similarities, such as being firstborn, rebelling against parental authority, and struggling for a highly valued independence. The problem is that there isn't much research, and what there is is based on a few cases. Besides, it's hard to know if the results represent things that preceded, followed, or developed in conjunction with the person's role as an ethnographer. And then we don't know about people with the same characteristics who didn't become ethnographers.

professional face-saving, personal anxieties, a desire to look "scientific," and so on.[6] While I can recognize all of these in my own experience, there is another reason that my own biases lead me to consider important—biases resulting from my interest in the study of human communication.

Imagine a trip to another place for a limited period of time. If you are an adventurous type, you move out into the local scene to learn something about it. You are overwhelmed with new sights and sounds. You find yourself acting and thinking in ways different from your ordinary life. Just to liven things up, let's say you also fall in love and spend more time than normal in various states of intoxication. At the end of your 2 weeks, you climb on the plane, your mind filled with images of partly understood, partly connected experiences. As you walk into your home airport terminal, a friend who has come to meet you smiles and says, "So how was the trip? What'd you do?"

Good luck with the answer. Most people confronted with this communication dilemma, resort to the language of intensive affect ("fantastic," "far out," "unbelievable") or go to specific descriptions that will make sense to the questionner ("Well, on Monday morning I . . ."). Only later, with much time and a lot of linguistic work, you might try to give your friend a better description—one that approximates more closely the richness, intensity, and variety of experiences that you had.

People in a branch of sociology known as *ethnomethodology* call this a problem in "indexicality." *Indexicality* refers to the amount of shared background knowledge necessary to understand a message. If you and your friend go to a party together, then you have shared the experience. When you talk later, you can say "Some party, huh?" and your friend will draw on the same experiences to interpret the message. On the other hand, if your friend wasn't there, then you have to describe several details before he can understand the point of saying "some party": "It was a good party because of some people I met"; "It was a good party because everyone got crazy and walked around in lampshades"; "It was a bad party because people only talked about boring things"; "It was a bad party because the host died before it really got going."

So when you got off the plane from your trip, you brought a resource of experiences that your friend had not shared. To describe the trip, you must describe those complicated experiences, your reactions to them, and do so in a way that makes sense in terms of the experiences your friend has had—a formidable task. Now consider the even more complicated situation of an ethnographer. I haven't really talked yet about what ethnography is. That will

[6] Freilich's (1970) introduction discusses some of the face-saving motivations. Wintrob (1969) covers some of the personal anxieties arising from doing fieldwork. Examples of critiques of an overconcern with being "scientific" can be found in Honigmann (1976), Redfield (1948), and Weakland (1951). Devereux (1967) shows the relationship between the psychodynamics of the researcher and the kind of "science" that he does.

come in detail later. But for now, it always involves long-term association with some group, to some extent in their own territory, with the purpose of learning from them their ways of doing things and viewing reality.

In part, ethnography resembles the common image of "social science"—questionnaires, tests, censuses, and so forth. But the ethnographer also eats with the group, works with them, relaxes with them, and hopefully comes to understand them. Meanwhile, he personally struggles with the interference from his own ways of thinking, feeling, and acting. Ethnography, whatever else it is, is an experientially rich social science. Compare it to many other forms of social science data collection—like a study based on questionnaires—and you get something like a comparison between Fort Knox and a quarter.

It is just this experiential wealth that presents a problem in methodology. When you attempt to describe some aspect of a group's life, you may be drawing from conversations, casual observations, 20 formal interviews, a previous ethnography, two novels, your general idea of the human condition, childhood experiences with your parents, and who knows what else. The problem in ethnographic method is to properly "de-indexicalize" descriptive statements. Throwing up your hands at the difficulty of the task strikes me as a perfectly sane response. Nevertheless, it's a problem that ethnographers must take seriously.

Reasons for Worrying about Methods

If ethnographers have gotten along so well for so long without being overly concerned about methodology, why worry? Well, first of all, they have not gotten along all that well. Consider the problem of cross-cultural comparisons. At Yale, the Human Relations Area File was developed in the 1940s under the leadership of George Peter Murdock. This file, called HRAF for short, is now available at many libraries around the country. Murdock and his associates attempted to take material from ethnographies and code them into content categories, like socialization practices, subsistence strategies, kinship systems, and so on. A codebook was published that indicates the many categories that were used to classify material.[7]

The idea, then, was that an anthropologist who wanted to compare socialization practices, for example, could look up the appropriate code numbers, go to the microfilmed file, and retrieve all the things that ethnographers have said about socialization. The problem is that ethnographers differed in their

---

[7] The codebook is listed in the References as Murdock *et al.* (1950).

interest in socialization, to stay with one example. Sometimes they all but ignored it. If they did discuss it, the discussions differed in the amount of detail. Even if they were similar in detail, they differed in their bias. One ethnographer might discuss socialization from a Freudian point of view. Another might discuss it in terms of learning theory. A third might focus only on the mother–child relationship. Another might emphasize mother and father but ignore sibling relationships. Yet a fifth might only examine birth to 5 years of age, while still another might discuss the socialization process through adolescence.[8]

How can one compare such widely different material? The problem gets worse when you examine the disagreements among ethnographers who work in the same area. Most famous among these disagreements is that of Oscar Lewis and Robert Redfield. Redfield had done a study of a Mexican village, as well as several other areas in that country. Oscar Lewis came along later and decided to do a restudy of the same village.

First of all, Lewis' behavior was a tremendous breach of etiquette. An ethnographer had "his village," and it was sacred territory. It was unheard of for another anthropologist to go in and do a restudy. Perhaps this unwritten rule of conduct partly arose as a form of methodological defensiveness. Such an attitude is certainly contrary to the spirit of scientific inquiry, where replications are routinely done to check the reported results of an individual researcher.

At any rate, Lewis came out with a description of village life much more negative than Redfield's. To oversimplify, Redfield had portrayed village life as harmonious and integrated, especially when contrasted with life in the city. Lewis, on the other hand, described the same villagers as displaying such unharmonious emotions as hostility, jealousy, and greed. In sketchy form, this is the famous "Lewis–Redfield" debate. The debate is something of a landmark event in the history of American cultural anthropology. Two competent, trained ethnographers produced dramatically different descriptions of the same group of people.

There are other cases of ethnographic disagreement as well. Margaret Mead and Reo Fortune disagreed over the nature of the male role among the Arapesh of New Guinea. An article written in 1946 describes a disagreement over the nature of Pueblo culture. On the one hand, Pueblo culture was described as harmonious and integrated; on the other, as full of covert tension. Then there's a Chinese anthropologist who studied the Zuni, and

---

[8] Many interested in cross-cultural research have developed ways to measure the quality of data in the HRAF. For example, see Naroll (1970) and other relevant articles in Naroll and Cohen (1970). The relationship between ethnography and cross-cultural research is also taken up in more detail in Chapter 9 of this book.

wrote an article in 1937 that was rather embarrassed at all the discrepancies between his experience and the reports of previous work among the Zuni. It's interesting that a common theme in many of these disagreements, including Lewis and Redfield's, is related to a differing emphasis on conflict or harmony.[9]

Still another example of ethnographer disagreement is the debate between Ward Goodenough and John Fisher. This one is even more striking because it involves the application of what appeared to be straightforward categories for coding postmarital residence patterns. Ethnographers have long discussed residence using such categories as "matrilocal" (residing with bride's family), "patrilocal" (residing with groom's family), "neolocal" (establishing a new residence), and so on. Yet when Goodenough and Fisher studied the same group on a Pacific atoll, they came up with different percentages of each residence type. Goodenough wrote a paper analyzing the problem.[10] He pointed out that in several cases, the residential situation was complicated and subtle, involving several kinds of relatives. One person might say they were "residing together" while other persons might say they were not. Because of the complexity, each ethnographer had to fill in some implicit assumptions in order to categorize the cases according to residence type. Since the two ethnographers differed in implicit assumptions, they came up with different percentages of each type. I think *implicit* is a key word here, and it no doubt bears some relationship to the mystique discussed earlier.

All sorts of things happen during fieldwork. Probably some of them will always remain implicit and incapable of articulation. But certainly not all of them need remain so. In attempting to make explicit the ethnographic process, we are contributing to the development of ethnographic method. To the extent we can do so, we might begin to understand how two professionals can be in such disagreement. Perhaps disagreement should be expected, given the complexity and personal involvement in ethnographic work. We'll return to this topic in Chapter 3.

Of course, there is a law that operates here that should be named after somebody. The more we insist that the experiential base of ethnography be

[9] The review of restudies comes from Naroll (1970). A discussion of the disagreement over Pueblo culture is in Bennett (1946). The Chinese anthropologist's article is cited as Li-An-Che (1937). Some examples of general discussions on the importance of restudies as a check on method can be found in Lewis (1953) and Herskovits (1954). On the other hand, Den Hollander (1967) argues that when restudies are done by the same person, or are based on the same original work, there is more agreement. Honigmann (1970) argues that although there have been differences, by and large ethnographers in the same area have reached similar conclusions. Den Hollander (1967) and Honigmann (1976), among others, argue that with the importance of the personal role of the ethnographer, it would be foolish to expect perfect replication at any rate.

[10] This case is described in Goodenough (1956).

made explicit, the fewer the experiences that can be dealt with adequately. Explicitness, in other words, carries with it a danger of trivialization. The strategy is to *selectively* narrow the focus within a previously explored broad field. A couple of sections down the road, you will be introduced to this as the "funnel" approach.

To sum all of this up, I am arguing that ethnographers have *not* gotten along very well by neglecting methodology. In the history of the field, problems in cross-cultural comparison, and the differences between ethnographers studying the same group, both point the damning finger at our failure to be explicit about what it is we do when we do fieldwork. As if these were not problems enough, there is another reason to worry about ethnographic methodology as well. That reason, to put it bluntly, is competition from other disciplines.

In a recent book on cognitive psychology, the author calls for more attention to "ecological validity"—the operation of cognitive processes in natural context. Another recent work offers a new perspective in social psychology, one that is essentially ethnographic. While some sociologists have always been active in ethnography, it seems to me that the pace has picked up considerably in the last few years.[11] In many cases, these ethnographically oriented authors from other disciplines do a better job articulating ethnography than we do. To give just one quick example, Glaser and Strauss came up with the elegant statement that in ethnographic research, data collection and analysis are done concurrently rather than being separately scheduled parts of the research.

In many sociological surveys, for example, a questionnaire is designed. Then interviewers go out and "collect the data." The data are then coded and keypunched. Only then does "analysis" begin, with the machine-readable data manipulated according to some statistical procedure. In ethnography, as we will discuss in more detail later, you learn something ("collect some data"), then you try to make sense out of it ("analysis"), then you go back and see if the interpretation makes sense in light of new experience ("collect more data"), then you refine your interpretation ("more analysis"), and so on. The process is dialectic, not linear. Such a simple statement, so important in capturing a key aspect of doing ethnography. An anthropologist should have said it long ago.

In addition to competition from non-anthropological ethnographers, another kind of rivalry is also important. Increasingly, ethnographers live in

---

[11] The cognitive psychology book is Neisser (1976), while the social psychology argument can be found in Harre and Secord (1972). A long list of sociological works are given in Note 15 of this chapter.

professional niches where they must compete for attention from granting agencies, publishing houses, and policymakers. Their competition consists of other social scientists who, for the most part, have a tradition of methodologies that are remarkable for their explicitness. These methodologies have their own problems, including their own brand of smuggled implicitness, but more on that later.

The point now is that these social scientists usually have little understanding of what ethnography is and how it is done. They usually find little to instruct them in the scarce methodological discussions in ethnographic research reports. If you are a policymaker and you have a choice between a survey that asked the wrong questions very explicitly, or an ethnography that asked the right questions but you cannot tell how they were asked and of whom, which one would you pick to base policy on? More and more ethnographers are concerned about the policy implications of their research. An increase in methodological sophistication will enhance policy credibility.

At this point, you may be warming up for the conclusion that ethnographers should just use the explicit methodologies already developed in other social sciences. My answer would be to applaud with one hand. Ethnographers ned to draw on procedures from other fields as part of the process of fieldwork, but ethnographers who just do surveys or administer psychological tests are not doing ethnography.

A few years ago, I was part of a symposium on "Ethnography and Criminal Behavior." During the discussion, a sociologist with ethnographic tendencies stood up and said, "The trouble with you anthropologists is that as soon as you start working in cities you look like sociologists." His point was that when faced with the large numbers and unbounded groups characteristic of the urban setting, many ethnographers flock to the methodology of survey sociology. In doing so, they abandon the unique features of the ethnographic process, and consequently sacrifice some important contributions they might make to the study of urban life. Although he ignored several important counterexamples, I quote him as a cautionary note. You cannot build a wooden bookshelf out of metal, though you might strengthen it with some steel brackets.

How This Book Was Written

Before I can tell you about this book, I first need to say something about how it was written. During the summer of 1978, I fled Houston for Mexico to study Spanish and escape telephones and memos. I began to think about ethnography for two reasons. First of all, my days in the drug field had taught me the political value of ethnography in humanizing stereotypes. Policy—and the treatment prevention, education, and law enforcement efforts that it logically implies—is built on assumptions of what "those people" are like. Yet a little ethnography quickly teaches you that the assumptions, at their very best, are oversimplifications. Ethnography, then, offers a social science metaphor within which the richness and variety of group life can be expressed as it is learned from direct involvement with the group itself. I also thought about ethnography because much of my career has been spent discussing it with nonethnographers. I learned that there were some fundamental differences in research world views, made more subtle by the fact that they were all included in the category of "social sciences."

I began to make some notes, and the notes eventually turned into the first draft of this book. My purpose was to produce something that a person could read to get a perspective of what it's all about—or at least my version of it. When I returned to Houston, I went to the library to see if what I'd written fit into the literature on ethnographic field methods.

By academic rules, you're supposed to go to the library before you write, but I'm glad I didn't. I was able to get my own conclusions straight before I encountered the mass of material I found when I got home. In anthropology we believe that there is not much literature on field methods. That's not quite true. There's an unbelievable amount of literature, but it's scattered widely through time and across many journals. I know there's still more out there. How do you know when you've reviewed enough literature? In these days of the information explosion, it's when you're exhausted, confused, and can no longer see straight.

Reviewing the literature was a humbling experience. I doubt if there are many things in this book that haven't been said somewhere by somebody. Take the title, for example. As far as I know, I invented it. Then I went to the library and found a book called *Stranger and Friend,* an article entitled "The Ethnologist as Stranger," and occasional references to essays dealing with "The Stranger." [12] I thought my discussion of ethnographic proposals would be unique, but then Pelto, Williams, and Freilich, for example, also discuss them, although not in the same way. [13]

On the other hand, the review was gratifying. It was pleasant to see that many of my conclusions were supported independently by the experience of others. It was fascinating to watch the issues grow. The opposition between observation and interview is there at the very beginning with the two founding

---

[12] The book is by Powdermaker (1966); the article, by Nash (1963). The two essays are by Simmel (1950) and Schutz (1964). Also, see Meintel (1973).

[13] See Pelto (1970), Freilich (1970), and Williams (1967).

fathers. Franz Boas stressed the interview as he tried to get descriptions of disappearing American Indian cultures from older informants; Branislaw Malinowski pitched his tent among the natives, learning their language and sharing their lives.

I watched the exciting collaboration between sociologists and anthropologists growing out of the community study orientation at the University of Chicago. Then, in 1949, under the editorship of Conrad Arensberg, the journal of the Society for Applied Anthropology (now called *Human Organization*) bgan regularly featuring methodological articles, a practice that has continued to the present. Finally, book-length treatments of ethnographic methods have begun to appear more recently, together with a growing number of personal accounts of the fieldwork experience.

It was especially gratifying for me personally to notice that two of the better personal accounts, by Powdermaker and Wax, were written by ethnographers who worked in U.S. settings long before the recent interest in U.S. ethnography. It was also interesting to see the continuing commitment of *Human Organization* to methodological discussions. In traditional anthropological circles, and to some extent still today, studying the U.S. or applied work is considered less prestigious than "pure" research on real "natives." There are some reasons for these biases (discussed later), but I think that work in niches where other professionals wonder what you're up to, and where you yourself are part "native," stimulates methodological reflection.

In fact, from the literature review, I now recognize two more books that should be written. The first would synthesize the voluminous scattered literature as a kind of state-of-the-art review. The second would treat the numerous personal accounts as personal documents, and analyze them for their similarities and differences.[14] That's not my purpose here, though. So what is my purpose here?

First of all, I hope to give a sense of ethnography as a special approach to understanding the human situation. I want to do this especially by contrasting

[14] Freilich (1970) attempts to analyze the personal accounts presented in his book, suggesting a model of fieldwork based on them. Pelto and Pelto (1973) do a similar analysis of personal accounts plus some questionnaire responses from professional ethnographers. Golde (1970) also reviews the personal accounts contained in her book in an attempt to define problems unique to women fieldworkers. We need more analyses of this type. Two of the best personal accounts, in my opinion, are Powdermaker (1966) and Wax (1971). Examples of others can be found in Henry and Saberwal (1979), Levi-Strauss (1961), Maybury-Lewis (1965), Middleton (1970), Romanucci-Ross (1976), Spindler (1970), Vidich *et al.* (1964), Whyte (1955), Beattie (1965), Casagrande (1960), Dumont (1978), Geer (1964), Golde (1970), Beteille and Madan (1975), and of course the now famous diary of Malinowski (1967). Other personal accounts can often be found as introductions or postscripts to published ethnographers.

it with hypothesis-testing approaches—not because I think such approaches are bad, but because to most people (including some anthropologists) hypothesis-testing is the core meaning of "social science." If you believe that, it leads you to ask questions that miss the point of what ethnography is all about.

Second, I want to contribute to a synthesis of some bothersome oppositions. In the literature, you will run across differences between "traditional" versus "problem-oriented" ethnography; between a "personalistic" versus a "standardized" approach; between ethnography as a "humanistic" versus a "scientific" enterprise. My goal is to try for breadth, but also depth in a few select areas; and to deal not only with the humanity of both ethnographer and group members, but to try to do so in a way that documents the experiences in a manner convincing to a skeptical outsider. Later in the book, this is called a "funnel" approach, with breadth and humanity at the beginning of the funnel, and then, within the context of that beginning, depth, problem-focus, and science at the narrow end. In a way, it's a "Why can't we all be happy?" strategy. But it's critical, I think. Without science, we lose our credibility. Without humanity, we lose our ability to understand others.

The book, however, will not be a compendium of methods that have been used in ethnographic research. Ethnographers have invented numerous methods appropriate to their research settings. They have also begged, borrowed, and stolen methods from most of the other social, biological, and physical sciences, as well as from the humanities. The design or theft of specific methodologies is, as I hope to show later, your problem. Rather than attempt a sort of catalogue, I am going to try to focus on the process in general—things that ethnographers worry about whatever their special interests.

Finally, I hope to provide a context within which additional research training will make sense.[15] There is little in the way of statistics here, but

[15] For an introduction to statistics written from an anthropological point of view, see Hurst (1976). Kay's (1971) edited volume illustrates several applications of mathematics in anthropology. A good introductory book on the topic of mathematical models is Lave and March (1975). Johnson (1978) introduces the topic of quantification from a point of view that considers traditional ethnographic concerns. Pelto's (1970) book discusses anthropological research within a general discussion of science. He then goes on to introduce statistics and several measurement techniques from sociology and psychology, as well as to discuss some traditional ethnographic field methods. Brim and Spain (1974) offer a blend of traditional ethnography and control-group research design adapted from Campbell and Stanley's (1966) work. While not an exhaustive list by any means, these works represent views of ethnography with the goal of furthering standardization and quantification. On the more qualitative side, in my opinion, the sociologists seem to be more active, as evidenced in the philosophical statements of ethnography by Glaser and Strauss (1967) and Bruyn (1966). Other book-length treatments by sociologists include

hopefully at the end you will have an idea of where statistics might be useful. Mathematical models are only hinted at, although you should see their potential and seek further training in that area. Research design in areas like survey research or psychological experimentation are occasionally mentioned, but it should become clear why you should master them. Likewise, I hope at the end that you will also explore methods from the humanities—techniques drawn from literary criticism, discourse analysis, hermeneutics, and so on. When you set out to do ethnography, the broader your research repertoire, the more creative you can be in developing research approaches to questions you didn't anticipate in a group you're just learning to understand.

A Research Biography

Before we start, I want to offer something of a research biography. Some of my examples will come from "real life," though I am not sure when a person is an ethnographer and when he or she is not an ethnographer. Some other examples will come from short-term consulting work I have done; these can be adequately described as the occasion arises. But a few experiences will be drawn on so frequently that it is worth giving a background sketch now. Besides, I want to illustrate the different roles an ethnographer can play.

Four of these examples are actual examples of fieldwork. One is from a village in South India; the next from a federal institution for the treatment of narcotics addiction; the third from a village in southern Austria; and finally, the fourth is from treatment centers and the streets of New York City. The fifth experience comes from a position in the "research establishment." For 4 years, I reviewed research grant applications for an agency in the Department of Health, Education and Welfare. The experiences are presented in chronological order.

SOUTH INDIA

In my sophomore year at college, I walked into an introductory anthropology course and decided to stay. In the course, I learned that ethnography was

Douglas (1976), Becker (1970), Cicourel (1964), Denzin (1970), Johnson (1975), Schatzman and Strauss (1973), Speier (1973), Junker (1960), and Bogdan and Taylor (1975). Though there are volumes reflecting a primary concern with qualitative analysis by anthropologists [see Edgerton and Langness (1974) and Williams (1967), for example], it strikes me that much recent anthropological writing is concerned with a move towards quantification, while many in sociology, coming from a tradition that emphasizes quantification, are concerned with formalizing qualitative analysis.

at the heart of it all, so I asked around and learned that Professor Alan Beals was going to India the next year. For reasons that I will never understand, I asked if I could go along, and he said, "Well, maybe." We worked out an arrangement where I would help supervise a team of genealogical interviewers part of the time. The rest of the time I would work in a small community nearby, with Beals supervising and teaching me what ethnography was all about.

Beals was returning to Gopalpur, a village he had described in an ethnography written from his earlier visit. "My" village was located about 2 miles away. It was populated by the Lambardi, a group of North Indian derivation now residing in the state of Karnataka. Previously, they had been a migrant group who served as the transportation system for goods in India. They would purchase goods at the point of origin, then migrate some distance to sell them at a profit. Partly for this reason, they are called the "gypsies" of India. In fact, they probably are distant relatives of European gypsies.

The settlement, or *tanda,* was located on government-owned wasteland. The Lambardi were poor by local standards. They had no irrigation and few owned much land or many animals. They had their own language from the North, but my work with them was done in Kannada, the language spoken throughout Karnataka. I rented a small hut there and split my time between Gopalpur and the *tanda.*

By the end of the 6 months that I worked there, I was on speaking terms (at least) with most of the *tanda*'s 200 inhabitants. With a few, I had very close and warm relationships. My work there was of the classic ethnographic type, where I tried to cover the entire territory, from crops to kinship to karma. Though this research occurred a while ago, in 1965–1966, it represents an important source for some of my notions of what ethnography is all about.

"NARCO"

The recent history of illicit narcotics use in this country is a stormy one. With the passing of the Harrison Narcotics Act, the subsequent Supreme Court interpretations in the 1920s, and the closing of the morphine clinics at about the same time, narcotics addicts were converted into criminals. In the 1930s the federal government constructed a "hospital" for addicts near Lexington, Kentucky.

The hospital, known as "Narco" locally, served federal prisoners convicted for narcotics related crimes, as well as volunteer patients who checked in for "the cure." By the time I arrived, in 1968, the name had been changed to the NIMH Clinical Research Center and the "patients" were civil commitments under the provisions of the Narcotics Addict Rehabilitation Act.

As part of its development as a research center, the hospital had opened a

Social Science Research section. The director of the section, John O'Donnell, wanted an anthropologist brought on to see what one would do. He turned to the applications for commissioned officer status in the U.S. Public Health Service just as mine crossed a Washington desk. When he contacted me and offered me a commission, I was delighted. It sounded like an unbelievably pleasant alternative to the choices then available to me and my male friends—the army, jail, or Canada.

The hospital, which also had many of the trappings of a prison, was a confusing place for a traditional ethnographer. Here was a group that was both part of and distinct from the rest of American society. They were localized, but only temporarily, and not by choice in most cases. They were all "dope fiends"[16] who differentiated themselves by age, ethnicity, residence, and so on. It was hardly the sort of group ethnographers deal with.

There were some interesting problems right away. For instance, the dope fiends had a name for people about my age who came around asking about life in the streets—"narc." Then I quickly learned that certain cherished pieces of ethnographic jargon, like the term *informant,* had to go. But in spite of such problems, as I compared my work at the hospital/prison with my work in South India, there were more similarities than differences. Even with such a different group, much of what I had learned about doing ethnography in South India worked in Lexington as well.

Lexington was important in another way. For the first time, I had left the family. I was the lone ethnographer among sociologists and psychologists. They often asked delicately phrased questions like, "Just what in the hell is it that you do anyway?" Or, more specifically, "Where is your instrument? What is the sample design? What is your plan of analysis?" No one I knew had worried about such questions, and it was embarrassing to know that somehow those were the wrong questions, but not be capable of explaining why.

Another first-time experience at Lexington was my entry into the world of government bureaucrats and policymakers. I went around telling the hospital staff the things I was learning, hoping to contribute to an improvement of the hospital/prison. But government bureaucrats constitute another culture, the implicit rules of which I did not know. I constantly said the wrong things to the wrong people in the wrong way during the first few months. While I had experience in doing ethnography, I had no experience in communicating the results of that ethnography to nonanthropologists for nonacademic purposes.

[16] In case anyone finds them offensive, terms like "junkie" and "dope fiend" are those used by street addicts themselves, aggressively so when faced with a straight person with a preference for medical, legal, or other euphemisms.

AN AUSTRIAN VILLAGE

In the summer of 1972, I joined a research team, led by John Gumperz, working in a bilingual village in the south of Austria. The study was a comparison case for Gumperz's earlier work in a bilingual village in India. In the Indian community, the two languages were of completely different families—one was Indo–Aryan, the other, Dravidian. Gumperz showed that speakers used one system of syntactic rules to speak both languages, and that the syntax differed from the standard versions of both the Indo–Aryan and the Dravidian language. Two separate syntactic structures, in other words, had been blended together over many years of bilingualism in the community.

The south Austrian village presented a similar case. For many years, the village had been bilingual in Slovenian and German. My job, as one interested in ethnographic semantics, was to do a study in the area of semantic structure. Did the villagers also have a single underlying semantic structure for both languages? I had about 8 weeks to learn something relevant to that question.

The Austrian experience was yet a different kind of ethnography. First of all, I had been an exchange student in Austria for 6 months, so in some ways it was like coming home. I knew the language, even speaking it with an Austrian accent. Second, I had never worked in a community occupied by two other ethnographers. Finally, I had never done so narrow a task. My job was not to "range" all over the territory as I had in previous ethnographic work. Rather, I was shown a particular limited task that would fill in a small piece of the overall portrait. Austria then, was yet another kind of ethnographic experience that contributed to my sense of how ethnography gets done.

NEW YORK

In 1973 I took a research position with the state treatment agency in New York. The agency bore the unfortunate title of New York State Narcotics Addict Control Commission (NACC). (It was later changed to Drug Abuse Control Commission, not much of an improvement, and then to Office of Drug Abuse Services.) In the beginning the position was a luxurious one. All I had to do was define research projects of an ethnographic nature, obtain approval from the research office, and do them.

Since I was an NACC employee, I had access to NACC-sponsored treatment centers, many of which were located in community settings around New York. I picked one center in particular in the Lower East Side of Manhattan. I had good rapport with the chief counselor there, and the neighborhood was interesting—a mix of ethnic groups and some remnants of the old East Village days. A second base in the area was a court referral program run by young Puerto Ricans. I told them who I was, that I wanted to learn about the neighborhood by hanging around, and that in return I would tutor kids in the program. No problem.

Using these two facilities as starting points, I eventually was invited into the streets. Both within the centers and in the streets, I became interested in the use of methadone. Since my earlier Lexington work, heroin had declined on the streets and the use of methadone had increased. Through informal conversations and observations, I began to try and learn why the change had occurred.

At about the same time, I met a remarkable individual. When I first arrived, I thought it would be interesting to do an ethnohistory of the heroin street scene in New York. I put out the word that I would like to meet some older heroin addicts, and the word came back that "Jack" (a pseudonym) would talk to me. Jack was something of a tribal elder. He was part of the early "beat" scene that included people like Burroughs, Ginsberg, and Kerouac. He was a mainstay of Kinsey's work in the Times Square area. Throughout his 60-some-odd years, he had been through almost every drug scene the country had to offer, beginning with his adolescence in Chicago.

When I met him, Jack was on a methadone program in New York. He agreed to be interviewed (little did I know at the time what an expert interviewee he was) and we began doing his life history. Our interviews ran off and on for 18 months. We still sometimes talk on the phone, and we visit whenever I get to New York. Our relationship is an important one; we are, I think, as close as "researcher" and "subject" ever get. Among many other things, he highlights an important paradox—it is hard to "do science" with people you like; it is also hard to "do science" with people you do not like; if you do not care one way or the other, it is hard to "do science" because you do not understand enough about the people you are doing science with.

The New York work was important in another way. I was able to take material learned in an isolated institutional setting (Lexington) and apply it in the streets. The Lexington material, by and large, held up fairly well, even though it was dated. Also, I learned that many of the descriptions I had recorded were overly optimistic, but more on that in Chapter 5.

REVIEWING GRANTS

The National Institute on Drug Abuse (NIDA) was created in 1973. It was assembled from pieces of the National Institute on Mental Health and from the Special Action Office on Drug Abuse Prevention. One of its divisions is the Division of Research, part of whose mission is to fund, by grant and contract, drug-related research from a variety of perspectives. One of these perspectives is called "psychosocial" research. So the Psychosocial Branch was born within the institute.

Most funding agencies have some sort of "peer review" process. When someone applies for research funding, their proposal is sent to reviewers with the expertise to comment on the quality and feasibility of the research design, the competence of the applicant, the appropriateness of the budget, and so on. In some cases, a standing committee, called an "IRG" (institutional review group) is appointed to conduct these assessments.

An employee at NIDA, the late Eleanor Carroll, had been arguing for ethnographic representation on NIDA's new IRG. In the "drug field," there is a bias toward the medical model. After that, in the area of social science, come people concerned with areas such as the sociology of deviance or psychopathology. Ethnography is a newcomer to the field by comparison. Ms. Carroll won her fight, and I was appointed in 1973 as the token ethnographer on the IRG.

During my 4-year tenure as an "ad hoc" member, I learned much about the bureaucratization and politization of social science research. I also learned, with an intensity that made Lexington pale by comparison, that nonethnographers have little idea of how ethnography works. Further, the IRG was a rough, sharp crowd. I saw their "tests" and "questionnaires" as encoding erroneous policy assumptions about the nature of drug use. They saw my ethnographic approach as so loose and uncontrolled that it could hardly be considered social science. Much heated and instructive discussion went on over those 4 years.

The NIDA experience taught me much about the politics of research—politics in the sense of research and federal policy, and politics in the sense of judging research proposals by a variety of disciplinary standards. The IRG also taught me something about "grant-getting," that old academic hustle. In Chapter 8 there will be a detailed presentation on the submission of ethnographic research proposals.

So much for the sketch of my own research experiences. I described them briefly now, partly so that you will have some background when I refer to them later in the book. But I also wanted to introduce you to the variety of forms ethnographic work can take—complete or partial; alone or with a team; with a village, a clique, or a person. Most of the discussion that follows assumes that you will be the primary ethnographer involved, and that you will start from scratch. If your situation differs, then, of course, modifications will be necessary.

Another purpose in stressing my own experience is that this book is written primarily from that experience. What I hope to do is describe a perspective on doing ethnography, one that I have been developing and articulating in discussions with nonethnographers since 1968. I wouldn't pretend even for a minute that it is "the" perspective on doing ethnography. It, hopefully, will contribute to some recent statements by others as to what ethnography is all about. By exploring the similarities and differences in such statements, we can continue assembling a coherent picture of the ethnographic process in its various forms, and begin to define the holes in our understanding of that process so that we can better articulate what we do.

2
Getting Started

Before the moment when you actually begin talking with people as an ethnographer, several preliminaries must be taken care of. First of all, you need to pick an area and a specific group to talk with. Then you should do a review of the literature to learn what other research has already been done. You must locate a network path from yourself to the group that will be more of a help than a hindrance. You could just show up, but, as elsewhere in life, the proper network can save time and make a helpful difference. Finally, unless you are independently wealthy, someone must support you.

Picking an Area

Sometimes anthropologists are categorized as "area" people or "theory" people. Most graduate training programs require a specialization in both, and if you talk to anthropologists, they will usually have a quick label for each. The area emphasis comes from a concept at the heart of antrhopology—the "cross-cultural perspective." The argument is that you cannot understand humankind by simply studying one society. A single society represents only one pattern among a number of possible ones, but we cannot define the universe of possibilities without examining the range of patterns that exist. This principle is itself an illustration of the yet more general idea of definition by contrast. One defines something by systematically contrasting it with what might have occurred, but did not.

The cross-cultural perspective is a critical part of anthropology. In the drug research area, for example, American policymakers have historically assumed that the use of Drug X is a necessary and sufficient condition for "abuse." By looking at the use of the chemical cross-culturally, one usually learns that Drug X is well integrated into other societies in various social, medicinal, or religious contexts.

By studying an area intensively, the student learns enough to have at least some material at hand for comparison with his own or other societies. This is reason enough for the importance of an area specialty outside of the United States during anthropological training. In addition to this general educational function, many come to anthropology with a primary interest in some area of the world. It might be sub-Saharan Africa, Southeast Asia, contemporary European society, or the urban United States. The interest might come from early travel experiences, a novel that caught the fancy, or a desire to study in one's own society.

Others may select an area with some theoretical purpose in mind. If you are interested in heroin use—either professionally or personally—then you obviously need an area where people are using heroin. If you are an economic anthropologists and you want to look at the *jajmani* system, then you very likely are heading for India. If you want to know the relation between family size and acculturation, then you'd better pick a place to work in that has some variation in both. A theoretical interest, in short, can constrain the possible areas you might choose.[1]

There is a potential problem, then, if Americans study the U.S., or Asians study Asians. What happens to the cross-cultural perspective that was so important a moment ago? This might explain the conservatism exhibited by some anthropologists when confronted with their students' growing interests in studying U.S. society. While that is a problem, the conclusion should not be that American anthropologists should avoid the States. It does mean that students should receive training in the details of another society before they become professionals.

Another problem related to the study of one's own society is the position, held by some, that *only* a member of the society should study it. The argument here is that only an insider knows enough of the subtle details of the life-styles. But an outsider's perspective is also valuable, especially since the enthnographer–informant relationship acquires some new characteristics when one works in her own society.

The distinction between "area" and "theory" interests may also help

---

[1] The *jajmani* system refers to the economic interdependencies among different castes in India. On the point of insuring that there is variation enough in a particular area of interest, see Levine (1970) for a summary discussion of theoretically motivated site selection.

explain why ethographic methods have been shoddily treated in anthropology. As an area person, one is interested in the details of some particular area. From this viewpoint, ethnography as a *general* process has little interest. One wants to find out what a group thinks and does; she is more concerned with the substance of the information than with the general procedures by which it was obtained. A reflective account of how the many conversations, observations, and interviews explicitly led to a conclusion is not a task with a high priority attached to it.

On the other hand, as a theory person one is more committed to issues generated by the theoretical language. The theory implies something about how people do things, and eventually one needs data to see if those implications are supported in some society. Ethnography is the way to get it. Unlike the area person, though, the needs are much more specific. In fact, the focus can carry with it the danger of missing other things that are relevant to the development of the theoretical language. But, here again, ethnography is not of interest in itself; rather, it is a means to get some specific information to fuel theoretical discussion. If there is some truth here, then ethnography falls into a crack between area and theory interests. In neither case does it receive the attention it merits.

At any rate, you may find your choices limited by circumstances beyond your control. First of all, American anthropologists are becoming undesirable aliens in some areas of the world. In U.S. society, some groups feel over-studied and want nothing to do with social scientists of any stripe. And then there is money. Currently, it is becoming more and more difficult to obtain research funds. In some agencies, obtaining funding is more of a problem when the research is to be conducted outside the U.S. Finally, an opportunity to work in a particular area may come along, constituting an offer you cannot refuse.

The latter was certainly true in my case. None of my early field experiences were in areas I consciously selected. I worked in South India because I wanted to do fieldwork and Alan Beals happened to be going there the next year. I worked in the hospital in Lexington because 2 years with the U.S. Public Health Service fulfilled my military obligation. I worked in Austria because India would not allow us to enter the border region where Gumperz had done his earlier studies. There were ongoing political conflicts that centered on the very language issue we intended to study.

But then I am not much of an area person. On the other hand, I don't like the distinction between theory and ethnography, either. There is a saying, attributed to William James, that you can't pick up rocks in a field without a theory. Ethnography is not simply "data collection"; it is rich in implicit theories of culture, society, and the individual. As I continue to try and articulate the ethnographic process in the name of methodology, there will also be an implicit articulation of cultural theory. At some point in the book, the relationship between these two articulations must be dealt with.

A Review of the Literature

Through your control or through kismet, you now know where you want to go. The next problem is to read "the literature." The way some social science is written, I don't know why it's called "literature," but it is. In addition to learning something, you must also do this as part of several practical chores, like grant applications and bibliographies for graduate examinations. But there is a "perverse streak" in some ethnographers that literature will only cloud your mind with other people's mistakes and misconceptions.[2]

This bias is not as crazy as it sounds. Let me give an example from my early days at the Lexington hospital. When I arrived, I knew nothing about heroin addicts. All I knew about drugs was what had been floating around West Coast universities in the mid 1960s, and that usually consisted of marijuana and hallucinogens. So I went to the well-stocked hospital library and began reading about addicts and addiction.

Most social-science drug research at that time was done by psychologists and sociologists, usually with specific interest in pathology and deviance. Everyone agreed that the heroin addict was a social-psychological failure in U.S. society. No one agreed on how best to explain that failure status. Social scientists would talk about properties of the neighborhood in which the addict grew up, different kinds of peer associations, and the comparative availability of "legitimate" opportunities for economic success. Others would discuss inadequate superegos, the psychopathic deviate (PD) scale on the Minnesota Multiphasic Personality Inventory (MMPI), and that great explanation of so many things, the absence of a strong male figure in the household.

"The literature" did not leave me very satisfied. First of all, there was not much of a "heroin addict" in it. Someone had obviously taken a test, submitted to a clinical interview, or responded to a survey instrument, but I did not get much of a sense of what being a junkie was all about. How can

---

[2] For example, consider this quote from Arensberg (1954): "It means not that the student ignores extant information but rather that he cannot accept it as it stands: too many false or irrelevant assumptions incrust it." See also Bogdan and Taylor (1975) who suggest going to the literature after, or perhaps during, fieldwork. In his review of four personal accounts of entering the field (Cohen *et al.*, 1970), Cohen notes that one author stresses the importance of using the previous literature to formulate problems while another suggests that you not accept the literature without questions. My sympathy, as you can see in the text, is with skeptics.

you understand a phenomenon when you do not have a sense of what that phenomenon looks like?

Then, I was also dissatisfied with the way many studies ignored some obvious questions. If a group of junkies had had certain experiences or displayed certain attributes, what about all the people with similar experiences and attributes who were not junkies? Finally, I wasn't much reassured by my clinical colleagues who tossed around labels like "psychopath, sociopath, and schizophrenic—chronic undifferentiated type."

This was a classic example of a nonfunctional literature review for the beginning ethnographer. I did need to know about this material when I began writing and speaking to other professionals who worked with heroin addicts, but reading it at the onset of my ethnographic work introduced a lot of unnecessary noise into my mind as I tried to learn about being a heroin addict from "patients" in the institution.

As I listened to patients talk with one another, there was not much social-psychological failing going on. They characterized themselves as being superior to straight people since they could survive in the streets by their wits, whereas straights needed the protected environments of mainstream society. They talked about their abilities at hustling money and drugs, and some of the hustles were rather sophisticated procedures that needed to be learned over a period of time. They discussed elaborate strategies: finding the best heroin, avoiding arrest, and getting a break from police and judges when the inevitable bust did come along. Discussions of social-psychological failures with elevated PD scores and blocked opportunities seemed to miss the point.

Later, when the different aspects of the informant are discussed in Chapter 3, this contradiction will be treated in more detail. For now I just want to note that my early ethnographic work at the hospital suggested some tentative conclusions that did not harmonize well with the current literature on heroin addiction. In fact, I began to feel like the subject in the famous Asch experiment, where everyone else in the room says that two different-sized lines are the same, and you wonder what is wrong with your perception.

Part of the problem here was that almost no ethnographic work had been done with heroin addicts. As studies slowly began to appear in the mid-to-late 1960s, I realized I was not as crazy as I thought. Other ethnographers also pointed out that the social-psychological failure status attributed to the addict didn't necessarily reflect what they had learned in their ethnographic research. Perhaps if there had been ethnographic literature on addiction, and I had reviewed that, I would have learned more useful information about heroin addicts before I began working. No doubt. But I still would have been cautious.

First of all, recall the general principle from the discussion of restudies in

Chapter 1. Different ethnographers may disagree in fundamental ways about the correct description of similar groups. This happens in heroin addict ethnographies now that the population of ethnographers has increased in the late 1970s. To give just a couple of items that are fought over, there is the degree to which junkie groups constitute a subculture; the variety of junkie lifestyles; the manner and effect of the use of other chemicals by people addicted to heroin; similarities and differences between male and female junkies, and so on.

I do not mean the preceding example to suggest that you should not review previous works. Use the increasing number of abstracting services, write to and talk with people who have worked with the groups you are interested in, and learn what you can. But I think you should view it all with a skeptic's eye, taking everything you learn, hanging a flag on it, and then testing the conclusions when you begin your own ethnography. Others may have worked with an atypical group, or they may have caught them at a peculiarly stressful time in their history; their biases may have led them to seek some details while neglecting others, or they might have just flat made a mistake. The way many ethnographies are written, it is impossible to tell.

Before leaving this discussion, there is one other kind of literature that should be mentioned. When budding ethnographers reach advanced graduate standing, and their minds are sufficiently polluted with ambiguous and vague social science jargon, someone will often call them aside and say, "By the way, be sure and read so and so's novels." Alan Beals did that for me, for example, before we left for India. He recommended all the novels of R. K. Narayan, who writes about Malgudi, a town in South India. Several junkies at Lexington suggested a number of novels and autobiographies to me shortly after I got there, including things like William Burroughs' *Junkie,* and Iceberg Slim's *Pimp* and *Trick Baby.*

Good novels often provide that elusive "feel" for the lifestyle of a group better than a social-scientific description. When I went to New York to do my ethnographic work, I saw the film *Panic in Needle Park.* Then I saw a play called *Short Eyes,* which has since become a motion picture. Then I reread *Junkie* and *Blueschild Baby* by George Cain.[3] In a way, it was a depressing way to begin fieldwork. I think that part of the ethnographer's role is to give

---

[3] For a discussion of more literary styles of ethnography, both in terms of doing research and in terns of presenting the results, see Edgerton and Langness (1974), Bruyn (1966), Redfield (1948), and Bennett (1948). Spradley and McDonough (1973) recently produced a reader that explores ethnographic learning through literature. I did a short paper (1977) analyzing a couple of addict autobiographies. Angrosino (1976) also discusses the use of autobiographies in ethnographic work. Heider (1976) and Hockings (1975) are good sources for discussions of both scientific and artistic aspects of ethnographic film.

some sense of different lifestyles to people who either do not know about them, or who are so bogged down in their own stereotypes that they do not understand them. If that is a reasonable, partial goal of ethnography, then what could an ethnographer possibly contribute that would add to that collection of one film, one play, and two books? Perhaps we should abandon that partial goal, or pursue it only in collaboration with those who have the artistic ability to construct messages in evocative language. Perhaps we should limit our role to producing messages with explicit empirical support and publicly displayed reasoning. Or perhaps we might learn from such material how better to conduct our work.

The Network "In"

Having done your homework, you must find a social trail from yourself to your first informant. One strategy is simply to "show up" but this often will not work for several reasons. First, working with some groups may require an institutional affiliation in the area. One of the changes in policy in several countries, for example, is to require American anthropologists who work in the country to affiliate with a local research institution, train local graduate students, and so on. You will not get a visa and permission to do research without such an affiliation.

A second reason is accountability. Assuming you have a research grant of some sort, a university or consulting firm will administer it. One of the things that funding agencies and administrators of research monies like to see is some local affiliation—a professional setting in which you will occasionally participate. Yet another reason to affiliate is simply the value of a good introduction. While a good ethnographer can probably overcome the effects of an introduction from a poor source, he will benefit tremendously with an introduction from a good source.

To give you a powerful example, several years ago I worked with the research director of the Haight-Ashbury Free Clinic in San Francisco. He was interested in epidemiology; specifically, he wanted to estimate the heroin addict population in San Francisco that had never had contact with treatment or law enforcement agencies. He asked me to hang out for a couple of weeks and see if I could come up with any suggestions on how to get data for such an estimate.

My suggestion was to start with a few informal in-depth interviews. I was introduced to the staff of the heroin detoxification-counseling program, and then turned loose. I picked two male and two female clients to interview. The women preferred to stay in the clinic and talk; the men quickly said they wanted to move out into the streets. The first thing that amazed me was the openness of the four. No one questioned me about my background or interests; my questions were quickly responded to in detail with no suspicion overtly expressed.

All this contrasted dramatically with my previous work with addicts. It usually took a while for junkies to decide you could be trusted, and even then there was a period of time when the questions you asked were carefully watched, and answers were often abbreviated or loaded with a heavy dose of caution. I began to understand the difference the first time I went out on the street with one of the males. He introduced me to junkies on the street as we walked around, saying something like, "This is Mike. He's working on something with the clinic." From that point on, I could ask almost anything and get elaborate answers.

The clinic had a solid street reputation. It had emerged from and grown with the counterculture in the 1960s. It had continued over the years to provide services for street people in a supportive way. By definition, any straight person working with the clinic was trustworthy and involved in something ultimately helpful to the street community. Affiliation with the clinic simply cut away the two or three months it had taken to establish myself at the hospital in Lexington.

The difference was made more striking by contrast when I worked in New York. I would be invited out into the streets with someone I had contacted in a NACC clinic setting (remember, that stands for the Narcotics Addict Control Commission). He would introduce me, usually leaving out my institutional affiliation. People would then ask who I worked for, and I would say NACC. The reactions ranged from departure to hostility to caution, but never did "NACC" elicit openness or enthusiasm. I suppose there is a possibility that the difference has something to do with New York junkies versus San Francisco junkies, but I do not think that would explain it.

The two examples of introductions via a local affiliation contrast dramatically. In the one case (the clinic), the introduction opened the doors; in the second case (NACC), it created problems that needed to be overcome before the ethnography could begin. A poor introduction will not destroy your work, though it can certainly complicate it, especially in its initial stages.

There is another problem with just "showing up" that I should mention here. I mention it because I have, on occasion, been horrified to hear someone talk about how they are interested in doing ethnography with criminal subcultures in the U.S., for example, and they plan to just walk up to a street corner and introduce themselves. That might work, but in some neighborhoods they might be running unnecessary personal risks. A middle-class straight person (which many of these aspiring ethnographers are) is just asking for problems by walking into the territory uninvited. It makes good sense to establish some contacts outside the situation first, and then go in with someone trusted and known in the area.

So, a general strategy emerges. Rather than contacting the group directly, an introduction from a person or institution that is well thought of by the group can be helpful. The mediating person or institution may be more like the ethnographer than group members—more professionals, higher education level, and so on. Since these persons will also be in direct contact with the group of interest, or know people who know the group directly, they can be an ideal bridge into the situation.

There is another problem here that will condition your choice of a trail in. In traditional ethnography, one worked in a bounded community. The community had a sample of most of the roles defined in the region as a whole; it continued through time; its members had a sense of community cohesion.[4] In other words, the group stayed put, and once you were in, the important initial stage of introductions and rapport (discussed further in Chapter 3) were over.

But recall the forms that my ethnographic studies have taken. Two of them—India and Austria—were in communities. But others—Lexington and New York—did not have the bounded permanence of a village. I even described a situation in New York where I did some ethnographic work "with a person." When ethnography is characterized in Chapter 4, you'll see that my sense of it is that it involves a perspective of understanding the human situation that does not require sharp group boundaries.

However, some ethnographers have worried about the loss of sharp community boundaries. One, for example, writing of her four field experiences, disliked one of them because they was no sense of "community." Another anthropologist, reviewing studies done recently in Africa, noted that a key problem for ethnographers was to stop asking "village" questions and begin to look at urban Africans as living in a different kind of social setting that required some new lines of investigation.[5]

At any rate, for now note that networks into dispersed urban populations may be more difficult because there is no neatly gathered clump of folks as the final destination. You may be meeting new people throughout your work, rather than just at the beginning. But in my experience, once you have a reputation with a few people in an urban niche, their introductions to others passes that reputation along so that you don't have to start again from scratch.

Still another problem that will be discussed in Chapter 9 has to do with the

[4] Arensberg (1954, 1961) offers particularly clear discussions of the "community" as a method and subject of research in anthropology.

[5] There is much discussion of changes in anthropology resulting from the "natives'" move from a village community to the city. The two examples cited here are from Powdermaker (1966) on the comparison of four field experiences, and from Gutkind (1967) on the changing focus in African studies.

ethnographer as an employee of an agency rather than as a free floating academician. In the previous examples of working for the Haight-Ashbury clinic in San Francisco and NACC in New York, I could not choose an affiliation for entree into a group—I was already stuck with one as a consequence of my job. This sort of situation, called "working for the man" by one ethnographer,[6] means that your problem is to figure out how to present your agency affiliation without lying, but at the same time trying to counter any negative assumptions that a person may make about people who work with that agency. That's a tricky bit of business that will be discussed more in Chapter 3.

Now, working backwards, you need to identify the right mediating group or person. You need a link from your immediate professional peer group to the appropriate mediating institution or individual. Other ethnographers who have worked in the area can be invaluable sources of information. With any luck at all, if you are a student, one of them will be on your faculty. Even if you do not have that direct contact, there are plenty of alternatives. For example, once you have done a review of the literature, you should be able to identify people to contact. Write them, or better yet, go visit them. Even the heroes, remote on the heights of Olympus, are sometimes remarkably friendly and accessible.

This "colleague connection" is also one of the things professional meetings are good for. Anyone who thinks that the only function of professional meetings is the presentation of papers probably has not been to one. There is an item of professional folklore that if a paper is any good, you will read it in a year or so anyway. One of the most important functions of meetings is for like-minded people to find each other and talk. You can meet people from whom you can learn and to whom you can communicate information that they want to know.

Now we are back to you, the starting point. You find people locally or at meetings or by correspondence who have worked in the general area that interests you. You learn from them good local persons or institutions to affiliate with. Then, using this as a base, you get introductions into the specific group with whom you hope to work. You are now ready to start.

Getting Funds

Of course, you are not going to last long without some kind of financial support. Among other things, you will need travel money, living expenses,

[6] The phrase is taken from the title of an article by Chambers (1977).

perhaps some money for field assistants and a tape recorder or two, and so on. We now approach the area of "grantsmanship," which academicians view with everything from disdain to enthusiasm. Obtaining research support brings the freedom to do one's work and adds prestige to one's reputation. On the other hand, it involves salesmanship and public relations work as well as scholarship.

Some anthropologists avoid the problem, or at least convert it into another form. One professional I know tired of dealing with funding agencies. He decided his knowledge was marketable. He did private consulting to earn money, then quit for awhile and did his own research. In some ways, of course, he traded one set of hassles for another, but he felt more comfortable as an individual entrepreneur. Another way to avoid the grant game is to get a full time research job. I have been fortunate enough to have had two of these. And, needless to say, they carry their package of hassles as well.

If you decide to pursue research funding, there are a number of chores ahead of you. First of all, you must explore the territory and find out who might be interested in your project. If you have access to a university research office, they are one good source of information. They usually have a staff who continually monitor the interests and funding levels of different federal, state, local, and private agencies. Good research offices will provide you with a counseling service to guide you through the maze and pinpoint specific agencies with whom you should correspond.

If you are not treated well in such offices, then complain. Many granting agencies provide something called *indirect costs*. The percentage varies, but the University of Houston, for example, requests 50% of salaries and wages listed in the grant as indirect costs. That means that if you apply for a grant and it is awarded, the same agency that gives you the salaries you request gives an additional 50% of that figure to the university. The research office *should* help you; you represent a potential source of indirect cost revenue, not to mention prestige.

In addition to the research office, your network of like-minded ethnographers can also be helpful. The elders can alert you to the agencies that have been interested in their work in the past. It is critical to learn the name of a specific staff member at that agency with whom you can correspond. In my four years as a grant reviewer, one of the most important attributes of many successful grant applicants was prior contact with a staff member.

At the National Institute on Drug Abuse (NIDA), for example, there are professional researchers on staff and one of their primary duties is to communicate with interested potential grant applicants. They can react to a concept paper and tell you if the agency is interested or not, and possibly recommend alternatives. They can read a draft of your proposal and critically react to it. Such reactions are invaluable because they know their peer review panel and the kinds of questions they ask. Then, when your grant comes up for discussion during the review, they can give some background information on you as an applicant that will help contextualize the application. It is a tremendous improvement over the cold bureaucratic trail that simply dumps a proposal onto the middle of the table with no background knowledge on the part of the applicant, the reviewers, or the staff.

In some cases, a staff member takes more than just a passing interest in particular kinds of grants. Eleanor Carroll of NIDA, whose recent death represents a great loss to anthropologists, devoted much of her time to encouraging grant applications from ethnographers. She wanted more ethnographies done of U.S. patterns of drug use, to counter stereotypes of drug abusers that underlie policy. She also wanted more cross-cultural research done, to put U.S. patterns of use into a broader perspective.

Eleanor Carroll attended several professional meetings, telling anthropologists about NIDA and encourageing them to submit research grant applications. She was the reason I was appointed to the review panel because she fought for anthropological representation in the new NIDA review group. She helped many anthropologists obtain NIDA funding, although she was not always successful. Her status among anthropological drug researchers is best described as "culture hero."

As you explore the research offices, learn from other ethnographers, and begin writing to agencies, you will notice that certain areas of research are currently "in." Then, if you watch for a few more years, you will see the "fashionable" areas of research change, just as they do in other areas of life. The changes, of course, are no accident. For any number of possible reasons, federal policy assigns a new priority to some areas—drugs, the aged, the Middle East. With a priority designation comes money, and often part of that money is slated for research—a new agency is created or an old agency reorients itself.

By piling gold around certain questions, federal policy tries to encourage researchers to address issues that are currently considered important. Your problem is to decide whether or not addressing issues where money is available represents your genuine interests. The problem is made more acute in a time of a shortage of research funds, a time that is currently ongoing.

My own bias is to have little patience with a stance of "academic purity." To me, such a stance represents naivete about the complex niche we occupy as producers and transmitters of knowledge. If the feds say aging is important, and you agree, and policy is being developed in that area, why in the world shouldn't you modify your research interests? To avoid a research topic because it is fashionable is as suspect as just doing a certain kind of research only because it is fashionable. In both cases, you are a slave to funding fashions.

Usually, you can adapt your interests to funding availability. Say that aging is the current fashion, but you are interested in the topic of social networks, and you want to work in urban South India. So, design a general ethnographic proposal around the idea of social networks among the elderly in Bangalore and see if you can locate some agency support. If you encounter new areas that are currently fashionable, and you share the assumption of the agency that the question is an important one, and the research is ethical (more on that later), then adapt and apply. Ask around about the agency among your colleagues, and contact a staff member for advice before you develop a full proposal. In fact, it is a good idea to travel to the agency to spend a couple of days meeting and talking with representatives. Many universities, for example, recognize the importance of such face-to-face preliminary contacts and provide travel funds for their faculty to make such trips before an application is submitted.

Once you actually wrap up the package (and by the time you are through writing, filling out forms, and Xeroxing it, it will be quite a package, representing a substantial investment of time and money) several things will happen to your proposal. (Again, I will use NIDA as an example because I worked with them, but the process will be similar in other agencies.) Your application is mailed to the Division of Research Grants (DRG) of the Alcohol, Drug Abuse, and Mental Health Administration (ADAMHA). When received, your grant will be "logged in" and assigned to a particular review committee. For this reason, you need to choose carefully when you create the title and the abstract with underlined key words. Such summary information is important in the process whereby grants are assigned.

Let us say the grant is flagged for NIDA research, and then goes into the Psychosocial Branch. At this point, it is given to a staff member in the branch. (I am not sure how the assignment is made—partly it depends on the expertise of the staff member, but that is not the only criterion. Some staff members, for example, were responsible for more grants than others.) Now the staff member assigns the grant to at least two committee reviewers. Again, assignments are made partly because of the professional background of the reviewers, partly because certain staff have "their" reviewers, and probably for other reasons I do not know. One of the reviewers will be "primary," and she will have responsibility for a complete description as well as a critique. The "secondary" reviewer will only be responsible for a critique.

The process occurs three times a year and culminates in a review meeting in Washington, D.C. Before the meeting, each reviewer receives two huge packages. In one are all the grant applications for the upcoming meeting. In the other is the additional background materials for each application to which he has been assigned. The background material is often extensive, including appendices, publications, past grant applications, and final reports. No one can actually read all the applications as thoroughly as they should. Reviewers do carefully review those assigned to them, and try their best to at least read other applications where their professional skills are relevant.

Some applications may be scheduled for "site visits" before the review meeting. At a site visit, the two reviewers and the staff member, and possibly some outside reviewers, travel to the applicant's home base for a meeting that can last anywhere from half a day to two days in the case of an elaborate application. Site visits are made for a number of possible reasons. First, if the grant requests a large amount of money, say $500,000 over a few years, a site visit will be conducted if it looks like the grant may be approved. Sometimes a grant is site-visited if it is on the edge of approval-disapproval, but lies in an area that NIDA is particularly interested in. Finally, site visits may be made to applicants new to research because, although they have an interesting proposal and obvious promise, their lack of experience created problems with the grant application. Finally, the entire committee convenes in Washington, D.C.

Committee membership changes. Each member has a maximum tenure on the committee of 4 years. After that, he or she must sit out a year before again being eligible for committee membership. Most of the members have a history of drug research. They are drawn from sociology, psychology, and psychiatry. Although I was the lone ethnographer for the first 2 years, an ethnographically oriented sociologist joined after that, and there are now two anthropologist-ethnographers on the panel.

As each grant comes up, the staff member gives a short background talk, offering the history of the proposal and their contact with the applicant. Then the primary and secondary reviewers read their descriptions and critiques. The critiques assess not only the research design, but also the budget, staffing patterns, past performance of the proposed staff, the kind of support the home institution is offering, pilot studies that may have been done before the application, and so on. If written reviews from outsiders have been requested by the staff, these are read, and then . . . .

If there is general agreement on the committee that the proposal has so many problems that it cannot be funded, there is often a quick move to disapprove. Anything else usually generates discussion, where members of the committee ask questions and raise issues. Because of the differing biases of committee members, the discussions can be heated. There will be a couple of sample stories later in the book when ethnographic research proposals are discussed further. If you are getting an idea that part of successful grantsmanship is learning something about the committee that is going to review your grant, you are right. And if you think proposal reviews are conducted impersonally using a single set of agreed upon standards of scientific research design, you are only partly right.

Let me give you a hypothetical example of review politics. This case never actually happened, but it represents a possible problem case distilled from my own experience and from that of people I've known on other review panels. A community based group in an urban poverty area wants to compare participants and graduates in two treatment programs. One program is run by the state; the other by a local radical political group. The community group wants to conduct interviews to find out how clients view the cause of their addiction to heroin, how they view the treatment process, and how they are doing after the program. The proposal is laced with terms like *oppression* and *capitalistic society,* and their methodology is based on "informal interviews."

This example is intentionally a difficult one. There are numerous methodological problems here. One requirement of social science methodology, of whatever stripe, is that it have the capability of demonstrating the investigator wrong. Informal interviews can be used, not necessarily with this intent, to support a position that the investigator is already committed to, both by the way the interview is conducted and by the analysis.

My first problem as the primary reviewer is to make a personal decision about my review. I decide that the proposal needs more research sophistication, but that it should be encouraged as something innovative in the tradition of drug research. I have a few options available: (a) Disapprove with communication—tell the applicant "no," but point out the research problems and encourage them to resubmit. I can almost certainly get that from the committee. (b) Defer with a site visit—put off a decision until the reviewers and staff can visit the group, and then reconsider the proposal at the next meeting. To get that, the committee must believe that the research is important, and that a personal visit will impress upon the applicant the critical need for more research sophistication, with some advice perhaps on how to obtain it from local resources. (c) Defer without a site visit—defer the proposal until the next meeting, and send a written list of questions to the applicant for his or her response. I do not think this will work, however, because the proposal already displays a lack of the very research sophistication that would be necessary to decode the questions and prepare a reply. (d) Approve with reduced time and/or money with communication—give them some money and some time to do a small pilot study and involve more researchers, and send it with a message indicating the problems with the application. This is not a bad alternative, but it leaves them adrift in the research area. If they have demonstrated good potential research contacts, though, it might be a good choice.

(e) Approve in time and amount with communication—give them the grant, and send a message telling them what the problems in the grant are. This probably will not happen, and I don't think it should.

To understand why this will not happen, I need to explain priority scores. Each reviewer has a vote—approve, defer, or disapprove, with or without communication. This vote is publicly made by a show of hands. However, each reviewer also has a priority vote that is written on his or her voting sheet, and this is private. Priorities range from 1 to 5, with 1 the highest. When funding time comes, grants are awarded according to their priorities. An approved grant with an average priority of 1.5 will almost certainly be funded; a grant with an average of 4.5 almost certainly will not. So, if approval is my goal for this grant, I have to "read" the committee and calculate from their reactions what sort of priority they will give it.

A second consideration is time. An advantage of the deferral over the disapproval is that the grant automatically is scheduled for the next meeting, roughly four months later. If the grant is disapproved, the applicant must prepare a new application and resubmit it over again. Practically, this means that it will probably not be considered until two meetings later—8 months hence, roughly.

Weighing all this, I decide to try for approval of a pilot grant if it looks like the priority vote will be adequate, or deferral with a site visit if the priority does not look good. Now, because of the political bias and methodological problems with the proposal, I know that several of the committee will be critical. In my view, they will be justified in the case of the methodology, but unjustified in the case of the politics. Many of them, my reasoning goes, would gladly support proposals whose political tone supported mainstream U.S. drug policies.

Hopefully, the other reviewer will be sympathetic. I check the assignment sheet and know that she is. That resolves one problem. Now I pick two or three of the other reviewers whom I know will be antagonistic. The proposal is scheduled for the first day, and I know that first day reviews are always longer and more elaborate, because no one feels the time pressure. So I could ask that it be postponed until later. I make a point of having lunch or an evening beer with the primary antagonists. I introduce the proposal as a topic, listen to their complaints, and try to reinforce some of the strong points and the social significance of the application. And that is about all I can do.

Comes the review, I will argue for my most favorable recommendation—approval in reduced time and amount in this case. Deferral with site visit will be my alternative position. There will be much discussion, and it will unfold in unpredictable ways as we argue over the construction of a context with which to evaluate the proposal. You win some you lose some.

I should note that seldom are proposals this much of a problem, and seldom do they involve the political manipulations that I decribed here. I should also say that, by and large, I was impressed with my colleagues on the review panel, with an exception or two, naturally. They were, for the most part, intelligent, honest, and fair people. Although the procedure is hardly perfect, good research is usually approved and bad research is not. Besides, the drug field is an area subject to particularly strong political currents.

However, political biases and professional background do make a difference, and if your application is on the edge of mainstream social science, you may have problems. Ethnographic applications to review committees dominated by nonethnographers usually fall into this marginal status. In such cases, a little help from sympathetic members of the committee can't hurt. And it is only fair, as an outsider to the process, for an applicant to know that.

Let us say that you apply and are approved with a good priority score. At NIDA, the rest of the process is *almost* automatic. NIDA, like other agencies, has a council with "community representatives." I am not sure how these representatives are chosen, but the NIDA council seemed like a diverse one, with different ranges of experience in drug research and treatment. The council reviews the actions of the committees and gives their own approval or disapproval, but seldom do they reverse the action of the committees.

After the council reviews the grant, assuming they also approve, it enters the machine for funding. It will take some time for the grant to be awarded, depending on the availability of money and the backlog. There is also, along the way, another opportunity for refusal. The staff of an agency has the final say in funding, depending on "program needs." If the staff feels that a proposal represents an investigation that is not in an area relevant to current program goals, they can administratively hold it up in favor of other grants that more effectively address those goals.

In my experience at NIDA, grants approved by the Psychosocial Committee were turned back in only three cases. In all three, I was the primary reviewer. The common denominator was a focus on drug research in non-U.S. areas. They dealt with patterns of traditional use of psychotropic substances in the sorts of nonindustrialized small communities that anthropologists usually study. The primary reason given for the failure to fund was the lack of relevance to program goals.

I'm still not sure what happened. On the one hand, NIDA sponsored contracts for some pioneering work on the use of cannabis in Jamaica and Costa Rica. Through grants they funded studies on topics like kava in the South Pacific, *qat* in Yemen, and coca in Peru. However, under the pressure of congressional critics, especially Senator William Proxmire's "golden fleece" awards, NIDA had become sensitive to funding additional cross-cultural research. Since one of the cross-cultural studies had won NIDA some fleece, and since they did not see such work as immediately relevant to the U.S. drug problem, cross-cultural research dropped low on the list of program priorities.

Internal agency problems like this can cause headaches for researchers, and not just at NIDA. In her book, *Doing Fieldwork,* Rosalie Wax described a site visit where the reviewers were given a copy of an application that she and her husband had submitted previously, rather than the application currently under consideration. Imagine the awkwardness of that situation until someone figured out the mistake. One of the applicants to NIDA for cross-cultural research got "on-again, off-again" messages that eventually inconvenienced, embarrassed, and embittered him. Again, the importance of staff contacts becomes apparent—you, the applicant, need some people on the inside who can keep you posted on internal agency events that may affect the fate of your application.

Hopefully this brief sketch will give you some sense of the process of getting funds. NIDA is only one agency, and its procedures will be idiosyncratic to some extent.[7] But the moral of this story is simply to encourage you to do some research before you submit an application.

This is not the last you will hear of research grants. In Chapter 8, there is another section on research grant design. There we will take a hard look at the actual sections of a standard research design and delve into the way that those sections are evaluated. For example, there is a section on the protection of human subjects that is independently submitted and reviewed, and that has not even been hinted at yet.

Finally, there are other ways that research is supported other than research grants. There are contracts, for example, that specify a particular task that the agency wants accomplished. When you are interested in contracts, you check the agency's Requests for Proposals and design a document that essentially is a bid for the contract. Other ethnographers are automatically supported because they are hired as part of a research staff or a private social science research firm. In their roles, they may still apply for grants or bid for contracts, but they may also do research automatically as part of their positions.

Let us move on to worry more about what happens when one actually

---

[7] Things do change in the review process. For example, under the Freedom of Information Act, applicants can now learn more quickly if their proposal was approved or disapproved in peer review. The likelihood of a site visit has declined with decreasing budgets. Staff roles changed over the years I was on the committee—on the one hand, they did not want to influence the peer review; on the other hand, both NIDA and the reviewers wanted them to give some background on the applicant. This discussion is only one of a number of possible forms the review process can take. You have to do your homework for each funding agency you deal with.

enters the field. Sometimes it takes a while to actually enter the field. There are items of folklore about ethnographers who spend the first few months in the field hiding in a hotel room and reading everything Agatha Christie ever wrote. Other stories tell of ethnographers who decide to do "language training," spending a lot of time at it as a way of doing something useful without actually talking to anyone. But with or without delays, finally one actually approaches the group, and the first problem is telling them, and knowing, who you are.

3

Who Are You To Do This?

Ethnography is really quite an arrogant enterprise. In a short period of time, an ethnographer moves in among a group of strangers to study and describe their beliefs, document their social life, write about their subsistence strategies, and generally explore the territory right down to their recipes for the evening meal. The task is an impossible one. At best, an ethnography can only be partial.

To some extent, the area covered depends on the ethnographer. On entering the community, an ethnographer carries more baggage than a tape recorder and a toothbrush, having grown up in a particular culture, acquiring many of its sometimes implicit assumptions about the nature of reality. And within that framework, he or she developed personal idiosyncrasies, and later went through some professional training, learning a set of biases about which areas of the human situation were worthy of attention.

As if that were not bad enough, a social category will be assigned to the ethnographer by the group members. The category may change over time, but one will always exist. As the ethnographer's role is defined and redefined, it will guide group members in their dealings with him or her. Their expectations of what the ethnographer wants to learn—and their decisions about what should be told—will derive partly from their sense of who he or she is.

These aspects of "who you are" deserve some careful thought. They raise problems for ethnographers, and for all social scientists. Even at this early stage, they show that ethnography is much more complicated than collecting data, and that "objectivity" is perhaps best seen as a label to hide problems in the social sciences. The problem is not whether the ethnographer is biased; the problem is what kinds of biases exist—how do they enter into ethnographic work and how can their operation be documented. By bringing as many of them to consciousness as possible, an ethnographer can try to deal with them as part of methodology and can acknowledge them when drawing conclusions during analysis. In this sense, ethnography truly is a personal discipline as well as a professional one.

Personality and Cultural Background

Before psychoanalysts are considered competent to analyze others, they must first go through analysis themselves. If they do not understand their own personalities, the argument goes, they will not be able to understand others. A statement made about a patient could be more a function of the interpretation of the analyst rather than anything the patient expressed. By going through analysis, the analyst can hopefully bring some personal background to consciousness and better control the interpretation of the patient.

Ethnographers, on the other hand, are allowed to go into a situation with no awareness of the biases they bring to it from their own cultures and personalities. This simply does not make good sense, but I am not sure how to correct it. For one thing, what constitutes the ethnographer's "culture"? In the case of an American ethnographer, he or she comes from a diverse society. What is "American culture" anyway, and what relationship does it have to all the different subcultures in U.S. society? Then consider a quotation attributed to Clyde Kluckhohn, that "Each man is like all other men, some other men, and no other man." How do we disentangle the many parts and hand the ethnographer–student some information that says "Here are your cultural biases; for the rest of it, go see a shrink."[1]

[1] There are several comments on the psychoanalysis of ethnographers. Devereaux (1967) and Sullivan (1937) argue strongly that the psychodynamics of the ethnographer are critical in understanding the research both as a process and as a product. There is a saying that I have heard that "all social science is autobiographical." After reading Devereaux, I realize how much truth there is in that statement. He shows how in some ways methodology is a response to the particular anxiety that the research situation elicits in the researcher. Blau (1964) offers a case study to illustrate his argument. Among others, Campbell (1961), Nadel (1953), Langness (1965), and Bell (1955) all call for the psychoanalysis of ethnographers. Powdermaker (1966) notes that her understanding of fieldwork changed for the better as a consequence of her personal analysis. Lewis (1953) notes that two ethnographers personally communicated to him that their fieldwork improved after analysis. On the other hand, Herskovits (1954) states that a comparison of work by students who have had analysis and those who haven't shows no differences. And Pelto and Pelto (1973), in their analysis of 51 questionnaire responses from anthropologists, note that the presence or absence of experience with psychoanalysis seems to make no significant difference in the experience of "moderate or severe" psychological distur-

Yet the problem is important. How many times have you heard a person describing someone else, and had the feeling that by substituting "I" for all the "he's" and "she's" in the description, the person would be talking about himself? As an exercise, read some ethnographies and try to analyze what the statements say about the ethnographer rather than the group under discussion. You will have to guess. Important as that information is, seldom do you learn anything about it in the text.

One folk theory in anthropology to explain the differences between Lewis's and Redfield's work has to do with the differences between the two ethnographers. Redfield, so the story goes, romanticized rural peasant life. It was closer to a "natural state" than modern urban life. Therefore, his description of village life, especially when contrasted with urban life, emphasized the more harmonious aspects. Lewis, on the other hand, had a personal view of the world that allowed for, if it did not emphasize, the darker side of life. When he went to the same village, things like hostility, greed, and jealousy were stressed.

This concern with the personality and cultural background of the ethnographer becomes even more critical when you consider that the ethnographer's background is the initial framework against which similarities and differences in the studied group are assessed.[2] Appropriate to Lewis and Redfield, one article argues that the ethnographer's attitude toward his or her own culture conditions the evaluative tone of the description of the studied group. The article suggests that the less the ethnographer likes his or her own culture, the more favorably the alternatives may be viewed.[3] Redfield, living and working in the Chicago area, might have gone into rural Mexico with the idea that "his" culture—urban America—represented a deterioration of the human condition.

The importance of the ethnographer's background is also emphasized in some of the discussions of ethnographers working among their own people. Now the ethnographer's framework is not as different from those of the group members, and the similarities and differences are not as striking as they might be. For example, Joan Ablon, working with middle-class Americans, also

---

bance during fieldwork. The results are obviously sketchy and inconclusive at this point. While I have never been psychoanalyzed, I have worked around practitioners since I began doing drug research. I agree with the discussions in the literature that an ethnographer has much to learn about the notions of "transference" and "countertransference." And Devereaux's book is a good dose of reality therapy for anyone who believes that one human dealing with another is similar to a physicist studying photographic plates from a cloud chamber.

[2] For sample statements about measurement against one's own cultural background, see Den Hollander (1967) and Wolff (1945).

[3] Braroe and Hicks (1967).

stresses the problem of the ethnographer's attitude toward her "own" culture, and also mentions related problems, like the difficulty in judging significant behavior and her own vulnerability as a member of the same society.[4]

Another kind of discussion also emphasizes the importance of the culture–personality background of the ethnographer. In Chapter 1, the argument about whether insiders or outsiders should study a group was mentioned. In increasing numbers, the "natives" are becoming ethnographers and reviewing the past work of their American and European colleagues. There is a recently formed association of third-world anthropologists that is posing some basic questions about anthropological culture, grounded as it is in Euro–American society.

For example, an African anthropologist recently published a discussion of some previous ethnographic research. His article had the rather unflattering subtitle of "the usefulness of the useless." He argued that some of the classic studies displayed fundamental misunderstandings of the group under study by the ethnographer. Among other reasons for this, he mentioned the colonial context, the loose methodology, and the tendency to rely on a few key informants. But the mainstay of his critique is the inability of the ethnographer to understand and communicate in the vernacular. Because of all these various background factors, the descriptions of African society reviewed are, at best, oversimplifications, and at worst, flat wrong.[5]

After reading all this material, I get the dizzy feeling that an ethnographer (or any social science researcher) is like a drunk pretending to walk a straight line in a dark room with a gale-force wind blowing though it. It's clear that the ethnographer's culture–personality background, though increasingly acknowledged as critical, is a great unknown in ethnographic research. To make things worse, it's not clear how to integrate it into discussions of ethnographic methodology.

Let me give a couple of examples from my own research. Eye contact is something that varies from group to group. There are times when you look people in the eye and times when you do not. I did not know that when I went to South India. I was not aware that that particular area of behavior was culturally variable, and that my rules were only one set of a number of possibilities.

When I arrived in South India, I was horrified. Gopalpur is in an area that was formerly administered as part of the princely state of Hyderabad. The

---

[4] Ablon (1977). For examples of similar discussions, see Colfax (1966) and Cassell (1977).

[5] Owusu (1978). For an earlier critique of African studies involving the cultural background of the ethnographer, see Maquet (1964).

ruler, called the *Nizam,* signed a treaty with the British, and they, by and large, left internal affairs to him. Unlike other areas of India, then, the villagers were not used to the presence of Caucasians. A young Caucasian, running around in a *dhoti* and *chappli,* [6] without the expected ornaments of a wristwatch and a row of fountain pens, was indeed an unusual sight. Of course, I did not know that; I thought I was "acting normal."

The villager's reaction was a friendly curiosity, so they would come up and stand a few feet away. Then they would clasp their hands together behind their backs, lean slightly forward, and stare. In time I would become annoyed at such obvious rudeness and say, *"eenappa?"* ('What do you want?'). They would change posture, look a bit startled at such an irrelevant question, and say, *"eenilla"* ('Nothing at all'), and then sometimes resume staring.

My rules said such eye contact was rude in the extreme. It was so unsettling in the early days of fieldwork that sometimes I would hide and read or write rather than go out and deal with it . When I did go out, I would try to ignore it, but it usually made me impossibly self-conscious. While struggling to look controlled externally, my mind would be screaming, "Quit the staring. If you want something, what is it? Go away." Actually, my mind was screaming things much more colorful than that.

It took some time to get over the noise introduced by that small piece of my cultural baggage, and that is only one example. Similar problems occurred in New York, my "own" culture. For example, consider the simple area of question-asking. The way I grew up, there were certain things one did not ask questions about, things that were defined as "personal." But there were a great many things you did ask questions about. In fact, you were *supposed* to ask questions—it showed you were "interested" in the other person, and a well-phrased question showed your "intelligence."

For the ethnographer, question-asking is vital. In fact, as we will see later, ethnographic question-asking is a special blend of art and science with a variety of subspecies. As you begin to learn from a group, you need questions—both to add to your knowledge and to check things that you think you understand. Ethnography without questions would be impossible.

In the streets, though, I learned that you don't ask questions. There are at least two reasons for that rule. One is because a person is vulnerable to arrest by the police, or to being cheated or robbed by other street people. Questions about behavior may be asked to find out when you are vulnerable to arrest. Or they may be asked to find out when or in what way you can be

---

[6] *Chappli* are the sandals that villagers wear, while a *dhoti* is several yards of cloth that men wrap in different styles to cover their lower body.

parted from some money or heroin. Even if one sees no direct connection between the question and those outcomes, it might just be because one has not figured out the questioner's "game" yet.

The second reason for not asking questions is that you should not have to ask. To be accepted in the streets is to be hip; to be hip is to be knowledge-able; to be knowledgeable is to be capable of understanding what is going on on the basis of minimal cues. So to ask a question is to show that you are not acceptable, and this creates problems in a relationship when you have just been introduced to somebody.

No wonder people were hestitant to talk with me, or I should say to answer my questions about what was going on. I had to learn to avoid questions initially, to allow people to watch my behavior for a while. Then I had to carefully explain why I was about to start asking questions. Often I would introduce a question by saying something like, "I know this is a dumb question, but . . .," or "I don't know whether or not it's cool to ask this, but . . .". As people came to accept my role as a curious straight and decided I was not a cop, the problem lessened. Also, as time went on, I could behave knowledgeably, in some areas at least. If I "layed back" first, and then asked questions, it also reduced the problem.

That was another small example of interference from my own cultural background. These two areas—eye contact and question-asking—are be-haviorally minor but powerful in their effects on the relationship between ethnographer and informant. Your own culture does not only influence you at this level, it can also guide your interest toward different topics at the expense of others.

As one example, there is a proliferation of ethnographic studies of women's roles in different societies, and an interest in women's speech in linguistics and its hyphenated relatives. The emergence of this new interest is clearly part of a larger change in American culture, or at least the part of it that self-consciously talks of traditional women's roles in U.S. society and the need to change them.[7] Another example would be drug research. Until not so long ago, ethnographic studies of drug use (excluding alcohol) were almost nonexistent. Now there are a growing number of studies in this area, covering a variety of psychoactive substances in a number of cultural settings.

When I went to South India in 1965, I had never had any personal experience with marijuana. While I was working in the *tanda* ('village') with the Lambardi, they had a ceremony at the nearby Hanuman temple. The

[7] Golde (1970) has collected a series of personal accounts of female ethnographers. In her introduction, she suggests that women in the field have different problems than men. For example, they may be more concerned with protection, less subject to suspicion, and more pressured into conforming within the group studied.

temple was only a remnant of a building that stood in an abandoned village, but the Lambardi used it to make offerings to Hanuman for the continued fertility of the women. The entire *tanda* walked to the temple behind the priest who had come especially for the ceremony, with everyone singing religious songs to Hanuman. As I was moving around trying to watch everything that happened, someone handed me a clay pot full of liquid. It tasted sweet, though it had things floating in it. The clay pot came around more times, and I drank from it each time.

A short time later, I stopped trying to watch everything. I found myself caught up in the music and singing and the smells of the burning incense. The red and yellow decorative powder took on a deeper color, and I stared at the image of Hanuman. I remember this very well because I began wondering if I had gone too far into the culture. As a committed agnostic at the time, the feelings I had made me wonder if I was being converted.

I was stoned. Only after returning to the U.S. did I learn about *bhang* and its use on ceremonial occasions. It did not occur to me to make a connection between the drink and my involvement in the ceremony. I think I attributed it to the hypnotic effect of the music. That may sound naive in retrospect, especially to younger readers of this book, but I'll tell you one that is even worse.

In Gopalpur, sometimes a group of village men would gather for a *bhajani*. One man would play a single string instrument made of a gourd and a bamboo stick, while others would play finger cymbals. The songs were religious in nature. At times, I would notice that one of the men would pack a short, cone-shaped pipe and light it, and then pass it around. There was nothing unusual in this since that is the way men usually smoked tobacco, though they did not often pass it around. I think I remember thinking something like, "Isn't that nice. They're short on tobacco, so they're sharing it."

I didn't get that one straightened out until many years later, when I became a "drug researcher." In conversations with Alan Beals, he reminded me of the marijuana smoking at the *bhajanis*. I had that feeling you get when the elevator stops too fast—I had missed an important part of a common village ceremony. The reason, of course, is related to the lack of ethnographic studies on drugs. Drug use, again excepting alcohol (*our* drug), was not something to pay attention to. I had no background knowledge to lead me to isolate it as a significant topic. I did not know enough to begin asking questions about it, or to make "marijuana use" the basis of interpreting the behavior I was observing. Now, of course, if I saw some Indian villagers smoking something during a religious songfest, I would wonder if it was marijuana. But then things have changed in my culture since 1965.

In addition to your personal and cultural biases, you also have been "programmed" with some powerful professional ones. What have you been taught to look for? Mother's brother and sister's son? Expended calories? Nature versus culture? Or a voluntary association? Have you been told to hang around and keep notes? Conduct a survey? Or ask people to sort things? It is quite likely you have been through a funnel, coming out at the narrow end as you finished your graduate training.

To some extent, the narrowing is impossible to avoid. First of all, there is an obvious information explosion going on. Just recently I received notices of two new journals that I should read, and heard of another by word of mouth. We are getting to the point where you will not pick journals to subscribe to. Instead, you will pick the several library search services that you want to use.

Second, the old disciplinary boundaries are crumbling—except as they survive, and will for centuries, I am sure—as established bureaucratic divisions within the university. Who has time for anthropology journals when there are all those things one should know about in the journals of other disciplines? The increased information flow is approaching overdose proportions. As one professor (with tenure) was heard to say, "Stop publishing or we will all perish."

However it is explained, the narrowing of one's focus will obviously be carried into the field. I can't tell you much about the economic behavior of the Lambardi. I know a bit about sources of cash, the role of reciprocity, and the kinds of crops they grow, but that is all. At that time, I had no training—and no particular interest—in economic anthropology. Professional training further widens the blinders of bias.[8]

This discussion circles around a general point. Whether it is your personality, your rules of social interaction, your cultural bias toward significant topics, your professional training, or something else, you do not go into the field as a passive recorder of objective data. During fieldwork, you are surrounded by a multitude of noises and activities. As you choose what to attend to and how to interpret it, mental doors slam shut on the alternatives. While some of your choices may be consciously made, others are forced by the weight of the personal and professional background that you bring to the field.

First of all, this background is another good reason to worry about methodology. Methodology will not help if you do not know to ask the

---

[8] Den Hollander (1967) argues that as a consequence of professional training, ethnographers tend to overrate the influences of beliefs on behavior, to overemphasize homogeneity, to overdo order and coherence and underplay exceptions and contradiction, and to emphasize structure at the cost of process.

question. But if you do document your learning with some procedure that publicly displays some of the experiences you had that led to the conclusion, and that potentially might have *falsified* that conclusion, you can at least show that your bias was supported by something somebody did or said.

A second strategy, as hinted at earlier, is contained in the idea of a discipline. Think about what you are doing. Force yourself to look at the same material in a completely different way. Use Descartes's method of systematic doubt and reduce yourself to basic premises. As you gain more experience, you will become conscious of more and more of your biases. As you bring at least some of them into awareness, you can describe them to others, show how they guided the kind of work you did, and suggest alternatives that might emerge if the ethnography had been done with another set of biases.

A third possibility is to have bias-awareness programmed into ethnographic training. In my field methods class, we do an exercise where students ask someone to describe a physical setting. Then they go to that setting and do their own description. They usually come back with a different description, so they go back to the informant and explore the reasons for the differences. Sometimes the differences are trivial, but it makes the point. Different personal biases lead to different descriptions. Perhaps a more sophisticated series of exercises could be assembled to refine the consciousness of professional ethnographers.

Yet another possibility would be to borrow the analyst's training model and require someone to study the ethnographer before he or she studies anybody else. At a minimum, an elaborate life history interview could be done with the prospective ethnographer. The material could be analyzed by anthropologists of both cultural and clinical persuasions. The results might then be fed back to the trainee. Besides, it would be good for the ethnographer to experience the role of informant.

A final strategy is to use more than one ethnographer. If several people examine a similar area, the differences in their biases will generate contradictions in their reports. Contradictions, rather than being viewed as threatening, should be seen as the beginning of a better question, a signpost pointing to a more sensitive understanding. Too many potentially rich contradictions get lost in the politeness rules of academic rhetoric.

Some of your biases will be jolted into awareness; some will only slowly emerge; and some will always lurk unrecognized in dark corners. Fieldwork presupposes an interpretive framework; and an interpretive framework cuts into the world like a jigsaw, leaving much of the wood behind. On the other hand, maybe some frameworks slice more "naturally" than others. That raises an interesting, and hopeful, idea that will be explored in detail in Chapter 9. But while you work on ways to climb out of this hole in the sand, treat yourself to a little self-indulgent arrogance. Some social scientists think that objectivity is an accomplished goal.

Ethnography and Personality

Besides the background of personal experience discussed so far, there is an elusive "something else" relevant to the makeup of the ethnographer. This "something else" has to do with those features of one's personality that are particularly adapted to ethnographic tasks. This is something different from, yet related to, the background experiences you acquire as a member of a particular society. In fact, certain aspects of personality may be human universals. I mention this because the aspects of the ethnographer I want to discuss are probably things that vary within any group. While they are certainly not totally independent of society and culture, some aspects are probably found in them all. There may be something here to help you identify the best key informants and field assistants.

One of the things ethnographers must deal with is "culture shock." The shock comes from the sudden immersion in the lifeways of a group different from yourself. Suddenly you do not know the rules anymore. You do not know how to interpret the stream of motions and noises that surround you. You have no idea what is expected of you. Many of the assumptions that form the bedrock of your existence are mercilessly ripped out from under you. The more you cling to them, the less you will understand about the people with whom you work.

One of the more interesting discussions of an ethnographer's adaptation to culture shock is an article by Dennison Nash. One way to understand ethnographic research, he argues, is to understand how the ethnographer adapts to the stranger role. As a stranger, he is cut loose from his former significant others. He has a strong sense of increased possibilities, and is overwhelmed by perceptual chaos.

One response to this situation is *authoritarian closure*—when central premises of existence are strongly asserted and contradictory information from the new situation is denied. Like-minded strangers might establish "enclaves" for mutual protection. But another type of response is what Nash calls "autonomous man," one with a high tolerance for ambiguity and uncertainty. He thinks that ethnographers are of this second type.

Nash, like others in the literature, uses the phrase "detached involvement" to characterize the successful ethnographic role. One is, at the same time, part of and distant from the community. One struggles to understand with involvement in the society; at the same time, one stands back critically to examine what one has learned. However, this detached involvement—this stepping into and out of society—is a strain in its own right.[9]

There are two obvious ways to lessen the strain. Either keep your distance or "go native." You keep your distance at the risk of failing to understand the complexities of a human situation different from your own. You go native, but then stop functioning as a social scientist. Actually, real ethnography represents some of both these strategies as the ethnographer moves around the goal of detached involvement.

Recently, the diary of Bronislaw Malinowski was published. During World War I, he was interred on the Trobriand Islands. While he was there, he did some ethnographic research, subsequently published in several volumes, that is still considered an admirable piece of work. But when his diary came out, many were shocked. In it, he sometimes called the Trobrianders "niggers," and made other comments that were cruel and hostile as well.

How could this be reconciled with the sensitive Malinowski who talked of the magic moment when, just for a few seconds, you saw the world like the natives? I think he was "distancing"—taking a psychic vacation from the intense involvement of living like a Trobriander. He sometimes dipped a bit heavily into the involvement side, and balanced the scale with some detachment. Some ethnographers I have talked with, like me, were not surprised by the contents of his diary.[10]

Once, in the *tanda,* I looked up and saw a villager approaching me. This occurred at a time when I felt particularly unhappy with my work and particularly distant from the Lambardi. I smiled and said (in English) something insulting. At that moment, I hated the Lambardi, hated the *tanda,* hated India, and wanted nothing more than to be on a vinyl seat in a neon-lit, air-conditioned coffee shop eating a hamburger. I could tell similar stories

[9] See Nash (1963). Meintel (1973) also discusses culture shock, characterizing it as a form of self-discovery that should be sought out rather than treated as a problem. She also stresses the "shock" of returning, as does Williams (1967). Andersen (1971) analyzed some of the dreams of American academics travelling in India. She outlines a change in dream content from an initial retreat to earlier life events, followed by the establishment of a "secondary identity" that allows dreams with mixed, but clearly distinct, American and Indian elements. Many others discuss the notion of detached involvement, including Jones (1973), Powdermaker (1966), Freilich (1970a,b), and Pelto and Pelto (1973). The "stepping into and out of society" phrase is taken from Powdermaker's book.

[10] Malinowski's diary is listed in the References. There is an interesting exchange on the diaries between Geertz (1967) and Powdermaker (1967) in the *New York Review of Books.* Geertz, in his review of the diary, concludes that Malinowski was distant and aloof during his field work. Powdermaker's reply was to balance this conclusion by noting that Malinowski stressed participant observation and understanding the native point of view. As his former student, she remembered that he called everybody names, and she wonders about the translated "nigger" from a diary written in Polish.

about my work with heroin addicts. It was a "harmless outlet" for the personal strain of the moment. I would hate to have my entire field experience judged by that bit of behavior, especially when compared to other moments of warmth and intimacy. Detached involvement is a winding path.

You might think that doing ethnography in one's own society would be less stressful. I find it more so. During World War II, an anthropologist was asked to find out why fighter pilots had more mental health problems than the infantry. He noticed that fighter pilots sit around the officer's club with a drink, then suddenly run to their planes and find themselves in combat. After they land, they are back in the comfortable officer's club.

The infantry, on the other hand, rested for a period of time in a noncombat area. Then they slowly geared up and marched into combat. They remained there for some time, then slowly marched back for more rest and recuperation. So, thought the anthropologist, the dramatic changes for the fighter pilot were probably more stressful; hence, a higher incidence of problems.

In ethnography of the traditional sort, there is a period of travel and adjustment of the field setting, followed by a long period of time in residence. After the fieldwork is over, one travels home and readjusts to the home culture. When you work in your own society, you cross the line between the field and home often and rapidly. While this does have some advantages, it can also produce "fighter pilot" stress.

One day in New York I had a particularly good few hours in the field. By that time, I knew several people in a particular neighborhood in the Lower East Side. My competence in "street talk" had returned. It was a pleasant fall afternoon and evening. I sat on a stoop to drink a can of beer and talk, went into the corner store and exchange friendly insults with the proprietor, and spent some time talking with youth in the local court-referral program.

Later in the evening, I had a dinner engagement with a friend on the Upper East Side. During the short subway ride, I thought continuously about the warm experiences I had just had. When I surfaced near the restaurant, I was jolted by the differences. The differences between the two neighborhoods is best explained in terms of money, with all that that implies. I walked into the restaurant, and it and the people in it were a mid 1970s self-conscious imitation of someone's idea of the 1960s. As I greeted my friend and looked around, the scenes seemed to shift like the jumping frames of an old silent movie. I had to leave and regroup for a couple of minutes before I could sit down and talk comfortably.

Changes were seldom that dramatic, but once in a while they were. Sometimes jumping that boundary once or twice a day is a bit much. While working in your own society, you still have the stress of detached involvement, compounded by the substitution of frequent repeated minidoses of culture shock in place of the one huge jolt that you usually get in more traditional forms of fieldwork.[11]

An ability to handle this kind of stress is obviously a desirable one for an ethnographer to have. Without it, anthropologists are going to view ethnography as something they are forced to do to get their union card. They will keep their distance or hide in enclaves to avoid culture shock. Then, after going through some kind of minimal adjustment, they will remain well on the detachment side of detached involvement. The folklore has it that this sometimes happens. Such people should not be forced to do ethnography. There is plenty of room, and much need for nonethnographic anthropologists.

There are other aspects of personality that are no doubt adaptive for ethnographers as well. John Price speculates that ethnographers are not "men of action"; rather, they tend to be shy and nongregarious. The Peltos think fieldworkers are flexible, humble, and sensitive, with an ability to meet on the basis of face-to-face human universals. Wax says the most important attributes of an ethnographer are luck and *manvit,* a term meaning "intelligence manifest in common sense, shrewdness, and flexibility." She also notes the importance of the ability to appear the fool. Powdermaker writes that the fieldworker should be outgoing, should like himself, expect others to like him, and be able to communicate easily and directly. In addition, the fieldworker should have an ability to be psychologically mobile among different social categories and be able to handle tension.[12]

That's quite a list, and its only a sample. Further, the authors always carefully qualify their list of attributes, noting that they are just speculating on personality features of ethnographers. As I review the list, and think of my own experiences, some things do clearly appear to me as critical. The ability to tolerate uncertainty is one example. Uncertainty creates anxiety. Yet in field work especially in the beginning, one does not know how to interpret or react to much of what is going on around him. This particular aspect of culture shock is unsettling, to say the least, but to learn a new way of viewing the world you have to rebuild from the gound up.

Another desirable personality feature might be a willingness to make mistakes. I suppose that this is really a tolerance for uncertainty with a personal cost attached. Ethnographers must take new bits and pieces of knowledge and test their understanding of them using their own behaviors. If they err, people will

[11] My experience is contradicted by Pelto and Pelto (1973) who note that less tension was reported by those who worked in North America, including those who worked with American Indians. Perhaps those reports are from ethnographers who entered situations different from "home" and stayed there until work was finished. My description is based on a field situation where the line between fieldwork and life is blurry and traversed frequently.

[12] See Price (1973), Pelto and Pelto (1973), Wax (1971), and Powdermaker (1966).

react with concern, sympathy, embarrassment, or laughter, but the message will be clear. Mistake-making is an important method in informal ethnography, but you must be able to handle the potential threat to your self-esteem.

Pity the poor ethnographer. And we haven't even considered some of the other sources of strain. For example, some note the professional importance of fieldwork. There's a lot of professional reputation riding on these efforts, and the inevitable mistakes can shatter an emergent professional identity. Some discussions of the ethnographic role conclude that there are few set rules. In my opinion, that's a realistic conclusion, but it only adds to the uncertainty. Then ethnographers must often conduct themselves with several reference groups simultaneously in mind—their own society, their study society, and their professional society—and the demands are not always consistent. [13]

At this point, we might review the entire psychological literature and speculate on which parts apply to the practice of ethnography. In fact, much of social science applies to social scientists, something that is not discussed nearly enough in the literature. It would be an interesting exercise to assemble a portrait of the perfectly adapted ethnographic personality (or personalities), and perhaps someday someone will.

Of course, no one person would match it. As I think of a particular individual who is one of the best ethnographers I have ever known or read about, even he is not immune to culture shock or the problems of overdistancing, and even he sometimes suffers the anxieties of uncertainty and the mortification of the unaware fool suddenly exposed. [14] No one is immune, but some are, or become, more adapted to the task than others.

Presentation of Self

When you begin doing ethnography, group members are going to wonder who you are. They will listen to you and watch your behavior, and they will draw on their own repertoire of social categories to find one that fits you. At

---

[13] Just as examples, Wintrob (1969) discusses the professional importance of fieldwork as a source of strain. Cohen et al. (1970), introducing four accounts of entering the field, note that there are no hard and fast rules. And Kloos (1969) discusses the role conflicts of the fieldworker.

[14] The Peltos (1973), after analyzing their 51 questionnaire respondents, reported that about half reported at least "moderate" psychological disturbance. Presence of spouse, prior fieldwork experience, and psychoanalysis seemed to make no difference in presence or absence of stress. Of the 51, they classed 19 as quantifiers, 19 as mixed, and 13 as nonquantifiers. They then noted that field research training was related to a reduction in stress among the nonquantifiers only. Quantifiers, they reported, often reported more tensions.

the beginning, you will offer some explanation of what your interests are and what it is you intend to do. This initial presentation of self leads us right into the issue of research ethics.

Until recently, there was not much of a formal statement of ethics for social science research. Then several things happened. Within anthropology, a scandal erupted at the 1970 meetings of the American Anthropological Association.[15] Some anthropologists were accused of doing "counterinsurgency" research in Thailand on the basis of records stolen from an anthropology professor's office. The business meeting, usually sparsely attended, was mobbed and continued for two nights. There was much heated discussion, followed by committees, investigations, and reports.

In my opinion, there were no heroes. I am still not sure exactly what happened in Thailand, though some individuals did collect information potentially harmful to their informants. At any rate, partly as a result of this event, the association adopted a more elaborate statement of professional ethics and formed a committee to hear complaints of unethical behavior on the part of its members.

At about the same time, the federal government began worrying about the rights of people who served as subjects in research projects. Their concern was also motivated partly by other events, like the scandal of using prisoners in high-risk medical experiments. From this came some guidelines for the protection of human subjects. Evaluating how well protected research subjects are now constitutes a separate part of the grant-reviewing process.

For these reasons, explaining who you are is more than a local methodological problem. It is an act for which you are held accountable by your profession and your funding source. There are many implications for ethnographers in the code of ethics and the guidelines. For now, the implication that concerns us is that people must be informed of your role—who are you and what do you want.

I would think that most ethnographers have always done this anyway. But there are different ways of explaining your role. For example, if you say, "I am an anthropologist and I am here to study your culture," the description, though technically correct, may not be very informative, especially for a group who has no idea of what "anthropology" and "culture" are all about.

On the other hand, suppose you say, "I'm here to write a book about you folks." Though devoid of references to social science, the statement may be more informative for some groups. It implies that you are going to explore

---

[15] Prior to this event, the Project Camelot disaster had occurred in Latin America, involving anthropology as well as other social sciences. Wax (1978), in his discussion of Deitchman's (1976) book, writes that it represents in social science the analogue of "the fall of man." For other discussions of Camelot, see Beals (1969) and Horowits et al. (1967).

different aspects of their life and eventually publish something about them in the public domain. Yet, I can imagine a reviewer who would accept the first statement and reject the second.

Let me give an example from New York. In the beginning I would say, as I was introduced on a street corner, that I worked for the Narcotics Addiction Control Commission. Often, people would discover that they had other things to do, and I would be left talking to a mailbox. Then I began saying, "I'm a social scientist, and I'm interested in the life in the streets." Then if I was asked who I worked for, I would say, "The state pays my salary, but I work on my own research projects." Then if I was asked who specifically paid my salary, I would say, "NACC, but I don't report to anybody on what specific people are doing."

The second method of presenting myself worked much better. Was it unethical? I do not think so. It was a way of dealing with expectations that I learned street junkies had. People from NACC were on the street to spot-check treatment clients or to attempt to locate clients who had disappeared from the program, possibly to return them to the criminal justice system. By just saying, "NACC," I allowed those assumptions to operate. By using my second approach, I countered the assumptions before they could come up.

Let me give you another example that raises more problems. A few years ago, a sociologist named Laud Humphreys published a book called *Tearoom Trade*. "Tearooms," homosexual slang for public restrooms where casual sexual encounters take place, were of interest to Humphreys. He had been counseling male homosexuals but, after reading the then available literature, he did not feel that he understood much about homosexual life. (Perhaps his problems with that literature were similar to mine with the drug literature, as discussed in Chapter 2.)

He then did an ethnographic study of a public park restroom known as a tearoom. However, he did not present himself as an ethnographer. Instead, he took the role of "watch queen," a person who does not actively engage in homosexual acts, but prefers just to observe those encounters. In return, the watch queen is expected to keep an eye out for police in particular or straight males in general.

Humphreys also wrote down the license numbers of the cars of males who stopped at the tearoom for casual sex. Using these numbers, he could then obtain their names and addresses, and ensure that data were collected from them during a large-scale sociological survey that was going on in the city at the same time. Using the survey, he could learn something about their lives outside the tearoom.

His study shatters the stereotype of the male homosexual. Though some of the tearoom homosexuals were "out of the closet," many others were not. In fact, many had all the trappings of straight male life-styles—families, suburban homes, and so on. Their major homosexual activity seemed to be limited to occasional stops at the tearoom. The book is an important piece of urban American ethnography. It is important, not particularly because of theoretical or methodological innovation, but because it humanizes a stereotype— something a good ethnography should do. However, the work generated a number of exchanges on the ethical issues.[16]

Should Humphreys have disguised himself as a watch queen? His answer would no doubt be that he could not have done the study any other way. The tearoom was nothing if not impersonal, and encounters were brief. Furthermore, the men were understandably nervous about the possibility of discovery and arrest. It was not the sort of situation that an ethnographer could introduce himself into and then work slowly to develop rapport with group members. If you wanted to observe the comings and goings in the tearoom, you had to be part of the situation. There was no time for a stranger to define a place for himself.

Humphreys identified the tearoom visitors without their knowledge and then maintained a list that identified them explicitly. Had it left Humphreys' control, a number of people might have had their lives devastated. Fortunately, it did not. Humphreys was conscious of the importance of the list, and he took great pains to keep it confidential. No one but him ever knew its contents. Anyway, he would argue, there was no other way to get background information on the tearoom men. If you tried to interview them at the tearoom, the possibility of being labeled homosexual would have caused them to refuse and leave.

So there you have it. Put it on the scale and decide what you think. By today's standards, Humphreys' study was clearly unethical. Yet the study was also clearly important—for counselors, for police officers, for policymakers, and, not least of all, for homosexuals. I wonder how a committee would have evaluated the risk to subjects versus benefits of the study? Most likely with too much weight on the risk side.

This discussion is meant to show that there are different ways of presenting yourself, but they probably do not fall into two discrete categories labeled "ethical" and "unethical." There are alternative ways of describing your role, and some are better suited to the situation than others. All this leads to a more general problem. Unfortunately, the guidelines for the protection of human subjects were not designed with ethnography in mind.[17]

---

[16] For an exhange of views on Humphreys' study, see the essays by Hoffman, Horowitz, and Rainwater in Hoffman *et al.* (1970).

[17] This problem will be discussed in more detail later. Wax (1977) has written a good critique of the guidelines for the protection of human subjects, noting that they are based on a model of biomedical and experimental psychological research that fits poorly into ethnographic research.

This will produce more problems for us later, but for now, notice that the hypothesis-testing social science research that underlies the guidelines is of a particular kind. The data-collecting situation is limited and neatly bounded. It involves something like an interview or a test, given by someone who is a specialist in that role. Ethnography is not so nicely packaged. People drift in and out of situations. The ethnographer is not always collecting data in interviews. Does one need to identify oneself to have a casual conversation with a stranger about the weather? If he is having a conversation with three informants about kinship and a stranger who is related to one of them enters the group, must everything stop until the ethnographic role has been described to the newcomer? If one is drinking in an urban bar and notices something interesting about sociolinguistic variation, must she announce that she is now doing ethnography by attending more carefully to intonation contours?

Those are silly questions, generated by a set of guidelines that do not take ethnography into account. Yet you must deal with them if you apply for a grant or go through a local committee for the protection of human subjects. Dealing with the bureaucracy will be covered when proposals are discussed in Chapter 8. But the bureaucratic procedures shouldn't obscure what is important—the people's right to know who you are. The problem is that whatever your explanation, you will be such an improbable kind of creature that people will have trouble believing you.

When I first began work in the *tanda,* I went through a carefully rehearsed speech about my interest in their customs and language, and how I was doing this as a university student from the U.S. Much later I learned that there were two somewhat similar explanations for my presence. First, I was a spy from Pakistan. Second, I was an agent of the government, there either to check their landholdings or to list all men capable of military service. Hardly a set of role-relationships within which rapport would flourish.[18] As you might imagine, similar kinds of things occurred when I began work in New York. On my first day in the field I was walking down a busy side street. Three young adolescents were sitting on a "stoop" drinking beer from a quart bottle. Their conversation silenced as I approached. One of them looked up as I passed and smiling, said, "Good afternoon, officer."

---

[18] Berreman (1962), working in North India, reports that a similar set of categories were applied to him initially. Freilich (1970a,b) notes that the "spy" role is frequently applied to ethnographers initially. Less frequently, ethnographers report a more benign initial categorization. For example, Powdermaker (1966), beginning her work in a small southern U.S. town, reports that because of her interest in blacks, a rumor began amongst them that she was really a Negro who was "passing." As you'll see in the text, sometimes I had a similar experience with junkies in New York.

In my experience, in the confusion that your presence initially creates, people restructure it with assumptions of your malevolent intent. I think this occurs because I am a complete stranger requesting the status of an intimate, an insider. What reasonable person would not be suspicious of someone like that? The ethnographer is asking for trust without yet having earned it. Little wonder that initial contact by the ethnographer is so often viewed with suspicion by group members.

The reaction will also depend on the sophistication of the group with whom you are working. Not long ago I did a short pilot study on an alternative-life-style rural commune. I was explaining my role to one of the residents, and he quickly interrupted with a question, "Who are you going to use for a control group?" He was a Ph.D. in biochemistry, with a sophisticated background in experimental research design.

Even if the group is not sophisticated in the literature of social scientists, they may have a history of dealing with them. In *Custer Died for Your Sins,* Vine DeLoria defined an Indian family as parents, children, and an anthropologist. A colleague tells a story that a graduate student was doing some linguistic fieldwork with an old Indian in the Southwest. The man was very helpful, finally saying, "You know, you're quite good. I used to work with Edward Sapir." Sapir, of course, is one of the founders of linguistic anthropology.

Or consider the case reported by Kendall Blanchard. He found a Navajo informant who had worked with anthropologists since the early 1930s. His associations became so permanent that he apparently added a room to his house for anthropologists to stay in when they came to do research. Blanchard discusses the impact of this long association in economic and psychosocial terms. For example, apparently the man made some economic gains from his associations, but, on the other hand, he followed the anthropological bias to preserve the traditional to the point that he is now considered one of the most conservative residents in the area.[19]

At Lexington, some of the older junkies who came into the hospital used to "game" on the clinicians. As the clinician was asking questions and giving advice, they would interrupt and critique their performance, sometimes pointing out things they did well, sometimes suggesting alternative strategies. The older junkies had been talking to clinicians in hospitals and prisons for years. The Lexington staff, for the most part, was fresh out of school fulfilling their military obligations. The role-reversal flustered the clinicians and amused the other patients.

Sophistication and background experiences with social scientists can make

[19] See Blanchard (1977).

a difference in how you are defined. The ethnographer can also make a difference, if she is not completely new to the group. If she can behave in a way that indicates prior insider status elsewhere, it will change people's interpretation of her role. In New York I met people initially in a community-based treatment setting and had the opportunity to talk with them for a while. I had worked in Lexington and knew something about how to talk from a junkie point of view.

I tried to tell everyone who I was but, as mentioned a bit earlier, in the flow of situations that ethnographers jump into, the message does not always get across to everyone. After I left, I later learned, two stories went around about me. One was that I was an old-time junkie who had gone to graduate school after cleaning up. The other was that I was a representative from Synanon. Both were attempts to label me—I knew more than a straight person should, but was obviously out of date. It was at least an improvement over being called a narc.

I guess I'm something of a fatalist about controlling the perception of your role. Some ethnographers talk of the importance of the early stages of forming your role, or write of the importance of the first days of fieldwork in conditioning the rest of your research. And there are some reports around of disasters that suggest that such advice should not be ignored. But then you read of the strain of maintaining what you think is the correct impression, which may be all wrong anyway, and you recall the earlier discussion of how there are no set rules for entree, and how at any rate everyone makes mistakes early in fieldwork.[20]

My own feeling is to agree with people like William Whyte and Rosalie Wax who conclude that people judged them on how they conducted themselves on a day to day basis rather than on any official explanations they offered. And I agree with Delmos Jones, who argues that there should be more emphasis on directness and honesty, more of a sense that one can be oneself. He gives a couple of examples from his fieldwork to show how changing from role-playing an ethnographer to more of a direct form of behavior was not a liability. It actually improved his fieldwork.[21]

Eventually, people come to accept you for what you are—a strange person who asks many dumb questions. Starting from scratch, it seems to take me about three months until some quantum leap occurs, and I am a functioning, accepted member of the community. While you are becoming adjusted,

---

[20] For some sample discussions of the importance of early role definition, see Geer (1964), Olesen and Whittaker (1967), Williams (1967), and Kluckhohn (1940). Though many mention the strain of behaving properly in fieldwork, Berreman (1962), Paul (1953), and Delmos Jones (1973) are good examples of such discussions.

[21] See Whyte (1955) and Wax (1977). The Jones article is cited in Note 20.

people watch you and find out (hopefully) that nothing harmful happens as a result of your presence. They notice that you do indeed ask questions about language and customs, write things down in notebooks, and tape record interviews.

When you are accepted, sometimes you are told what to do. After a few months in India, I was sitting in my hut reading a book by lantern, relaxing to the background noises of evening in the *tanda*. Suddenly the door opened, and taking great liberties with the translation, I heard, "Where's your notebook? We're having an important ceremony out here. What's the matter, you're not working tonight?"[22]

Similar things happened at Lexington. Once a patient came into my office and closed the door. "Listen," he said, "we just copped some blues ("numorphan") and we're going to get off. You want to come and watch?" Yes I did, but I declined. It would have put me in too much of a bind. That is another kind of ethical dilemma that we will get to later on.

Whatever you do, though, you are probably going to be regarded with some caution initially. You may be able to reduce the distance more quickly if you have worked with similar groups and can demonstrate that you have enjoyed insider status previously. But however you present yourself and are perceived, you should probably hang question marks on many of the things you learn in the early part of your fieldwork.

During my first month in the *tanda*, I took a census, thinking that was a fairly standard, harmless task. Later, I found out that much of the information was wrong. People laughed about it and that is when I learned that I had been seen as a Pakistani spy and a government agent. I found out that people tended not to tell me about young males living in the household, in case I was going to take them for the army. People also said they had less land than they did, in case I was from the accountant's office.[23] Ever since I have become an ethnographer, I have never been able to keep a straight face when people say things like "a 2-week fact-finding tour," though I should admit I've done a couple.

So, the goal is to begin your work honestly by presenting yourself and your task in some way that will make sense to group members. Then some group interpretations of your role will occur that may present problems in the early stages of your ethnographic work. Try to find out later how group members initially saw you. As time goes on, you will be accepted, at least by some of the group, and you will feel an exhiliration as people decide you really are

---

[22] Powdermaker (1966) also mentions that her presence with a notebook made an event "official." There are other similar accounts in the literature as well.

[23] For a similar account of problems with census taking, see Kobben (1967).

interested in learning how they think and what they do. Now it is only the baggage in your mind that is preventing you from understanding. That takes us back to the first part of the chapter. Having come full circle, it is time to discuss more formally what ethnography is all about. What are its goals and how does it differ from other kinds of research traditions?

4
Ethnography

Until now, problems surrounding doing ethnography have been discussed—its role in anthropology, getting connected in an area, presenting yourself as an ethnographer, and so on. But there hasn't been much talk about its goals and their accomplishment. You're getting a sense of what ethnography is all about—or, more accurately stated, getting a sense of what I think ethnography is all about—from the discussion of these issues. But it's time to refine the elusive idea of ethnography. First, it would be useful to discuss it in the context of mainstream social science.

The Mainstream

Most research in the social sciences pivots around the idea of the testing of hypotheses. Hypotheses are logically derived from some theory. *Theory* has many definitions, but in this case it is usually a loosely connected set of empirical generalizations. That is not the only kind of theory you find in social sciences, but it is no doubt the most frequent.

A *hypothesis* is a statement that has some predicted truth value, assuming the theory is correct. The point of the testing is to check the actual truth value among some group of people and see if the theory's predictions are correct or not. If they are, then your confidence in the theory increases a bit; if they are not, then there is something wrong with the theory, or perhaps with the test.

The hypothesis states a relationship among a group of variables. In the simplest case, a statement will conceptually link two variables. The higher the value of variable A, the higher the value of variable B, for example. To test the hypothesis, some kind of measurement is necessary so that values can be assigned to the variables. Defining how values are assigned is called an *operational definition*. The operationalization may be contained in a survey questionnaire, a psychological test, some entries in the census, or a game that is played in a laboratory. Social scientists worry about whether the operationalization is valid (Does it measure what you think it does?) and reliable (Does it measure the same way at different times?).

Before the hypothesis can be tested, a group must be identified who will be the subjects of the research. The social scientist specifies who gets to participate in the research and how they are chosen—the sampling problem. Assume that the group to be studied is the population of Houston. First of all, the social scientist must decide how many people to include to have an adequate sample, so that she can then confidently generalize to the whole population.

Next, she must worry about how to choose the sample. If every person in the city has an equally likely chance of being included in the study, then her heart soars like an eagle, for she has a true "random" sample (if you ignore the problems that philosophers have with the concept of "random" in the first place; can you call something a machine generates a random number?). She may want to "stratify" the sample by intentionally including more people within the freeway loop around the center city. Although proportionately few people live within the loop, the study focuses on that area, so the social scientist decides to "oversample" residents there.

If the sample isn't random, the social scientist must worry about the biases represented in the eventual sample she winds up with. Say she runs an ad in *Texas Monthly* magazine—her sample will probably be biased more to the political left than a sample from an ad in *Texas Parade*. In either case, she will miss people who don't read at all, or who don't read those particular magazines.

Once the sample is defined and the variables are operationalized, she is ready to collect the data. Often, hired assistants will actually administer the interviews or tests. Once the data are in, they are analyzed for the answer—as variable A increases in value, does B increase as well? No one expects the results to be perfect. The question is, Does the relationship hold strongly enough so that the social scientist does not completely reject the prediciton of the theory?

The plan of analysis to test the relationship might be based on a correlation between the two variables. The correlation coefficient that resulted would be an index of how well the increases of A and B approximated a straight line if the values were plotted on a graph. Or we might arbitrarily divide the values of A and B into high and low. Then there would be four ways to code the data—high A and high B, high A and low B, low A and high B, low A and low B. If the statement is true, then most cases should be in high A and high B, or in low A and low B. There is a simple statistical test that tells you how strongly the idea is supported by the way the cases fall into the different quadrants.

Right now, researchers who practice this tradition of hypothesis-testing are calling my ancestors evil things. This sketch is oversimplified and does not approach some of the more sophisticated procedures developed in the last few years. As I said in Chapter 1, there are a variety of sources for you to go to to learn about hypothesis-testing research. But I don't intend to introduce that approach fully here.

A specific study, however, might help illustrate the tradition. I'll use part of a study conducted by my friend of long standing, Richard C. Stephens. Dick and I arrived at the Lexington hospital at about the same time. Although both of us were graduate students working on our Ph.D. theses, Dick's was in the tradition of the sociology of deviance. The amazing thing about Dick is that he actually came to Lexington because he wanted to do his thesis there. Most of us were there to avoid Vietnam. Since our Lexington days, we have been arguing many of the issues discussed in this book. A lot of ideas in the book are undoubtedly stolen from him, though the best ones are mine alone.

Dick was working within a theoretical tradition in sociology known as *labeling theory*. Labeling theory argues that people, once labeled as deviants, will remain so partly because "significant others" in their social environment won't allow them to be anything else. So, he reasoned, labeling theory would imply that junkies who left Lexington and returned to their home communities would have a hard time staying "clean." Even if they tried to become "straights," their families and friends would know them mainly as junkies. They would have a tendency not to allow the returning patient to act like anything but a junkie. Straight behavior from a junkie wouldn't make sense to them.

So, Dick formulated a hypothesis: The stronger the labeling when the patient left the hospital, the more likely that he would relapse (return to using heroin). Dick broke down the labeling by groups, so one of the more specific hypotheses became: The stronger the labeling by the family, the more likely that the patient would relapse.

Now he had two problems. The first was to operationalize the variables. Relapse was easy. Since he was using patients released from Lexington, all of them had gone to "aftercare" facilities in their hometowns. As part of after-care, they periodically had to give a urine specimen which was checked for narcotics use. So he could just check the records of the urine tests and count the "positives" for narcotics as a measure of relapse. Of course he had to worry about no-shows and refusals to give urine, but by and large operationalizing relapse was not a big problem.

Labeling, on the other hand, was more difficult. Dick talked informally to junkies, read ethnographies and junkie autobiographies, and came up with a list of things that a family might do if they suspected that one of their members was using heroin. He came up with a variety of things. He asked how families reacted if they were in the bathroom a long time. The bathroom is a place where junkies frequently shoot up. He asked if family members checked their clothes for cigarette burns—junkies frequently nod after they shoot heroin, and cigarettes or hot ashes sometimes fall onto shirts, pants, and so on. He asked if the family would trust the individual to go to the store with a $20 bill. It wasn't a bad list.

He then went through the procedure of developing the items into a "scale" that measured labeling. The procedure is more technical and complicated than I want to deal with here, involving item–item correlations, cluster analyses, and so on. But he eventually wound up with an operationalization of labeling through the construction of a social-psychological scale that measured it. His sample was more or less defined for him since he was dealing with junkies who had left the Lexington program for at least 6 months. Although he visited some of the aftercare centers himself, most of the data were collected by people who actually worked there. Dick would mail them the questionnaires and someone at the center would do the interview.

When the data came back, Dick fed them into the jaws of a computer. With all the various kinds of labeling put together, it correlated about .50 with relapse. Statisticians say this suggests that about 25% of the variance has been explained. Roughly translated, the number means that labeling has something to do with relapse, but there are many other things going on as well that weren't taken into account.

Now, there are several things to notice about Dick's study in particular, and the hypothesis-testing approach to social science in general. First, several assumptions are floating around, like the focus on how people stay the same rather than how they change. Then there's a focus on external factors rather than internal factors that keep them the way they are. Next, the assumption is that these external factors are "social others" who are seen to have control over what behaviors the patient is permitted to display. The social other does this through an unarticulated blend of verbal and nonverbal messages that are only a small part of the emergent system that encompasses face-to-face interaction.

For the real Lexington patient returning to the community, the situation is, of course, more complicated. He changes as well as stays the same; internal processes are as relevant as external ones; other pieces of social interaction might be more important to relapse than those isolated by labeling theory. It's not possible to evaluate the simplifying assumptions without an understanding of what has been left behind in the simplification.

Next, where did the operationalizations come from? There is more to being a junkie than just using narcotics. What other things does he do when he returns to the community? We can only wonder if some of those other things might be better indicators of relapse into the junkie lifestyle than narcotics use. Then, the items in the scale tap the specific details of social interaction with family. Where did these details come from? Many of them came from informal interviews Dick held, similar to those used in ethnographic work, as well as from ethnographic studies that were published at the time Dick was developing the scale. Given the simplifying assumptions of the approach, they weren't bad.

Finally, consider the nature of the human relationship between interviewer and respondent. First of all, it is a short-term, highly specific relationship. Dick, or more often his representative in the aftercare agency in the community, met with the client for a short period of time to get some specific information. The relationship existed only for that purpose, and only for that length of time.

If there was more to it than that, we should know about it. If the relationship had other aspects—friendship, kinship, teaching, or counseling—there would undoubtedly be some tangling of the threads influencing the questioning and the responses. In Dick's study, if the interviewer was also the client's aftercare counselor, we should know something about the history of the relationship to fully evaulate the interview.

In addition to being short-term, the relationship was also asymmetrical. The interviewer was the dominant member in the relationship. He had the right to ask questions and the interviewee had the obligation of responding; he defined the appropriate topics of discussion and the linguistic style in which they would be discussed; he had the power to initiate and terminate the interaction. The social science member of the pair, in short, had control.

The control factor is justified by the demands of the method. The social scientist wants the same framework to be provided for each interviewee. By forcing the behavior of different individuals into the same framework, it can be compared on the same yardstick. Any differences in responses can then be attributed to the respondent, not to a change in the framework.

This argument is somewhat delusional. First of all, different people will have different strategies for fitting their behaviors into a framework that many of them will define as alien to the "natural" way they would deal with the same topic. Because the same questions are read in the same sequence, this does not, at any rate, necessarily mean that the framework is the same. Is the interviewer lumped in with welfare investigators, interested strangers, cops, or just plain nosy, rude people? The categorization will make a difference in the way the person responds.

William Labov did a study of the verbal behavior of black school children that makes this point well.[1] When brought in singly to a formal room with an adult black interviewer, the children behaved just like "verbally deprived" ghetto children should. When the interviewer sat on the floor, brought in kids who were friends, provided snacks, and introduced taboo topics, the same children exhibited a creative use of language. In short, the problems of who you are, discussed in Chapter 3, don't disappear just because you write down the questions. They might even get worse.

None of this is intended to mean that hypothesis-testing research is necessarily a bad thing. On the contrary, it is an important strategy that can play a role in the overall process of doing ethnography. It has many strengths, not the least of which is its explicitness. When one writes grant proposals or articles, he can lay out the hypotheses, operationalizations, and sample design before or after the fact. With this material explicitly presented, the skeptic can evaluate the procedures and criticize them if he wishes. The dedicated skeptic can even copy the procedures and replicate the study to see if he comes up with the same results.

But the people being researched don't get into the picture until fairly late in the research game, at the time of data collection. Then they only get in insofar as they are allowed by the framework that has been set by the hypothesis-testing social scientist. If they don't like the framework, they can't modify it and talk outside of it, except maybe over a beer after the interview is finished. If this were the only way social science research happened, the people studied would never have much of a vote. If they don't refuse to participate, they get to fit a piece of themselves to a framework selected as significant by the *a priori* simplifying assumptions and operationalizations of the social scientist. And the piece, more often than not, has to be expressed by the person in some way so that it fits an alien framework for its expression.

And yet, speaking from experience in the drug field, hypothesis-testing research is the fashion, the expensive, high-prestige section of research city. Policymakers turn to it for information, even when the simplifying assumptions of the research design are the same ones that support the policy. Such research sets the standards for the review of research grant applications, and an ethnographic grant application often looks bizarre by such standards. Of course, that's partly our fault because we have never developed much of a

[1] The article is by Labov (1969)

methodology to discuss. But I'm climbing onto my favorite soapbox a bit ahead of the game. First, let's discuss ethnography and find out where the incompatabilities lie between this tradition and ethnographic research.

Ethnographic Research Differences

When you think informally about ethnographic research, a few things strike you right away. First of all, there is an emphasis on direct personal involvement in the community.[2] As mentioned earlier, research of the hypothesis-testing type often relies on hired hands for direct contact with the people who are actually providing the data. I think most ethnographers would be nervous if they lacked a firsthand "feel" for the people they're working with. Later, in Chapter 7, I'll give an example of my own experience with "research assistant" ethnography.

Beyond the firsthand contact, though, there are other aspects to the relationship that enthnographers establish with group members. Recall that the hypothesis-tester was one-up in the asymmetrical relationship; he had to be to maintain scientific control. The ethnographer is also part of an asymmetrical relationship, especially at the beginning of her work. The difference is that she, not the informant, is in the "one-down" position.

This initial one-down position is reflected in two of the metaphors ethnographers sometimes use to explain themselves—*child* and *student*.[3] What is being said with such metaphors? Both child and student are learning roles; they are roles whose occupants will make mistakes, which is perfectly acceptable as long as they don't continue to make the same ones. They can be expected to ask a lot of questions. They need to be taught—both will look to established members of a group for instruction, guidance, and evaluation of their performance.

This discussion of the learning role should already have you nervously wondering, "How do I write a research proposal?" It's not necessarily that ethnographers don't want to test hypotheses. It's just that if they do, the variables and operationalizations and sample specifications must grow from

---

[2] For a couple of sample statements on the importance of direct personal involvement, see Plotnicov (1973) and Weakland (1951).

[3] For example, Crane and Angrosino (1974) mention the student role, while Cohen (1970) uses the metaphor of the child role. There are many other examples of the use of these metaphors in the literature. Burnett (1974) points out some interesting theoretical implications of the metaphor, noting that a concern with methods from this point of view also has to do with the study of the acquisition of culture in general. I should mention that much of the discussion in this section is taken from a short methodology paper I wrote for the drug field, cited in the Bibliography as Agar (1976).

an understanding of the group rather than from being hammered on top of it no matter how poor the fit. You can't specify the questions you're going to ask when you move into the community; you don't know how to ask questions yet. You can't define a sample; you don't know what the range of social types is and which ones are relevant to the topics you're interested in.

None of this goes over well with hypothesis-testing fanatics. Yet this devotion to the initial learning role is one of the major ingredients that makes ethnography the unique concoction that it is. Later on, we'll worry more about trying to make the learning process more systematic, and then discuss how what you do later in the ethnography may be something like hypothesis-testing, grounded in that critical early learning period.

To get to that later point, you don't stay one-down forever. Relationships will change over the time that you do fieldwork. Perhaps some group members will never let you go one-down: You are always in the dominant role as far as they are concerned. On the other hand, some relationships will move to symmetry. Or, to "dejargonize" for a moment, you'll make friends.

To "rejargonize," some of these people will become key informants or field assistants. You will rely on them intensely for assistance during fieldwork. Later in the fieldwork, if you do some systematic checks of your newly acquired knowledge, you will of course assume the one-up position. At this point, you'll look something like a hypothesis-tester, except that your one-up stance will be one moment in a relational history that allows other forms for the relationship as well.

That moves us into another difference in ethnography. Recall that hypothesis-testers established short-term, specific relationships with their respondents. Ethnographic relationships are long-term and diffuse. An ethnographer associates with people over an extensive period of time. Further, she associates with them in a variety of contexts—home, place of work, religious ceremonies, recreational activities, and so on.

There are many reasons why this is stressed. First of all, it takes a while for people to accept your role and begin to trust you. Then to achieve the kind of learning to which ethnographers aspire, much time is necessary. Finally, people have different sides of themselves that they display under different sets of circumstances, making it essential to see group members in different situations, not just during a brief interview.

For the same reasons, there is also an emphasis on the ethnographer going into the groups' home turf to do the research. People are usually more comfortable in their home territory, compared to bringing them into an office or laboratory, though there are times when an ethnographer needs a quiet place for personal interviews. Then, if one is interested in all the situations that a person ordinarily moves through and deals with, it only makes sense to be there when it happens. Finally, because much of ethnography can be translated as becoming part of a group, living with them is a usual correlate of being a part-member.

New problems have been introduced for the ethnographic proposal in the eyes of hypothesis-testers. Just on a practical level, there will be high-budget figures for travel and living costs, particularly if the group you plan to work with is some distance from your usual home base. Then all of this student-child learning is suspect to a group whose starting point for research is a clearly specified hypothesis. Finally, the intimacy with the community and intensity of involvement often produces a criticism of probable bias resulting from getting "too close."[4] So, you see the problem. Ethnography is a different sort of research process from hypothesis-testing. From my viewpoint, ethnography is the more general process of understanding another human group; hypothesis-testing is a minor, though potentially significant part of that process.

Let me give an example that helps illustrate some of these differences. A few years ago a social-science consulting firm was awarded a contract to do a survey of heroin addicts who had been in treatment programs. After interviewers were located in each of the cities included in the study, they were brought to a central location for training. I was asked to come in as a trainer. I told them I didn't know much about survey research, but they said they wanted me to talk generally about what "these people" were like. It seemed like a harmless enough way to pick up a little beer money, so I accepted.

My talk centered on the idea that junkies, like all of us, have different aspects of self that are presented in different situations. Sometimes they would present themselves as social failures; sometimes as social successes. I used that as a springboard into the importance of the relationship the interviewer establishes with an addict. I talked about rapport and stressed the importance of spending some time loosening up before interviewing if possible, or loosening up after interviewing and learning if you got the same picture as you did during the more formal interview. Finally, I tried to emphasize that this population was not like suburbanites who are stopped by a survey interviewer in a shopping mall. Junkies usually have been interviewed to death. For this and many other reasons, they are often not enthusiastic about another interview—in fact, they may be downright hostile.

After all the talks were over, speakers were asked to circulate among discussion groups. The groups consisted of interviewer trainees and staff

---

[4] Wolff (1960) points out that the influence of the researcher, or "personal equation," discussed in Chapter 3, is considered a problem to be neutralized in hypothesis-testing, while ethnographers are more likely to accept it as an inevitable part of the research process.

members from the research firm. It didn't take long for differences to become apparent. I was asked what to do if a junkie–patient were approached on the street and, after you explained the study, he or she seemed reluctant to participate. I immediately advised backing off from the formal interview and suggesting something else that would allow for some informal talk first, like "Let's go get a beer before we do this thing."

While some of the group liked the idea, the leader didn't at all. She said that it was company policy not to drink while conducting interviews. Among other things, it might offend the next person approached for an interview if the interviewer had alcohol on his breath. I had visions of junkies I've known saying, "Sorry, man, I don't talk to anybody who just drank some beer." Some of the trainees chuckled with me at the absurd image.

Shortly after that another person asked what to do if it became clear that the respondent did not understand the question as phrased. "Paraphrase," I said, giving some examples from a copy of the questionnaire sitting in front of me. Again, there was a horrified look from the group leader. She disapproved, noting that it was important for the questionnaire to be presented in the same way to each respondent. At that point, all I could think of was a quote from Charles Frake addressing a psychologist, "If you ask a question and people laugh, you say, 'Come on, this is serious.' If I ask a question and people laugh, I wonder if there isn't something wrong with the question."[5]

The next day, the training interviews started. There were rumblings about how some of the local junkie–patients who were serving as guinea pigs were not showing up as scheduled. Of those who did show, some were downright nasty. One trainee told of his bizarre experience. He had met "his" interviewee at the door, and had chatted amiably as they walked to the interview room. As soon as they sat down and he placed the clipboard on his lap, the interviewee became "sullen." At the end of the interview, as they walked out, they again had a pleasant talk, loitering on the front steps of the building for 15 minutes or so because they weren't ready to end their conversation. "Weird," said the trainee in summary.

Part of the junkie's reaction was no doubt due to the interview training session itself. I was asked to attend a couple. The trainee and the interviewee sat in the middle of an ordinary motel-type room. They were surrounded by other trainees, invited consultants, company representatives, and sometimes representatives from the university that had the main contract for the research. At the sessions I visited, this didn't seem to bother the junkie, but the interviewer–trainee didn't look very comfortable.

---

[5] The quote is paraphrased from a transcript of a conference proceeding published in a special issue of the *American Anthropologist,* listed as Romney and D'Andrade (1964).

In one unforgettable scene, an older female methadone patient sat quietly, a weary look on her face, while the interviewer nervously stumbled through the questions. I felt badly for the interviewer because the sensitivity that she displayed in her nervous reaction to the awful setting meant she might do well once she got out on her own. Finally the old woman couldn't stand it any longer either. She leaned forward, and with the kindest of eyes patted the interviewer on the knee and said, "There there, hon, you're doing just fine." So oppressive was the situation that there was hardly any reaction. The interviewer just plunged on ahead.

And then there were the questions. A chart was offered that had the preceding 5 years divided up by months. Respondents were supposed to locate events related to drug use, arrest, treatment, criminal activity, and employment. In my observations, they had difficulty doing so. The appointment calendar does not have the sacred value in the street life that it does in the life of survey researchers. It was interesting to listen to those who thought out loud as they tried to fit their history to what they saw as a bizarre framework. I can't remember exact samples, but it might have gone something like this: "Let's see. That would have been about the time Nixon was elected the second time. Right after I started working there, they had that thing about fight-fixing down at the stadium." People were locating events in relation to significant events in their own personal history. Their memory was not organized by the precision of the yearly calendar. However, their recollections might be transformed into an approximate position on the yearly calendar by locating the event of interest near events that had been reported in the public media. This simple time transformation was not provided, though. The respondent had to do the work, without access to verification of public event dates.

People also had trouble with the "time lines" that the interviewer was supposed to draw. To draw the line, they needed to know, for example, when the respondent "started" and "stopped" using heroin. But the respondent might say, "Well, I started about March, and then used quite a bit for a week or so, but cut down some, but later I got hooked, even though I tried to control it once in awhile, I think I kicked for a couple of weeks, but I went right back to it. Finally I had to stop in September when I got busted." Should that be a continuous line from March to September? If it shouldn't, it is difficult to know how to break it, especially when the respondent won't remember when the breaks occurred within that 5- or 6-month period. It's not that it's impossible to transform personal histories onto time lines. It's just that whoever designed the question did not understand the amount of work he was asking the respondent to do; nor was he sensitive, apparently, to the amount of "uncontroled," "unstandardized" information processing that was going on (assuming the respondent cared enough about the interview to bother at all).

That story hardly covers all the differences, but it hopefully illustrates some of the problems when ethnography and survey research interact. Many in the literature deal with the fit between hypothesis-testing and ethnography. Before moving on, I would like to discuss a couple of other critiques of hypothesis-testing approaches—ones that focus specifically on operationalization of variables. Using them, with the help of a couple of my own examples, we can make an initial foray into the goal of ethnography.

TWO CASES OF ETHNOGRAPHIC CRITIQUES

Edmund Leach is a British anthropologist who had done ethnographic work in Sri Lanka. He contributed to an edited volume on field methods by taking a hard ethnographic look at a survey done in that country. His chapter is a detailed critique of the results based on the manner in which certain critical elements of the survey were operationalized.

For example, he notes that a household was defined as persons who cook rice from the same pot. But then he goes on to consider additional information. For one thing, Sinhalese village girls marry young. However, they all have a separate cooking pot. Then he notes a second observation of village life—most property is handed on only when the original owner becomes elderly. The results? A household consisting of a married couple with their three married sons would, by the survey definition, be counted as one landed household and three landless households. So, Leach concludes, we can only wonder how many of the 335 landless households (out of 506) are actually young, recently married adults who are heirs to still living parents.

Let me give you one more example. Landholdings were classified into high-yield and low-yield. But cultivated lands, Leach learned from doing his ethnography, were of two types. One type, traditional lands, was estimated by using a rule of thumb that Leach describes in some detail. But the results, based on his work, usually overestimated actual acreage by about 50%. The other type of land, called acre land, was developed recently after purchase from the crown. These lands were actually surveyed by professional surveyors.

The conclusion is that traditional lands will always look like low-yield lands, since their acreage is overestimated by one-half. When you add the knowledge that acre lands are usually held by the wealthier villagers, it partly explains the apparent relationship between large holdings and high-yield lands.

There are many other examples in Leach's article. The debate is made even more interesting by the political implications of the results. If Leach is correct, then the situation in the communities studies is not as bad in terms of landholdings as the survey concludes. If Leach is incorrect, then he is erroneously contributing to a status quo that supports a few wealthy landowners. The political consequences of this kind of methodological debate, here as in the drug field, are often frightening.

Let me give you one more quick example. In an article in the same volume, A. J. F. Kobben talks about some problems in gathering census data in Surinam. For example, he notes that informants feared jealousy if they had a large number of kids, so large families lowered the number of children they would report. And mothers feared talking about children who had died because of possible connections with witchcraft. As a final example, the men were mobile, having more than one family in one village. In fact, they even joked among themselves about how hard they were to count.[6]

Kobben and Leach are both criticizing the interpretation of what would seem to be fairly straightforward "facts"—household composition, land yield, number of children, and so on. These facts were zeroed in on in one context—the informant's—then lifted out and placed in another context—the researcher's. But the meaning of the "fact" changed in the transition. In Kobben's critique, the meaning of "children" was connected to beliefs about jealousy and witchcraft for the informants. For Leach, land ownership was a poor fit with connected ideas about marriage, cooking pots, extended families, and customary inheritance.

As I think about my own experience and the literature I reviewed, I begin to realize how frequent is this ethnographic critique of other social science research. The critique highlights another difference between hypothesis-testers and ethnographers—one that has more to do with a fundamental difference in research world view. An ethnographer learns something new, and then tries to understand how it connects with other aspects of the situation in which the new learning occurred. As if that weren't difficult enough, he then tries to see if it connects with other things he has learned that are not immediately apparent—things like parts of the belief system, or the history of the group, or the wealth of the informant.

This formidable search for connections, this ethnographic belief that an isolated observation cannot be understood unless you understand its relationships to other aspects of the situation in which it occurred, is called a *holistic perspective.*[7] This perspective, of course, has its own problems, such as the *holistic fallacy,* when an ethnographer constructs a connection because of his

---

[6] See Leach (1967) and Kobben (1967).

[7] For a lucid philosophical discussion of holism, see Phillips (1976). The term *holistic fallacy* comes from Sieber (1973).

bias to find one without checking it out carefully. And holism does not mean that you can *never* lift things out of context and talk about them in isolation, though it does mean that this lifting is a more complicated process than most hypothesis-testers think it is.

Holism does help to understand, though, why ethnographers are cautious with the idea of a variable. For what is a variable but something that can be measured in a standardized way across situations, across people, across groups, and even across cultures. From a holistic point of view, the very idea of a variable is enough to make one skeptical. Yet in spite of its traditional importance, holism is reportedly on the decline as more and more anthropologists move towards problem-oriented research and increasingly argue for hypothesis-testing methodologies.[8]

Later in the book this will be discussed at some length. As you have noticed, I have mixed feelings. On the one hand, I am concerned with the development of a more explicit ethnographic methodology; on the other hand, things like the learning role, the long-term intensive personal involvement, and the holistic perspective are what set ethnography apart—they enable us to learn what people are like rather than seeing if a minute piece of their behavior in a context we define supports or does not support our ideas of what they are like.

A survey sociologist would no doubt read my account and give a point by point rebuttal.[9] His strongest rebuttal would probably come at the end of the argument, when he said, "So what do you have to offer as an alternative? Some self-serving anecdotes that support a conclusion you might have reached before you even started doing your research?" It's time to start taking

---

[8] For example, Johnson (1978) notes that the "contradiction" between holism and detailed measurement, which used to be resolved in favor of holism, is now beginning to be resolved more in favor of detail. Similar arguments can be found in Narol and Cohen's (1970) introduction to their edited volume, and in Kaplan and Manners (1971). As pointed out in Note 15 in Chapter 1, many of the recent methods books in anthropology emphasize quantification, standardization, and hypothesis-testing, although they do so in a perspective that includes at least some concern with the general idea of ethnography. On the other hand, Edgerton (1970), after reviewing a variety of methods used in psychological anthropology, notes that one problem is that such methods force us to "atomize" and lose context. He suggests that we develop our own methods that retain a sense of context, complexity, and interaction. That pretty well summarizes what I had in mind when I started work on this book.

[9] He could make an even stronger rebuttal by pointing out that surveys have been used very productively in some studies. Although I'll talk more about how ethnography can use surveys later, there are several good sources in the literature. Powdermaker (1966) shows how a survey was useful in her work in South Africa. Bennett and Thaiss (1970) review the anthropological literature and show many cases where surveys were productively used. Vidich and Shapiro (1955) also describe how a survey and ethnography interacted.

that charge seriously. We have to offer something in the way of methodology as an alternative.

Goals of Ethnography

Methodology is not something to be appreciated solely in terms of its internal esthetics. Methodology serves some purpose, some higher-order goal. A particular method is a procedure that is a part of the larger process of doing ethnography. What we need, then, is a sense of our goals—just what are we trying to accomplish when we do ethnography? Only then we can properly evaluate specific methodologies. After we use a method, we should be closer to the goal than before we used it. If we are choosing between two methods, and one gets us closer to the goal, other things being equal, we should select it.

All this is obvious, but it is important to remember to keep methodology in perspective. Several years ago I went to a conference on decision-making in natural context. Interestingly enough, the conference quickly broke into two groups. One group was fascinated with the methodological techniques available in the mathematical study of decision-making. Their guiding question was, "What kind of data do we need to collect to fit this elegant model?" The other group was primarily interested in doing ethnography. Their question was, "How much do we need to hammer and weld this model so that it fits what these people are doing when they make choices." The difference here is methodology as an end in itself, or in subordination to goals of doing ethnography. There's nothing wrong with working only with a specific method in isolation. It's just not what we're talking about here.

So what is this broader ethnographic goal? If it seems like I'm avoiding the question, it's because I am. I'm not sure what a precise goal statement would look like. In cognitive anthropology, some have suggested that the goal of ethnography is to be able to "behave appropriately" in a community.[10] You'd also want to include behave "inappropriately" as well, but that's not really a problem. Intuitively, I believe there's a kernal of an explicit set of goals in there, but it's simply too vague at this point. Where is the boundary of appropriateness, and who in the community is the judge?

What about the notion of "student–child" discussed earlier? Again, therein lies an implicit goal. The ethnographer's purpose is to learn—to acquire some knowledge that he previously did not have. But a cursory glance at the psychological literature teaches you what a simple-minded statement that is.

---

[10] The classic statement of this goal is in Goodenough (1957).

What kind of learning? What kind of knowledge? The structure of knowledge or the process of using it? What if the knowledge is not new for the ethnographer? And, as in the preceding paragraph, whose knowledge are you trying to learn?

If those are two of the clearer goal statements, we are in trouble. Perhaps with a bit of strategic oversimplification, we can establish a more explicit goal for now. It won't be broad enough, but it may serve as a beginning. The goal will hinge on the idea of *paraphrase,* which will stress the importance of interpreting the perceivable world of sound and motion.

Let's take an example of paraphrasing from my work in India. You stand with an informant in the *tanda.* You are about to leave, and someone is preparing a snack for you to eat on the trail. Just before he wraps the food in a cloth, he places a small piece of charcoal in the bundle. Now, you and the informant both saw the same stream of motion. If someone asked you what just happened, you might say, "Hell if I know. He just put a lump of charcoal in with the food. Maybe it's supposed to flavor it."

Suppose the same person now turned to your informant and asked what happened. The informant says, "It is midday, a time when spirits are especially active. People alone are particularly susceptible to spirits, especially when they are carrying food. Spirits are repulsed by charcoal. That's why he put the lump of charcoal in there—to protect you."

Consider another example. In New York I see a person going into a methadone clinic, as does an informant who is also a clinic patient. Someone asks me what he is doing, and I say "He's probably a patient in the program. He's an outpatient, so he must go into the clinic to obtain his methadone. He might also stay for a group session or a meeting with his counselor." Now the same person asks my informant. His reply is much briefer; "He's going to cop." Again, we both saw the same motions and heard the same sounds, but my statements were an official interpretation of methadone clinics, while the informant's statements interpreted the same behavior from a street point of view.

In both cases, the informant and I are giving different *accounts* of what we have seen and heard. We each took our sense perceptions, decoded them to assign some kind of meaning to those parts of the sound and motion that we attended to, and then on the basis of that meaning, we produced some statements that were our accounts.

Hence the relation between giving accounts and paraphrasing. The paraphrase is something that ethnographers have always used, whether or not they were primarily interested in linguistic matters. Paraphrasing is a powerful test of comprehension. If you hear a sentence, can you properly decode it? Do you understand it in one of the possible ways that the listener does? If you do, you should be able to encode it into a new sentence or group of sentences, such that the people around will say, "Yes, that's what I (he/she) just said, allright."

"It's hot in here" can be intended, and interpreted, as a request to turn down the heat, or a hint that going out onto the open air balcony might be a better place for an intimate conversation than a crowded party. So what happens when our ethnographer tries a paraphrase and says, "Oh, you mean the temperature is higher than you normally prefer?" Everyone collapses in hysterical laughter. In fact, sometimes I think the only reason ethnographers are tolerated at all is for their entertainment value.

This goal should serve to test our understanding and invite group members to comment if we are wrong. We will rely initially on sharpening the ability to paraphrase as a working ethnographic goal. But recall that we are using *paraphrase* in a boarder sense than its traditional use in linguistics. We are talking about the ability to decode rather involved sequences of verbal *and* nonverbal behavior, and then encode our understanding of the meanings of that sequence into some utterances to check whether or not we understood what just occurred. It is in this special sense that I speak of *giving an account.*

In the examples given earlier from the *tanda* and from New York, my account differed from that of a group member. My immediate goal is to reduce the difference between the two accounts, so that mine better approximates a group member's. Anything that helps me do this is a valuable ethnographic method.

Several objections to this goal came to mind. First, why the emphasis on language? The emphasis is on language as *metalanguage,* as far as the goal is concerned. One of the confusing things about human language is that it is both object language and metalanguage. As *object language,* it is part of the flow of behavior that occurs as group members do the activities they do. But it is also a *metalanguage,* used to talk about that flow of verbal and nonverbal behavior. An account is given using the group's language as metalanguage.

An ethnographer's ability to give an account might be modeled by some procedures that take as input the observation of behavior and provide as output a set of metalanguage statements that group members judge to be a correct interpretation of what is going on. Of course, there are problems here. For example, there may be more than one correct account, and group members may disagree in any case on which account or accounts are correct.

It strikes me, though, that such problems are informative, and it is a strength of the focus on the goal that they occur. The ethnographer wants to know about alternatives and disagreements within the group. Variation like that is only a threat to a social scientist committed to a monolithic portrait of group life. Unfortunately, the quest for "the normative order," deeply ingrained in

many social science traditions, has sometimes blinded us to the many important lessons for the ethnographer when confronted with variability as well as
uniformity.

But what if the ethnographer comes up with an account that no one ever
thought of before? All kinds of interesting things can happen here. You may
elicit an "aha" reaction from informants, showing them a connection they feel
is true but which they never previously consciously articulated. In fact, you
may contribute to account giving strategies among the very people you are
studying. That's a situation that some call "training" informants.

And what if the ethnographer has ideas about what is going on that differ
from group members' accounts? Good question, but wrong place to ask it. At
this point, I am just worried about defining a low-level ethnographic goal—
learning to give accounts of an event like community members do. Later on,
higher-level analyses of accounts will be discussed—like the relationship
between accounts of different events, and the problems when an ethnographer learns about and checks out accounts that may be contradictory to the
accounts of informants. But these larger-level analyses presuppose an ability
to give accounts, so right now we'll stay with that.

Another serious objection might be the passive role of the ethnographer
implied by the goal. Is he to become sort of a commentator, sitting on the
sidelines and giving a play-by-play account to a panel of assenting and
dissenting judges? This role would infuriate people like Richard Nelson, who
advocates a method of "direct participation."[11] In his work in the Arctic with
Eskimo and Indian groups, his philosophy was, "If you think you can describe
seal hunting, then you yourself should be able to successfully hunt a seal."

This direct participation goal makes me personally a bit nervous, since I can
easily imagine myself putting a spear through my right foot. There are other
problems. If I think I can give an account of a religious ceremony as group
members do, does that mean I must be capable of conducting it? Group
members aren't; the ceremony is done by a specialist. If I can give an account
of a wedding ceremony, does that mean I must be capable of going through
it? I hope not.

In spite of the problems, the sentiment is an important one, but I'd hate to
make the ethnographer's object language and behavior in the stream of
community life the ultimate test of ethnography. For one thing, he's had less
practice and must deal with interference with his own culture, unlike informants. For another, he may have problems for a host of personal reasons—
self-consciousness, shyness, or he may just generally be what in the jargon of
the social sciences is known as a klutz.

[11] See Nelson (1969).

At the same time, the goal of accounting is by no means intended to isolate the ethnographer. If for no other reason, he should be part of the flow of community life to learn to ask better questions. And nothing in the goal prevents an ethnographer from jumping in. If you want to hunt seals, more power to you. I'd make a lousy seal hunter, but that doesn't mean I'm not interested in understanding folks who do.

So, let's begin with the goal of giving accounts. It's not perfect, and it's oversimplified, but at least it's a start. We can't really discuss ethnographic methods until we have at least a tentative sense of what those methods are supposed to accomplish. To begin, this is what those methods are supposed to accomplish: They should add to the procedures used by the ethnographer to transfer observations into accounts that group members say are possible interpretations of what is going on.

Before plunging into specific ethnographic experiences again, some comment needs to be made about theory. Some of this section sounds like the beginning of some critical theoretical issues. What are those "procedures" that transform observations into accounts? Does an "account" have certain features that distinguish it from other informant utterances, and are these features more general than just what you find in your study of a specific group?

For the second time, we are confronting the relationship between methodology and theory. Can we sensibly treat them separately, or are they so intertwined that we separate them at the risk of obscuring rather than enhancing our understanding? Again the issue appears, and again we put it off until later. For now, let's accept the broad goal of accounting and return to the field. Now we can take up some specific problems that you will face as you begin doing your work.

5
Beginning Fieldwork

You arrive, tape recorder in hand, with a grin rigidly planted on your face. You probably realize that you have no idea how the grin is being interpreted, so you stop and nervously attempt a relaxed pose. Then you realize that you have no idea how *that* is being interpreted. Soon you work yourself into the paralysis of the psychiatrist in a strip joint— she knows she can't react, but she also knows she can't *not* react. It is little wonder that people sometimes hide in a hotel room and read mysteries.

This, of course, assumes the worst—that the group is a complete unknown to you. You might have read some ethnographies of such groups, but those sometimes have a disappointing lack of relevance when you're actually faced with a representative of the group that supposedly has been described. This early phase is, I think, the source of the mystique of fieldwork. You are adrift, trusted by none, and unsure of what is going on around you.

In this chapter, I want to consider some of the problems of the early phase of fieldwork. Several problems are relevant here. First of all, some people will be more likely to approach you than others. Then you have to learn to steer conversations in directions that cover areas you need to begin to learn about. You must also make some sort of decision on how and how much of these early experiences to record. Finally, as you begin to integrate into the community, or perhaps even before, you may want to add some community members to the research teach.

Who Talks First

Often an ethnographer bases much of her work on intensive discussions with a very few people. Rather than looking at the distribution of a few predefined variables in a large population, she is trying to learn the interrelationships of a large number of discovered variables among a few people. The ethnographer often comes up with a statement like, "There *exists* a pattern such that . . . ." But the reader gets no sense of how it is distributed in the larger population.

A good analogy can be found in linguistics. When the field linguist (as opposed to those who "introspect") works on a new language, he sits down with a few informants. He gets some data, and then comes up with some tentative rules that articulate the implicit structure in those statements. Then he gets more data, further tests the statements, gets more data, and so on.

Then along came the sociolinguistic arguments of people like John Gumperz and William Labov.[1] People speak differently from each other, something that becomes striking as soon as you leave your four informants and listen to the other 5000 people in the town. Traditionally, linguists often called this "free variation," meaning that things could be said in different ways, but that they didn't want to deal with it. They had enough problems just trying to account for a few informants.

So Labov, to take just one quick example, studied the way that the pronunciation of the r varied in New York City. He found that the more formal the situation, and the higher the socioeconomic status of the speaker, the more likely the r was to be pronounced. By studying distribution in a large population, Labov cut a piece of understanding out of the "free variation" wastebasket and began the process of adding it to linguistic theory.

The catch, of course, is that he would never have known which variable to look at without the blood, sweat, and tears of previous linguists who had worked with a few informants and identified problems in the linguistic structure of American English. All of which finally brings us to the point of this example—traditional ethnography struggles mightily with the existence of pattern among a few. It's a worthy, necessary, first-priority struggle, but it's not enough. A couple of chapters down the road, the problem of *distribution* of these patterns will be discussed. For now, the moral of the story is that when you do your initial work with a few people, you had better worry about who they are. If you had done linguistic work among New York's elite at museum benefits, you would come up with a phonological description that

---

[1] A recent collection of Gumperz' work can be found in Gumperz (1971). The example of Labov's work is listed in the References as Labov (1966).

said the r is always pronounced. The reviews of your work in the *Daily News* would be awful,[2] and you probably wouldn't get tenure.

In my own fieldwork, I find that usually the first people to approach are "deviants" and what, for lack of a better term, I'll call "professional stranger-handlers." Most groups have official or unofficial stranger-handlers to deal with outsiders. Such stranger-handlers are natural public relations experts. They can find out what the outsider is after and quickly improvise some information that satisfies him without representing anything potentially harmful to the group.

Among the Lambardi, the professional stranger-handler was an older man named Sakrya. He was the first who came up to talk with me when I entered the *tanda*. He pleasantly explained, for example, that the *tanda* was over-crowded. Therefore, I had to understand that it would be impossible for me to live there. It was Sakrya who suddenly appeared whenever I began doing something bizarre in the early days of fieldwork, like drawing a map or measuring the dimensions of a *tanda* hut. After a couple of months, it was partly Sakrya's decision that I was trustworthy that opened up the *tanda* to me. He was also quick to rent me a hut and provide me with *tanda* people to hire who were kin, but then that's probably a fringe benefit of being a stranger-handler.

When I first began working in Lexington, I was met by stranger-handlers there, too. One became a close friend. Like many Lexington junkie–patients, he reappeared a couple of times during my two years there. In fact, he used to joke, "I don't know if it's better to do your time 8 hours a day like you do, or a few months here and then a few months on the street like I do." Anyway, Jack was one of the first who approached me when I went on to the "unit" (the patient dormitory area).

I later learned that Jack, like Sakrya, enjoyed a solid insider's reputation. I suppose a professional stranger-handler would have to enjoy such a reputation since the position requires the trust of group members as a prerequisite. When he first met me, he bluntly said, "How do I know you're not a fed?" I said, "Try me." He later told me he couldn't turn down a challenge, so he began carefully guiding me through patient territory. He insured that I didn't see anything I shouldn't see. At the same time, he would introduce me into some settings to see how I acted and what kind of questions I asked. He gave me false information about violations of hospital rules to see if I would report them. Like Sakrya, his eventual approval opened up several new relationships in the unit. And, like Sakrya, he benefited somewhat by having control over some resources—magazines, books, food, and phone calls.

[2] For the non-New Yorkers, it is said that the *Daily News* enjoys a wide readership among working-class folks, while those who would go to museum benefits probably read the *Times*.

The "deviants" were another case altogether. *Deviant* here simply means members who are on the boundary of the group in some low-status position. When the ethnographer approaches, he represents a potential resource that the deviant might control to gain status. The deviant has nothing to lose and everything to gain by approaching the ethnographer and establishing a relationship.

The *tanda* presented me with my most unusual case of early encounters with deviants. Early on, a younger man came up and talked to me at length. He had several ideas about things to do in the *tanda* and he wanted my help. When he left, I asked Sakrya who he was. "Oh, he's the *naik* ('headman')." The man was a loner, and didn't appear to receive any of the respect I would have guessed a headman should receive.

Later, I learned that this *naik* was a bad character. His father had been a good man, but he died young. Since the position was hereditary, there was no choice. He was an embarrassment to the *tanda* because he had grown up stealing from other Lambardi, and he continued to do so, especially when drunk, which was as often as possible. It was tragic. An informal council of elders ran the *tanda,* and when a *naik* was necessary, they called a respected *naik* from a neighboring *tanda* to come and preside over the council. At such *tanda*-wide gatherings, the local *naik* would sit apart from the group, not participating in the discussion. He was one of my first informants.

In the hospital at Lexington, some of the "deviants" were like the staff. Although they were heroin addicts, they were of middle- or upper-middle-class backgrounds, often with college educations. Many of them felt out of place in the imported street world that flourished in the unit, so they would hang around the staff a lot and talk with them.

One of them played an ironic role in staff–patient exchanges. He was an articulate, intelligent addict who was "doing well" in treatment, actively participated in institution activities, and was generally held up as a "model patient" by the treatment staff. However, as I learned after I lived in the institution for two weeks, he was also a homosexual, going around the unit at night after the staff went home and having sexual relations with several patients. The patients enjoyed the staff's presentation of a person they would ordinarily define as "sick" as representing the goal they should all aspire to.

I don't mean to say that its *only* deviants and stranger-handlers who will approach you at first, but I'd be willing to bet that a large proportion of early ethnographic contacts are one or both of these types. The problem is even more acute because in the early part of fieldwork you probably don't know how to identify them. But, after all, what kind of person would run up to talk to a stranger with the bizarre intentions of an ethnographer? You should wonder.

There is more room for worry if you consider that these are the only people an ethnographer talks with. With too much distance, or too little time, this could happen. Imagine the picture you get of community life by just talking with its outsiders and public relations experts. It might be accurate, but one should get some information from the "regulars" to verify that.

There are some notable counterexamples to deviants and stranger-handlers in the literature. One of the most striking is William F. Whyte's description of Doc, his main informant in *Street Corner Society*. Whyte was introduced to Doc by a community worker who thought he might be helpful in the study. By Whyte's account, Doc didn't seem to care about his background and intentions, beyond asking if the book he planned to write would help "change things." He turned out to be a leader in the street scene. He more or less told Whyte to be quiet and let him do the talking. Among other things, he quickly taught Whyte such basic ethnographic skills as not asking questions too early in the game, since people would just "clam up." He advised Whyte to listen and he would learn almost everything. He also told him to be himself. It doesn't look good, Doc said, to try to act like a street corner boy.[3] By my reading, Doc was neither a deviant nor a stranger-handler. We should all be so lucky.

At any rate, as time goes on you will begin to widen your social circle. In Chapter 3 I suggested that one not worry about the "official" explanation of one's work, though as I noted then, some ethnographers do offer specific advice, sometimes stressing the critical importance of the early definition of the ethnographer's role.[4] My advice is to worry more about deciding which of the people you meet you want to work with intensively in those critical early days. How do you know when a person like that comes along?

The official term for a good relationship with an informant is *rapport*. At this

---

[3] See Whyte (1955), especially the methodological appendix where he discusses meeting Doc. Casagrande (1960) has edited a collection of articles by anthropologists about their key informants. In his introduction, he notes some common themes in their lives—they usually had contact with Western culture, sometimes intense, with both positive and negative consequences. They usually had some personal tragedy in their life history, and some occupied positions of authority. There are also numerous accounts of early contact with informants in personal accounts (cited in Note 14 of Chapter 1) and sometimes in the text of ethnographic reports.

[4] See Note 20 in Chapter 3. Also, Wax (1971) emphasizes the importance and difficulty of the early stages of fieldwork. Evans-Pritchard (1940) gives some excellent examples of difficult fieldwork, such as a transcript of an interview with a hostile informant, and a description of informants showing up and announcing that everything they have told you was a lie. I do agree that the earlier part of fieldwork is difficult, but mostly because of the strains discussed in Chapter 3. Though there are exceptions, I agree with Pelto and Pelto (1973) who state that, by and large, the "stranger" (that word again) is usually well accepted after a time and finds himself capable of doing his work.

point, I feel like a newcomer to an art museum—"I don't know anything about modern art, but I know what I like." As I try to think about the key people I've worked with in my different ethnographic studies, they strike me as a varied lot. Most of them, I think, had characteristics that would have attracted me to someone in ordinary life—though there's always that boundary problem. I'm not sure how to define *rapport*. The personal equation—the importance of the ethnographer's personality—suggests that the definition will be a variable one. Maybe we should read the social-psychological research on personal attraction.

Some in the literature do worry about why an informant would bother to enter into a long-term relationship with an ethnographer at all. There are arguments for the ethnographer as partner in a transactional exchange, ethnographer as exploiter, and ethnographer as exploited. The informant, then, depending on your point of view, gets "personal confirmation," is thoroughly ripped off, or acquires a resource to be exploited as a "Fort Knox, pawn, social expert, or technician." Then there is also the commonly reported ethnographic role as "druggist" and "scribe."[5]

I think there are several reasons why, once past the initial phase, an informant might talk with you. First of all, you're a person who's genuinely interested in and respectful of another's point of view. There usually aren't many people like that around. Second, most people enjoy telling their story to an interested listener. Third, rather than coming on like Hitler, you are interested in adapting to group life—sharing their living conditions, their food, and so on. And fourth, you are perfectly willing, probably insistently so, to reciprocate in reasonable ways with the people you work with.

You are a potential friend, though of a peculiar sort.[6] In fact, many ethnographers I know are uncomfortable with the depersonalized labels for the people they work with—somehow "natives," "informants," and so on seems too cold for the relationship they have. At the same time, the relationship is not really a friendship since the ethnographer is, after all, "doing research" and, once he leaves the group, he may have little or no further contact. The paradox of detached involvement appears again.

At any rate, as you begin fieldwork and encounter people with whom you have rapport, you must pick some to work with intensively. Here the choice becomes critical, for rapport with one person (or clique) may shut down

---

[5] Hatfield (1973) reviews the different models and uses the terms *Fort Knox*, and so forth. Lundberg (1968) describes the transactional model of fieldwork. Paul (1953) describes the "druggist" and "scribe" roles, and also cautions against the possible scapegoating of the ethnographer.

[6] Pelto and Pelto (1973) describe the peculiar nature of this strange "friendship."

alternatives.[7] For example, when Sakrya the stranger-handler gave me his seal of approval in the *tanda,* his faction opened up to me, but, the other faction in the *tanda* became more distant. Though I had cordial relationships with them throughout the study, and friendships with a few, most of what I learned came from Sakrya's group. Because of such problems, it's good to pick people to work with from different sections of the community. It's not easy to do that, since in the early days you're not sure what those sections are. It's because of this representativeness problem that issues of sampling and distribution will be discussed in Chapter 6.

Finally, you need to select informants who can inform. They must first of all have the time to do so. Then, as it was so succinctly stated in one article, the informant's job is to collect, retain, and transmit information, and to have the motivation to do so.[8] While I wouldn't advise ruling out others, especially later when observational work is discussed, it does suggest that inarticulate people who have poor recall, and who don't get around the community much, would be poor choices to work with. It's good to remember, too, that you're looking for a teacher with whom you have rapport.

Asking Informal Questions

Now that you've found people to talk with, what do you talk about? There are at least two possible starting conditions. The first assumes that you know enough about local talk to actually conduct an interview. When I began working with junkies, there were language differences, made more subtle because we supposedly shared the same language, but at least I could begin interviewing. In the *tanda,* on the other hand, though I had studied Kannada before leaving, I found myself incapable of participating in the flow of conversation, so I needed interpreter help and more language study. For the moment, assume you can, in fact, talk well enough to begin interviewing.

Since my immediate goal is to understand the informant's ability to give an account of a situation, my interest is in learning what the significant details of an event are and how they are connected. In short, I am after what one

---

[7] Morris (1973), Miller (1955), and Vidich (1955) all discuss this problem. Berreman's (1962) monograph is a thorough case study of how two different field assistants—one Brahmin and one Muslim—led to very different contacts in the village and very different kinds of data. Wax (1971) gives a similar account of how the choice of a family to live with on an Indian reservation was disastrous both in terms of the control over information that the family exercised and in the range of social contacts they allowed.

[8] The article is by Back (1956).

anthropologist calls "experience near" concepts. I want to learn how informants interpret the world through which they move. There are other ethnographers who emphasize the direct observation of behavior, recording that behavior using concepts that they define—"experience distant" concepts—and they, of course, would write a methods book from that point of view.[9]

There is a meeting ground for these two points of view that we'll discuss later in the chapter. But my bias is to take the informal interview as a central form of data in the early part of ethnography and use observation in a supplemental role. So let's begin with a discussion of the *informal ethnographic interview*. It's called "informal" for a variety of reasons. First, you don't have a written list of questions. Rather, you have a repertoire of question-asking strategies from which you draw as the moment seems appropriate.

It's also informal because you are not taking on the formal role of interrogator. The ethnographer is very much in the one-down position discussed earlier. He doesn't know enough to ask the appropriate specific questions. In this early dance, the informant takes the lead. The ethnographer's role is to look interested and suggest a couple of turns toward the other side of the ballroom so that he can check the view from there.

Finally, it's informal because it happens in many different situations besides a one-on-one isolated talk. You might ask informal questions while working with an informant on a harvest; you might ask during a group conversation over coffee; or you might ask while watching a ceremony. If used with tact, the strategies suggested in this section can add to your ability to give accounts while doing minimal harm to the natural flow of events into which your questions intrude.

The general idea distinguishing formal from informal interviews is, again, the idea of control. In the informal, everything is negotiable. The informants can criticize a question, correct it, point out that it is sensitive, or answer in any way they want to. Compare this to a Likert-type item, where the social scientist defines a question and forces the informant to respond on a seven-point scale: "How close are you and your best friend?—1. Not close at all, 2. Somewhat close," and so on. There's quite a difference.

At the same time, formal versus informal is not a neat dichotomy. There are degrees of control that can be exercised. Whyte, for example, offers a typology of interview directiveness.[10] At the least-directed end of the scale are expressions of interest. You simply encourage the informant to keep talking by word or gesture. Next comes a simple reflection back of the informant's

---

[9] Experience near and experience distant concepts are discussed in Geertz (1976).
[10] See Whyte (1960).

last statement. He says something, and you simply repeat it as an invitation to elaborate. Then there is a "probe" on the last remark. You ask some specific question about the last statement, inviting elaboration in a specific direction. And so it continues, through probes on earlier material up to an interviewer-requested change in the topic of the interview.

Beyond Whyte's typology of informality, even more structure can be imposed on the presentation of questions to informants. For example, in Chapter 7 structured ethnographic questions such as "frames" and "hypothetical situations" will be introduced. But that comes later, when you know enough to begin to more systematically document your ethnographic work. For now, we'll stay at the informal end of the scale.

As you sit down with an informant, what do you talk about? Since the goal is to learn about informant accounts, it makes sense to start with informant descriptions of situations. It might be something you both saw occur in the flow of life. Or, you might begin by getting an initial characterization of a range of situations from an informant point of view. To do this, you might use interviews on the informant's daily routine, or you might begin asking for a life history. In either case, you begin to learn what sort of situations exist and how they are interpreted.

To give you a sense of how to formulate questions, we can talk either at the level of *general guidelines,* or at the level of *specific question formation* in response to what an informant just said. To discuss the first level, we again flirt with the boundary between theory and method. Until recently, most people who were interested in theories of talk worked with single sentences as the maximum unit. Now we are again in an epoch when there is interest in long sequences of talk and the relationship of those sequences to their social context. Any of this work can profitably be consulted for guidance in that particular sequence of talk called "the informal ethnographic interview." At this point, another book could be written on the methodological implications of recent work in sociolinguistics, discourse analysis, semiotics, and computer simulations of natural language. I'm not going to do that here, but let me take a well-known example and show you how it might work.

The example comes from Dell Hymes' work on the "ethnography of speaking." Hymes views talk as a piece of behavior in a situation that includes many other features as well. There is no way to tell what aspects of the situation will be significant, a priori, but Hymes offers you a list of things to get you started.

The mnemonic for the list is represented by SPEAKING—setting, participants, ends, acts, key, instrumentalities, norms, and genre. Each aspect represents some potentially important part of a speech event, and by a bit of metaphorical extension, any social event at all. Before you start using it as an inspirational source of informal questions, note that you can apply the framework to analyze the informal interview of which you are a part as well.

Hymes' work must be consulted to understand the full range of possibilities.[11] It does not automatically generate specific questions, but it suggests areas within which you can creatively improvise some questions. Let's say you're standing with an informant watching two people work in a field. Just take the first two aspects of *speaking*. *Setting*—what kind of field is this? Who does it belong to? What are the special characteristics of this field, if any? *Participants*—who are those two men? Why are they here? Is there any reason why those two men in particular should be in this particular field?

Of course this, and any other, framework also generates questions that you can use in interviews when you're distant from the behavior you're talking about. Imagine you're talking to a street junkie and she says, "Yeah, and then I started going to the clinic across town." *Setting*—what neighborhood is the clinic in? How is the clinic designed inside? How is it different from other clinics the informant had seen? *Participants*—what kinds of junkies go there, or is it just frequented by junkies? Who is the staff, and are there different kinds? Again, *speaking* generates general questions that begin to range over the territory of how your informant accounts for events.[11]

This is only one example of a framework for large chunks of talk representing a theoretical area with strong methodological implications for ethnographers. There are many others, and not all of them are from the social sciences. Both my parents worked in the newspaper business, and I remember their "five W's and an H"—who, what, when, where, why, and how. This guideline was intended to help reporters remember to get all the necessary information when they collected a story. If that suits you better during the early days of ethnographic work, then use that instead.

In addition to general guidelines such as these, there are some specific question-forming strategies that an ethnographer might find useful. The situation will arise when the informant just said something, but you need to learn something else, and one of these strategies can request an extension of the informant's talk from where he is to some unexplored territory. It's up to you to pick the opportunity and the strategy, or to develop new ones. Sometimes I think ethnography is to social science as jazz is to music.

Here are some examples of possible strategies. The items are neither mutually exclusive nor exhaustive, but they should give you the general idea.

---

[11] See Hymes (1972).

BAIT

Some social scientists worry a great deal about whether or not a question "leads" the informant. I've never understood what a "nonleading" question would sound like. It is not whether or not a question leads, but whether or not the ethnographer controls it enough to know where it is going. Besides, the informant may or may not follow. He at least has that option when the ethnographer is one-down or symmetrical in the relationship.

Sometimes it might be sensible to lead, and lead strongly.[12] Questions that strongly suggest an answer are called *baits*. They are particularly important, because they are one way to *falsify* emergent conclusions in informal interviews. The ethnographer takes a statement made by the informant, especially when it fits his idea of what is going on in the community, and then does everything possible to get the informant to modify, contradict, or weaken the statement.

Here's an example from my work in New York. I'm talking with a methadone patient in a coffee shop. (Throughout the examples in this section, "I" will indicate "informant" and "E" will indicate "ethnographer.")

I: *It's fucking ridiculous, man. Everybody on the street's doing methadone. Look at that dude over there, man, methadone and goofballs. I mean, you can't get a decent bag of stuff anywhere, man.*
E: *C'mon, man, there's got to be some stuff somewhere.*
I: *Yeah, well, maybe some of them rocks once in awhile, but that shit's hard to find unless you know the right people.*

I should note that you've got to be careful about contradicting your informant this way. Where I worked, street rules allowed for such verbal assaults. With other groups, you might need to be more subtle.

This example, or a variant of it, happened several times in New York. I was interested in the way that methadone had become a popular street narcotic. It seemed to be replacing heroin. The informant in the example was going my way, so I tried to get some counterexamples. In this case, I suddenly became aware of "rocks." Rocks, it turned out, were a strong form of narcotic smuggled in by illegal immigrants from China (or so the story went). When I left New York, rocks were still increasing in popularity, as was heroin from Mexico and other sources in Asia. Though the "French connection" had been

---

[12] See Nadel (1939). He argues that for some informants, and for some topics, what he calls a "bullying" technique can be used.

disrupted, and though the street scene had turned to methadone, it appeared that other sources were beginning to fill the gap. My learning about that all began with the use of simple baits to falsify the then common statement that "everyone's into methadone."

A couple of ethnographers actually did a study of baiting, or "leading questions."[13] They found that seven interviewers judged as good and experienced used leading questions 22–40% of the time. They also studied 20 student-conducted interviews and found that "proportionately more" leading questions elicited additional volunteered information, and that the amount of misinformation was the same for leading and nonleading questions. There's not enough in the article to get a full sense of how they made those judgments, though.

At any rate, they went on to classify leading questions into three types: (1) When the question correctly anticipates the informant's answer, it gives an impression of friendliness and interest and encourages volunteered elaboration. (2) If the question is clearly incorrect, it gives the impression of a misinformed ethnographer and elicits corrected information. (3) If the question is partially correct or incorrect, it gives the impression of inattention and lack of comprehension, and the informant may fail to correct the ethnographer. This last type, they argue, is the "bad" type of leading question, since you don't know what's coming back.

Baiting, in short, is not a problem to pretend you're avoiding. It is a strategy to use to encourage informants to continue, or more importantly, to encourage them to disagree with what you think you've learned.

DISTRIBUTION CHECKS

In Chapter 6 the problem of testing the distribution of patterns will be treated. Before we get to that, though, an ethnographer can get a check on distribution from the informant's point of view during informal interviews. Every language has so-called "quantifiers," and such terms are among the first you should learn. Quantifiers, in English, are words like *none, a few, some, many, all.*

If the informant makes a statement that interests you, try to get him to estimate how many people in the group the statement applies to.

I: *The other day, I was talking to a kid, the only thing he's ever done is methadone. He doesn't know anything about heroin.*

E: *Does that happen a lot now?* [Or, "That doesn't happen much, does it?"

[13] See Dohrenwend and Richardson (1964).

or "How often would you say that happens?"—depending on whether you want to bait, and in which direction.]

I: *Yeah, well, not a lot, but you sure never used to see shit like that 10 years ago.*

Note that this question allowed for a distribution check with or without baiting. I wanted to show how strategies can be combined, though this is the only time I'll construct an example to make that point.

FOLK ESTIMATES

When asking for a distribution check, or when asking other questions requiring estimates of proportion or value on the part of informants, an ethnographer should try to learn folk methods for giving those estimates. Among the Lambardi, for example, I wanted to ask how well their crops had produced that year. I kept trying to get estimates using awkward questions like, "If your crop was perfect, let's call it 100. So how much of 100 did you get this year?" I got answers, but there was a long pause while informants fit their estimates into my unfamiliar framework.

Later, I learned the folk method of doing the same thing. Rupees are the main currency in India, and each rupee is divided into 100 *naye paise*. Not long ago, though, the rupee was divided into 16 *annas*. In fact, there were specific expressions for the values of 4, 8, and 12 *annas*, and people used the *anna* along with *naye paise* when they discussed purchases. When they made proportion estimates, they used the old *anna* system. I finally learned that when I overheard a Lambardi talking to another about his "12-*anna*" crop. From that point on, I had no problem with my question.

In matters of value, the junkies at Lexington hospital also had a specific way of evaluating material goods. Material goods were seen, logically enough, in terms of their monetary value. They would sometimes characterize goods in terms of how many "bags" they would bring. It was a popular game to look around my office and talk about how many bags my typewriter and tape recorder were worth. As time went on, I learned not to laugh quite as nervously as I had at first.

CONTRAST

This strategy is borrowed from linguistics. In phonology, for example, one learns something about how to characterize a unit of sound by comparing it to other units of sound to see if it differs. Compare *p* and *b* and the contrast is that one is voiced and the other is voiceless. The trick here is that the two items must be similar enough to compare. If I ask you to contrast *p* and *dog*, you would look at me strangely and say one was a word and one was a sound. You couldn't compare the two.

So you get two possible lessons with one question. Are the two items comparable? If so, then how do they differ? Here's an example, again from my research on methadone.

I: *Yeah, so I was on methadone, but my partner was doin' speed.*
E: *What's the difference between methadone and speed?*
I: *Oh man, they're completely different things. Methadone is a narcotic, you dig, and speed is an up.*
E: *So what's the difference between methadone and heroin?*
I: *Well, the methadone comes on slower. You know, like there's no rush. And methadone's harder to kick if you get strung out. But the high is pretty much the same.*

The first comparison taught me that I was asking about apples and oranges; the second got down to specific differences.

SELF AND OTHER

This type of question is really a specific form of a contrast question. It is singled out for special attention because it throws a switch that personalizes or depersonalizes a question. The strategy can go either way. For example, you might want to depersonalize some question that gets into a sensitive area. Instead of asking a Lambardi,

E: *Did your wife ever leave your house and return to her father's?*

You would do better, and be more tactful, to ask,

E: *Does it ever happen that someone's wife would leave the tanda and go to her father's house?*

A wife's departure is an important statement on her part, a call for help in arbitrating a situation that she finds intolerable. It happens sometimes, and people will talk about it, but it is an embarrassment for the parties concerned.

On the other hand, you might want to personalize other questions to learn if an informant's personal experience includes some of the activities being described.

E: *If the "ideal bride" ['cross-cousin'] exists, can a boy refuse to marry her?*
I: *Yes, but he will be fined and everyone will be angry with him.*

E: *Do you know anyone yourself who actually refused?*
I: *No.*

These are only two examples of where this strategy might be appropriate. The self–other choice is one you should always be sensitive to. It has attracted other social scientists as well. There are psychological scales, for example, that ask the subject to say whether some attributes are true of people in general as well as of himself. Among other things, a large difference might be used as a measure of alienation. Psychiatrists watch the self-other distinction as well. Often when a patient talks in sensitive areas, the pronouns change from "I" to the general "you" or "he/she." There are other examples as well.

LINGUISTIC LINKS: PART I—ETHNOGRAPHIC SEMANTICS

There is a subfield in anthropology variously called *ethnographic semantics, ethnoscience,* and *cognitive anthropology.* It appeared in the late 1950s and is now floating off in different directions as it merges with different issues in anthropology and linguistics. One of its concerns was, and still is among some, the structure of the lexicon—how are different lexically labeled concepts interrelated. Contrast is one of the relations talked about, but that was sketched earlier.

There are a variety of other relationships explored as well. Among them are the following: X is a kind of Y ("A cat is a kind of animal."); X is used for Y ("A knife is used to cut."); X is part of Y ("A piston is part of an engine."); and, as a final example, X is a stage in the process of Y ("To cook, you first have to pick out a pot."). Again, one should consult the literature to get the full picture.[14] The relations discussed suggest some strategies for question-formation in response to items mentioned by the informant.

Here is an example illustrating a couple of the relations.

I: *So then he grabbed his works and split, man.*
E: *What are works?*
I: *Works, you know, gimmicks, outfit* [is the same as]. *You use them to shoot dope* [used for].
E: *Are there different kinds of works* [kind of]?
I: *Sure, there's the regular rig and then there's a gun* ['regulation hypodermic syringe'].
E: *What are works made of* [part of]?

---

[14] Some of the classic articles in the field are collected in two volumes—Tyler (1969) and Spradley (1972). I wrote a short monograph to introduce the perspective in introductory anthropology courses—Agar (1974).

I: *An eyedropper, the bulb from a baby pacifier, a spike* ['needle'] *and some thread or paper for a tight fit.*

Sometimes the informant made the links himself, and sometimes they were requested by the ethnographer. But in both cases, a knowledge of the relations is useful in the informal interview.

LINGUISTIC LINKS: PART II—LOGIC

Many in linguistic theory are currently interested in explaining the logical relationships among sentences in a given language.[15] While this is not the time or place to review the issues and explain the logical notions, let me give an example. If A "entails" B, then if A is true B must be true. To put it another way, A is a sufficient condition for B.

Entailment can be a useful tool in guiding the formation of questions. Supposedly, the ethnographer is putting the pieces together as he learns. New bits of knowledge are integrated into a growing structure that he is trying to build. Entailment is one way of checking if you've put the new piece in the right place.

I: *At Mangya's daughter's wedding there was only one drummer.*
E: *He must be very poor.* [Ethnographer has learned that financial status is a key to explaining differences in wedding ceremonies, so he tests the statement that little money entails fewer drummers.]
I: *No, he just doesn't have many friends.*

The ethnographer has just learned that lack of money may not entail fewer drummers (it is not a "necessary" condition)—he'll have to check that later. But he has also learned that social isolation has something to do with ceremonies as well, and this opens up a whole new area of questioning that must be pursued.

LINGUISTIC LINKS: PART III—CASE GRAMMAR

In 1968 Charles Fillmore came up with a new way to represent the underlying structure of a sentence.[16] The verb is central, he argued, and hanging from it are a variety of slots, some of which *must* be filled, and some of which may be *optionally* filled. These slots stand in certain relations to the verb. One slot, for example, may require an "agent," a doer of the action

---

[15] See Kempson (1977) for an introduction.
[16] See Fillmore (1968).

encoded by the verb. Another slot may be optionally filled with an "instrument," a specification of the means through which the action was carried out.

Like everything else in this section, one should consult the literature. *Case grammar* has undergone many changes since its first appearance (in its new form) in 1968. But still, even in the simple form presented here, it suggests a strategy for question formation. By attending to the verb the informant just used, the ethnographer can run a quick check for unfilled case slots. If there are any, he can make the unfilled slot the focus of the next question.

E: *So then what happened?*
I: *The dude was busted.*
E: *Who busted him* [agent—no pun intended]*?*
I: *This snitch named Joey set him up.*

Or, to take another street junkie type example:

I: *So I went ahead and opened the door.*
E: *How'd you do that* [instrument]*?*
I: *With a regular set of picks, you know.*

Not only is case grammar useful in formulating specific questions, but it also can serve as a broader framework, like SPEAKING. The main event under discussion in the interview is represented by a verb or verb phrase, so case relations can guide you to get a complete account. In fact, many of the cases bear some resemblance, at this level, to the old five W's and an H that newspaper reporters use to guide their interviews.

FRAMES

Though "frame" is an idea with different uses in different disciplines (not to mention in the streets), I use it here in the sense developed in cognitive anthropology. A *frame* is simply a statement with a hole in it that can be filled in a variety of ways. It is a more general strategy than those considered earlier. In fact, most any of the relations discussed in this section could be used to develop a frame. "Toys are used for _____." is a frame. Different informants might fill in the slot in several ways, and in ways that differ from person to person. For example, if an informant said "gifts," he would be responding in the relation mentioned in the discussion of cognitive anthropology. If, on the other hand, he said "having fun," he would be using the relation in the sense of the case relation "instrument."

An ethnographer should always be on the lookout for frames. They are perhaps less useful in immediate question formation, and more important for the systematic testing that will be developed later. Nevertheless, here's an example of one possible use: A Lambardi says, "You need a wife to wash your back." (I was often teased about that, being single at the time. It was said that I had the dirtiest back in India.) The frame that you quickly spot is, "You need a wife to _____." There are other possible frames—"You need a _____ to wash your back."—but they don't look as interesting. You make a note for possible use of the frame later, and then use it to form the question, "What else do I need a wife for?" If nothing else, you'll learn some folk wisecracks, an important attribute of your status as an ethnographer.

So there you have a sample of strategies for forming specific questions based on what the informant is saying. There is a wealth of additional suggestions in literary criticism, computer science, and linguistics, not to mention the social sciences. You may also come up with some that are group-specific as well. But to remind you of where we started, one begins at the informal end of Whyte's scale, expressing interest and reflecting back the informant's statements once she begins giving an account of some events. Then one uses more general frameworks, like SPEAKING, or the five W's and an H, or Fillmore's cases to begin to get more details in the account. Finally, one gets pushier, using specific question-forming strategies to obtain details, learn connections with other kinds of accounts, and attempt to prove yourself wrong in what you think you've learned.

Actually, the process may not be this linear at all. As you sit listening, something bewildering may be said that launches you into detailed specific questions. No problem, as long as you keep a record of where you've been, so that you can come back later. In the long-term relationships established during fieldwork, there is plenty of time to ask questions that might have been missed earlier. There is no need to panic and try to get everything in a few sessions. That would be impossible anyway. If you're always asking questions, you'll drive an informant crazy and exhaust yourself.

The problem, and the challenge, of the informal interview is that questions are not prearranged in some linear way. Their use depends on where the informant leads you in conversation. An ethnographer should not self-consciously monitor informant statements, and then pause for a few seconds while he ticks off a list of alternatives, comes up with one that fits, and uses it to ask a question, for that would deprive the talk of its spontaneity and informality. The way out is for us to do more work on the structure of the informal interview, and then train students before they do fieldwork. It would be something like learning a limited language. At first the student would be self-conscious and awkward, but with practice the different strategies would become habit.

Finally, these strategies are useful not only in forming questions, but in analyzing transcripts of informal interviews that have been tape recorded and transcribed. These and other strategies can help you understand what you've done, even if you didn't know what you were doing at a conscious level at the time. Of course, not all of your talks will be taped and transcribed. Some of it will occur during an event that you are at least observing and perhaps participating in. (More on that shortly.)

But how does one interview if one doesn't speak the language? One of the most interesting results of my trip through the literature was the scarcity of discussions I found on the topic of translation. Many authors emphasize the importance of language competence in ethnography, and they also note the new problems that are introduced when one must rely on an interpreter.[17] Yet the literature is eerily quiet on the subject. I get the image of nervous ethnographers who are far from fluent trying not to bring the subject up.

That problem would characterize my own research. In South India, my Kannada was fair after a few months. I could pass the time of day and ask questions about things. But when it came to rapid speech or specialized topics (which requests for detail usually get you into), I was in trouble. And then the Lambardi native language is of North Indian origin. But since I had learned some Kannada before I left the U.S., I worked in that. We were all operating in a second language. When things shifted into Lambardi, I was totally lost.

I relied heavily on two interpreters. The first was an ex-untouchable, Christian high-school graduate who sometimes worked with me, but he knew no Lambardi. The second was my cook, a Lambardi who figured out what I was generally doing. He would take a butchered Kannada sentence, add some intent, and rephrase it for me in either Kannada or Lambardi. In neither case was I as in control of the situation as I should have been, but I expect that's not unusual.

In Austria I was in a different kind of situation, using a language that I once spoke fairly fluently. By the end of my 6 months in a small Austrian town as a high-school exchange student, I was fluent in the role of obnoxious teenager. When I went to college, I took a year of additional German, so that by the time I stopped off to visit my Austrian family in 1964, I was babbling away, making wisecracks, and able to get definitions easily for words that came up that I didn't know.

But by the time I worked in the Austrian village, it had been about 7

---

[17] See, for example, Pelto and Pelto (1973), Paul (1953), Williams (1967), and many others, all the way back to Rivers (1913). Powdermaker (1966) talks about the problems in the one field setting where she did not know the language, as compared to the other three where she did. Naroll (1970) uses as one of his key measures of the "quality" of ethnographic reports the ability of the ethnographer to use the local language.

years since I had used German. My language ability was returning quickly, though it never approached the previous level in the short time I worked there. I was able to work without an interpreter, though, but I was doing a much narrower task in Austria, working as part of a team to look at the question of bilingual semantics. The focus of the study was on the language itself.

That, by the way, is one of the reasons why I was attracted to ethnographic semantics in the first place. I think most ethnographers would agree that learning the language and learning the culture are far from independent tasks. In ethnographic semantics, the focus is on developing an explicit set of relationships between language and culture so that the study of language becomes a systematic exploration of the conceptual system that underlies it. The basic premise of the field—the learning of how people think about the world by attending to how they talk about it—pervades the methodological orientation of this book.

The problem doesn't disappear when you work in your own society. In fact, it is sometimes more complicated because the partial sharing of the surface forms of the language can create the illusion that you understand when in fact you don't. It's too easy to interpret informant statements into your own framework, missing the fact that the informant framework that produced the statement is quite different.[18]

Let me give an example from my work with junkies. Take the word *square*. When I first heard it, I thought it was a derogatory label for a socially acceptable, unadventurous orientation to life. That's the way I had learned it. In the next stage, I learned that as junkies used the term, it was not necessarily a derogatory label—its core meaning was "nonheroin user." There could be "hip" squares. But then as time went on, I learned more about the meaning of *square*, which derived from the contexts in which junkies encountered them. Squares were hypocrites, since they often frequented the streets to obtain goods and services that they ordinarily would say were illegal or immoral. Squares were larcenous, since their desires to get something for nothing made them a seller's market for stolen goods and a likely target for confidence games. *Square* was a complicated term to learn, and my initial belief that I understood it only got in the way.

Just to add more complications, consider a critique of ethnographic work mentioned earlier. In one article, an African anthropologist shows some key misunderstandings in a couple of classic works in the field. He argues that the misunderstandings are grounded in an inability to understand the vernacular. The few studies that I did find are impressive documentations of the amount

---

[18] James (1972) also makes this point.

of time and energy necessary just to get reasonable approximations in transla-tions.[19]

I don't know how to resolve this problem. On the one hand, some prior language study is essential to get at least a basic idea of syntax and a rudimentary lexicon, even if only to have a basis for modification.[20] The problem also makes one year in the field look like a ridiculously short time to do ethnography. Finally, though I'm biased in this direction, it suggests that training in ethno- and sociolinguistics is a must for ethnographers. And it gives you a better understanding of why this book emphasizes the details of informant talk as a way to get at their interpretation of the world around them—to learn how informants give accounts is to learn the language. They become inseparable tasks.

Analysis of Informal Interviews

Once you have some cassettes full of talk, they must be analyzed. Under the general term *content analysis,* there are a variety of techniques for doing this. To take just one example, B. N. Colby codes folktales and then does a computer analysis of the themal structure, looking for *eidons,* to use his term. Louis Gottschalk, a psychiatrist, codes clinical interviews for affect, then does an analysis with interest in the relation between affect and content of talk.[21]

These are only two sophisticated methods for dealing with informal inter-views. There are others that ethnographers should familiarize themselves with as well. For now, I want to point out some obvious things to do with informal interviews whatever your interest. The procedure described here only in-volves the analytical tools known as pencil and scissors.

In the initial stages of fieldwork, it's a good idea to transcribe tapes com-pletely. Transcription is a chore—with a clear tape and a good typist, it might take around 6 hours for each hour of tape. Later, selective transcriptions may be adequate, but at the beginning, one should lay out the entire stretch of talk to see what one has. It goes without saying that the first thing to do is to read the transcripts in their entirety several times. Immerse yourself in the details, trying to get a sense of the interview as a whole.

Having done this, you, the analyst, now seek to categorize the different segments of talk. The categories will allow you to pull different pieces of the

---

[19] The article by the African anthropologist is Owusu (1978). The two studies of interview translation are Phillips (1960) and Werner and Campbell (1970).

[20] There are some introductory treatments of linguistic fieldwork, such as Lounsbury (1953) and Gudschinsky (1967).

[21] See Colby (1973) and Gottschalk and Gleser (1969).

interview—and pieces from different interviews—together into one place. The trick is to try and develop categories from the way the informants talked, rather than imposing a set from outside. There's nothing necessarily wrong with imposing categories—you may do that later. But that's not what the early phase of ethnography is all about.

The simplest way to begin is to take a pencil and go through the transcripts, marking off stretches of talk that cohere because they focus on the same topic. This is not an automatic procedure by any means. For example, you may be able to mark off statements at different levels of generality—topic, subtopic, and so on. Or there may not be a clear transition from one topic to another. But for the most part, ethnographers and informants—like everyone—orient their talk around some focus. They keep it there until one or the other changes that focus, and the change is usually obvious in the transcript.

As you go through the transcripts, you'll begin to notice that some topics recur. These recurrent topics are prime candidates for categories to code the information in the transcripts. You will need to give the topic some kind of name for your own purposes, and you can then go through the transcripts again and mark which sections fit the new category.

The goal is to come up with ways of marking off topics that cover as much of the transcribed talk as possible. Again, the method is hardly foolproof, but it allows for categories to grow from the way the informants talked during the interview. In almost all of my fieldwork, I've done this as part of the research, and it has never failed to teach me some important things about the pattern that underlies the talk.

Once the material is categorized, you apply the next analytical device—scissors—and cut up a copy of the transcripts according to the new topic-oriented code. Each group of talk can then be read to check for consistency within each informant and variation across informants. You can also see what was talked about and, more importantly, what was *not* talked about. With the luxury of time, you can also sketch out some other types of informal questions that you would like to use in each area in the next round of interviews.

At this point perhaps a specific example would help. When I began working in New York, I was struck with the frequent use of methadone as a street narcotic. My first strategy was to conduct several informal interviews—some with individuals and some with groups—in three different treatment centers where I had spent some time. I began by talking about how things had changed in the streets since my work at Lexington. Then I either expressed interest or used some of the questioning strategies discussed earlier.

After typing the transcripts, I did the kind of analysis described above. At one point, my apartment floor was covered with piles of butchered transcript. But as the topics emerged, they were remarkably similar to the analyses I had done of tapes focusing on heroin use at Lexington. In other words, ways of talking about methadone in New York were similar to ways of talking about heroin in Lexington in 1969. There were, of course, differences, but they were interesting as well.

In this particular case, the methodology was the message. The analysis suggested the continuity of the heroin subculture in the process of adaptation to a shift in the chemical ecology of the streets. The results of that analysis have been published elsewhere.[22] Though I didn't set out to code the transcripts the same way, the results can still be questioned on the basis of out-of-awareness influences on me from my past work. But then that's where the systematic check of my conclusions comes into play, a topic that will be treated in more detail beginning in Chapter 7. In fact, one of the specific examples used in that chapter will be a small survey done to check some of those conclusions.

But that's jumping the gun. For now, I just wanted to illustrate a simple procedure to begin dealing with the data of informal tape-recorded interviews. From this simple beginning, you begin building a map of the territory that will help you give accounts, and subsequently begin to discuss what "those people" are like.

Types of Informal Interviews

About now, the idea of an informal interview may be changing into an amoeba. The concept includes a variety of kinds of talk that the ethnographer engages in. On the one hand, the ethnographer may do nothing more than suggest a broad area and sit back while the informant talks for half an hour. On the other hand, the ethnographer may get downright pushy, interfering frequently in an attempt to steer the informant's talk in a particular direction. There is a rough correlation here with how much you have learned. The more you know, the more specific questions you can ask.

Earlier in this chapter, daily-routine and life-history interviews were mentioned. The daily routine is an old standby of ethnographic work. The basic idea is to get the informant to outline the events that he moves through on both typical and special days. Then, based on his outline, informal questions are used to encourage him to provide richer accounts of daily life. One version of this that I found in the literature is the *diary-interview* method. In this version, the ethnographer first works with informants to develop a guide

---

[22] For a discussion of continuity and change in the shift from heroin to methadone, see Agar (1977b).

for diary keeping. Then the informants are turned loose, recording the flow of events in some sample of their life. When they return, informal interviews are conducted and they expand on the diary entries.

In another type of interview, called *network serials,* the ethnographer was interested in learning from informants who they encounter in daily life, in what settings, and in what kind of activities. With these three particular kinds of topics in mind, he conducted informal interviews with a sample of informants for a sample number of days. He then used the results to better understand the kinds of social networks that the informants were involved in in an urban setting.[23]

In contrast to the daily-routine interview, the life-history approach encourages the informant to talk about his or her own life in a chronologically ordered way. The life history has been more elaborately treated in the literature than the daily-routine interview.[24] Everyone agrees that life histories are important, but no one agrees on how they should be analyzed, beyond a simple presentation (edited in unknown ways) of the informant's narrative. For our present purposes, it is sufficient to suggest that the approach is a useful way to begin obtaining informant accounts of events, since that's the data we're after at this stage.

Another kind of informal interview is based on the use of videotape recording equipment. The use of visual documentation in ethnography is something that I have neglected here. I have no experience in the area, and the field has mushroomed into a subdiscipline with its own professional society. But one application that fits into the methods being discussed here is the use of videotape to elicit informal interview material. A recorded event is presented to informants, singly or in groups, as the basis for interviews focusing on their interpretations. There are several advantages to this way of relating observation and interview—the observational material is the same in each interview, and the wealth of detail is preserved in the recording. While I have never used the method, I intend to the next time I do fieldwork.[25]

There are of course other kinds of informal interviews. You might sit down with an informant to talk about some recent event that you observed. Or you

[23] The diary-interview method is described in Zimmerman and Wieder (1977). Network serials are discussed in Sanjek (1978). For another discussion of diaries, see Axinn and Axinn (1969).

[24] See, for example, Allport (1942), Gottschalk *et al.* (1945), Dollard (1949), Mandelbaum (1973), Langness (1965), and Watson (1976). The Langness reference is particularly good for a review of the literature and a historical sketch of the uses of life histories, together with a methodological critique.

[25] For sample introductions to visual anthropology, see Heider (1976), Hockings (1975), Scheflen (1973), and Collier (1967). The use of videotape as an eliciting device is discussed in an essay by Bellman in the Hockings (1975) volume.

might have learned of a particular topic that you want to explore with somebody. Or you might make a compilation of categories of activities, like the codebook of the HRAF or the guide to fieldwork known as *Notes and Queries,* and work up informal interviews based on those.[26] But, as promised earlier, the purpose here is to talk about doing ethnography in general rather than providing an exhaustive catalog of methods that have been used elsewhere.

Interviews and Observations

Now it's time to come to an issue that anthropologists love to talk about— the relationship between what people say and what they do, or the relative importance of talking to informants as opposed to watching them. Imagine a world where only two positions are possible. If you take the first position, you would argue that the only way to learn about people would be to talk with them in private in an isolated room. If you take the other, you would not listen to anything people say about what they do, but just observe their movements. Ridiculous choices.

Yet sometimes anthropologists have arguments where these seem to be the corners they work themselves into. Every ethnographer, in saner moments, realizes that you take what you can, especially in the early phase that is of concern to us now. Most would also agree that sometimes people do what they say, and sometimes they don't, and that, at any rate, one needs both kinds of data. But my bias is to take talk as the primary area for systematization, and use behavior as input into talk and as a test of the result of talk. Before I get into that, we need to clarify some confusion about the dichotomy of talk versus behavior.

Aren't people behaving when they talk, and don't they talk when they behave? Of course, yet in some discussions this problem is ignored as if everyone knew what they were "talking" about. The real problem, I think, is whether the talk is about something remote in space and time, or whether talk is part of what's currently going on.

Perhaps we should fall back on the distinction discussed earlier between language as object language and language as metalanguage. But then what if I write this: "It's a bigger job than I thought writing this book." Is that a comment on the book, part of the book, or both? And is the comment I just made a comment on the comment, or part of the book, or both?

[26] Williams (1967) discusses this strategy. The field guides are in the Bibliography as Murdock *et al.* (1950) and Royal Anthropological Institute of Great Britain and Ireland (1951).

I know intuitively that there are important differences in the sources from which an ethnographer learns. I also know that if you watch people doing things, you learn something you can't get by just talking with them, although you can't learn much unless you do talk with them before, during, and after the event. I don't mean to ignore the problem, if only I could clearly define it.

I think it might be more profitable, in the underdeveloped state of ethnographic methodology, to take the transcribed informal interview as the methodological core, and then ask how other kinds of things ethnographers do relate to it. These other things, then, either provide material on which an informal interview is based, or provide natural experiments for the testing of things analyzed from those same interviews.

Let me give one example. You go to a couple of funerals in South India, and you notice that all the bodies point in the same direction. Later, you ask a couple of Lambardis who are sitting and talking with you why that is. They say, "Because Hanuman is in the south." You begin to ask more questions, and you learn that in the epic, *The Ramayana,* Hanuman did indeed wind up in Ceylon (now Sri Lanka). You put this together with your earlier observations in the Hanuman temple, and you begin to realize that the Lambardi have a special relationship with Hanuman that you must learn more about. Without this simple observation, you would probably never have thought to ask the question, and it would probably not have been volunteered by an informant discussing funerals.

Notice that this observation fed informal interviews in two ways. First of all, it suggested something to ask during the ceremony itself. If it had been appropriate, you might have turned to someone next to you and asked why the bodies pointed south. Before you ask questions during the event, though, you must be sure that the asking does not disrupt the very event you are observing. Sometimes informants would motion me to be quiet, or give a curt answer and turn away.

But there is always time later. In this case, I brought up the subject again in a conversation that was going on anyway. I might also have asked an informant for an interview and taken him into my house and turned on the tape recorder. This would have allowed for a more uninterrupted focus on the funeral and Hanuman, and might have freed the informant from immediate social pressure so that he could say some things that would have made him uncomfortable among his peers.

Let me now use some junkie experiences to illustrate the other role of observations—to test the results of interviews. When I worked at Lexington, I was particularly interested in the study of events. I wanted to learn the junkie theory of events by attending to how they talked about them. One event that I heard discussed was "hanging out." By listening and later asking questions, I learned that hanging out was a filler, a sort of nonevent while waiting for other things to happen. The middle-class equivalent, I thought, would be like two strangers waiting for a plane—"Where you from? What do you do? Rotten weather, isn't it?" And so on. I ignored it in favor of other events like copping and using heroin.

When I worked in the streets in New York, I found myself actually hanging out with junkies on streetcorners and in coffee shops. They were usually waiting from something else to occur, but hanging out served many useful purposes. While they hung out, they exchanged information critical for "getting over" on the streets. Hanging out served as a context for talk of news. Who had the good stuff today? Where was so and so? Jack just got busted. Rick is back on the streets. "The man" is hanging out over by a particular dealer's place right now. The street scene was a social environment that could change rapidly because of outside pressures beyond one's control. Hanging out was used to keep posted on the current state of that environment.

In this case, then, the observation in the streets corrected the account I received in the hospital. To pursue an understanding of the event, I now needed to talk with more informants, observe some more, and so on through the dialectic until I felt I could give a more thorough account of the event. I did not do this because I was focusing on other topics. There is always that problem—the more you zero in on one area, the more you must neglect others.

So, observation and interview mutually interact with each other, either simultaneously or sequentially, in the course of doing ethnography. Perhaps this frequent mutual interaction is one reason why they're so difficult to separate. Following my own biases, I would advocate making talk the central source of data in informal work and pulling in other data to interact with it in a more dependent role. Other ethnographers would strongly disagree with that bias. The test for all the biases, though, will be how well key statements are supported in later, more systematic checks of the informal part of the research. That's a topic we'll take up in Chapter 6.

To sum all this up, then, observation is critical in enriching our ability to give accounts of events. Informants, giving accounts in interviews, may leave things out.[27] They may do so for any number of reasons. Informants, like

---

[27] For related evaluations of informant reliability and precision, see Young and Young (1961) and Poggie (1972). For discussions of lying, see Passin (1942) and Salamone (1977). General discussions of informant error in ethnography are in Dean and Whyte (1958), Whyte (1960), and Vidich et al. (1964). Cancian (1963) shows how informant error can be used to demonstrate the correctness of an ethnographic statement. Killworth and Bernard (1976) compare informant statements with communication data to look at accuracy in reporting network data.

ethnographers, have their "personal equation" that influences how they see things and what they report. Within his relationship with an ethnographer, an informant may judge that certain parts of an event account should be left out while others should be stressed. Some details of the account may be left out as "unimportant" or "obvious" when, in fact, they represent important things for the ethnographer to learn. The informant may just flat forget some details, or perhaps be misinformed, or, on the basis of limited experiences, give an idiosyncratic account.

The informant may be giving an account that is covered in part by the rules of the group that apply to account-giving. In one group the rule might be to downplay one's personal wealth, so in an account from an informant, you don't hear that a lot of what's going on has to do with his position as a wealthy member of the community. On the other hand, in another group the rule might be to stress personal control over others, so you get an account that makes it sound like the informant engineered and directed the entire flow of events. Or the informant, after repeated contacts with you, may become trained into your way of looking at situations, and give you accounts that fit your own developing ability to do the same. Or he may just decide to put you on.

Notice how much more complicated this all is compared to the discussions of "reliability" and "validity" in the hypothesis-testing literature. In many of the ethnographic discussions that deal with differences in informant accounts and observations, the differences are not seen as a problem to be eliminated. Whether they are called problems of "reliability," "error," or "lying," the tone is that differences between reports and behavior are a normal part of human interaction. Just because one human is an ethnographer and the other is an informant, there is no reason to expect it not to occur. The problem is to understand it, not to pretend that it doesn't happen, and then to include in your methodology some procedures for dealing with it.

As an ethnographer, your involvement in personal relationships with informants and your participation in community life will provide you with rich information to evaluate informant interviews. As time goes on, you will begin to learn about idiosyncratic and systematic differences between informant accounts and actual events, and it will largely be your observations that enable you to do so.

Since I'm advocating interviews as the core of ethnographic fieldwork, and since there are other ethnographers who would argue with this, it might be well to consider the other side of the question, though with a view towards supporting my bias. As already noted, most ethnographers use a blend of interview and observation, and many would agree with the kind of strategy advocated in this book. But others would emphasize the data of direct observation as an end in itself.[28]

John and Beatrice Whiting have done an interesting piece discussing situations where systematic observation might be necessary.[29] In some cases, they note, informants may be unable to give relevant information in areas of interest to the ethnographer. Further, ethnographers may want some kind of standardized data from a variety of different settings. They then go on to illustrate the development and use of a scheme for the direct observation of children's behavior.

Even here, though, they note the importance of a sense of the community as a prerequisite for the design of a successful observational study. And they caution against trying to record everything. They also note the need for other "measures" of the sorts of things one obtains from observational data, and conclude that systematic observation is "laborious and time-consuming." They advise doing it only if informant reports are not reliable.

Other ethnographers have also developed observational schemes to systematically record ongoing behavior.[30] But again, a charting of motion through space without a sense of the meanings of those motions to group members doesn't seem to me to be what ethnography is all about. A major way to learn those meanings, especially in the early stages of ethnography, is to ask people what they are about. It is for this reason that I emphasize informal interviews as the core of ethnography, with observation in a supplemental role.[31]

Field Notes

Field notes are considered the traditional core of data from ethnographic research. Usually, a discussion of participant observation, field notes, and

[28] Harris is one of the better known critics of what he calls "mentalist" positions. In his book (1964) he attempts to develop a scheme for the description of the structure of behavior without recourse to the meanings the participants assign to it. In an article (1974), he argues that an ability to give accounts like an informant does not mean that you can describe all the things that happen in an event.

[29] See Whiting and Whiting (1970).

[30] For example, see Guest (1960), Hall (1963), and Wolff (1960). Webb et al. (1966) in a related vein, advocate the use of "unobtrusive measures" to study human behavior without actually interviewing informants. Even here, as they note, the development and interpretation of those measures depend on a prior understanding of group perceptions of their world.

[31] There's nothing new here. Many earlier statements emphasize the interaction between interview and observation, as in for example Nadel (1939) and Paul (1953).

informal interviews constitutes field methods training in anthropology. *Field notes* are the record of an ethnographer's observations, conversations, interpretations, and suggestions for future information to be gathered. They are so central traditionally that often anthropologists refer to analysis and publication as "writing up your notes."

In my opinion, field notes are the most overrated thing since the Edsel. Part of the reason such significance is attached to them, I think, is because they are all we have. Yet in my own fieldwork, I rapidly became disillusioned with the idea. Let me use some experiences to tell you why. By the time I first went to India, I had heard the professional folklore about writing in your notebook. For example, one story has it that an anthropologist who did not want to write in front of his informants would learn something and then run off into the bushes to scribble furiously. No one said anything, but eventually the folk herbalist visited him with a cure for diarrhea.

That gets us to the first problem. Since you do not yet know what is significant, you don't know what to record. As we'll see shortly, since there is a problem with memory, it is best to write things down as quickly as possible. But it takes much longer to record everything you can remember about what just happened than it did for it to happen. In one field methods book, it is suggested that the ratio of recording time to participant observation time is six to one! So while you're scribbling furiously, other things are going on that represent the continuity between when you left and when you return.[32]

Of course you can write everything down at the end of the day, but then you must contend with long-term memory problems. A colleague of mine once held a graduate seminar where he decided to do some ethnography of remembering. One student had four friends who were starving graduate students. They saved up their money for a month, and then went to dinner at a very fancy restaurant.

The student waited until after they had gone out, and then she interviewed each separately about the meal. They all described the *maitre d'*, the waiters, the piped-in music, the potted palms, and so on. But when the ethnographer went to the restaurant, the *maitre d'* was a woman, the waiters were waitresses, and there was no music, nor were there potted palms. But it was a *very fancy restaurant*.

The problem is that long-term memory recall often produces distorted results. And the distortion is not random, but rather alters in a direction away from the details of the specific event and towards the more general stereotypi-

---

[32] Among others, Wax (1971) and Williams (1967) both suggest that early notes are not worth much. The suggested six to one recording ratio is in Bogdan and Taylor (1975).

cal conceptualization of that event. What the four diners "erroneously" remembered were some details from their shared idea of a very fancy restaurant.[33] This kind of primary method of recording is far from desirable.

Field notes, then, are a problem. In their worst form, they are an attempt to vacuum up everything possible, either interrupting your observation to do so or distorting the results when retrieving them from long-term memory. Not that you shouldn't keep notes, but they should be more focused in topic, and they should eventually be made obsolete.

The more specific focus indicates that you are no longer trying to capture everything. At any given time during your early informal fieldwork, there will be a couple of topics you are focusing on. Center your informal interviews, conversations, and observations on those topics. When you are not learning anything new, you are ready to move on, unless something remarkable occurs to cause you to reevaluate what you think you learned. Or, you may choose this reevaluated topic as one of the few you will later research more systematically. Of course, no one would advise ignoring everything that is not related to the current topics of interest. That would be destructive in the unique openness of informal fieldwork. When something interesting appears, *note* it. But don't lose the focus on the topics currently under consideration.

Field notes will consist, according to this scheme, of two kinds of things: First, some ideas from observation to follow up with interviews, or some observations/questions to follow up that came from interviews; second, some things you've noticed that you want to be sure to get to eventually. Field notes, then, are *working* notes. They are a step on a ladder used for an ascent towards an understanding of some group. Once you've used a rung to get a little higher, you don't need it anymore. Observational and interview material centered on a particular issue can be gathered into working papers as a first step in the analysis. At least you won't have boxes full of stuff that you will never look at in 100 years, except for nostalgia.

On the other hand, a personal diary is a record of another sort. Diaries focus more on the reactions of the ethnographer to the field setting and the informants, the general sense of how the research is going, feelings of detachment and involvement, and so on. It is just this sort of material that goes into "personal accounts," bringing the ethnographer's role more explicitly into the research process. Personal diaries would profit from more careful development as an ethnographic method in their own right.

---

[33] D'Andrade (1973) has published an article documenting and discussing this problem. His work is also discussed in Johnson (1978).

Ethnographic Goals Revisited

Before moving on, it would be good to step back for a moment from all the talking and watching and get a sense of how it relates to the ethnographic goal discussed in Chapter 4. Though used in a variety of ways, perhaps the best cover term for all this activity is *participant observation*. [34] The term suggests that you are directly involved in community life, observing and talking with people as you learn from them their view of reality.

As I've repeatedly warned, though, the preceding discussion has not inventoried all methods that one might use in this initial participant observation phase. For example, in some traditional communities kinship is an important system for organizing social relationships. Because of kinship's traditional importance, there is an abundance of literature on working with genealogical material. There is also another, more recent perspective on social relations that involves the study of networks. [35] But in spite of these and other holes in the discussion, you hopefully now have a sense of the kinds of activities that ethnography involves, together with a sense of what these activities are intended to accomplish.

But still there has been no sketch of the process through which all this activity accumulates into an ability to give accounts of events as informants do. I don't feel too badly about this since this higher level analysis of ethnographic materials is difficult to explicitly discuss—there haven't been too many attempts in the literature. [36] In fact, in the first draft of this book, I jumped from the discussions of interviews and observations into the next chapters, where systematic checks of what you think you've learned are suggested. The implicit message was, "Well, you do all this, and then you sort of get some ideas about how things work, so you test them out."

Perhaps much informal work is right-hemisphere activity that's difficult to translate—the intuition and pattern perception that is another part of the ethnographic mystique. Or maybe it's a series of procedures that have just

---

[34] The notion of participant observer has been elaborately discussed in the literature. See especially the reader edited by McCall and Simmons (1969). Much of the literature discusses the nature of the research role, with variations depending on the amount of involvement. See Gold (1958), Furk (1955), Jones (1961), Junker (1960), Kluckhohn (1940), and Becker and Geer (1957).

[35] For discussions of the genealogical method, see Barnes (1947), Conklin (1964), and Schusky (1965). For an introductory overview of network approaches, see Whitten and Wolfe (1973).

[36] For general statements of ethnographic analysis see Weakland (1951), Wolff (1945), and Bruyn (1966). Some of the more specific discussions of grounded theory and analytic induction will be taken up in Chapter 6.

not been made explicit yet. There is a history of change from intuition to explicit analysis in the sciences in general, so perhaps right now we're in the midst of that process in ethnography.[37] At any rate, although some of these issues will be discussed under "culture theory" in Chapter 9, it won't hurt to think a bit about them now.

The first issue has to do with all the bouncing around between accounts and events. An informant may be inconsistent in the account she gives; then two informants may disagree in their account of the same event; finally, there may be discrepancies between an informant's account and your observations.[38] The first thought to keep you from going over the edge is that all of these are normal. Informants, as mentioned earlier, bring their own personal equation and notion of your relationship into interviews, and the hidden agenda in all of that can produce problems in their descriptions. Besides, their inconsistencies may reflect an honest effort to report variation in the events being discussed. Then two informants can be expected to disagree on some counts, but then again there should also be some agreement—a shared framework within which two informants, and eventually the ethnographer, can talk about events. Finally, who in the world could report all the details of an actual event? If your observations don't teach you something new, you're probably not paying attention.

My own goal, as I wander through the maze, is to build some kind of theory of events. The test of the theory, in informal ethnography, is that it should allow you to take a particular slice of behavior and interpret it by putting it into context. In other words, something occurs, and you are able to talk with informants about what it is and how it is related to an ongoing event and other events to which that event may be related. The theory you put together may be nothing that you obtained directly in any interviews, but it should serve as a resource for you to talk with people in the group about "what's going on."

The next step, in my view, is to take the ability to give accounts, define that as data, and look for patterns across events. Say I can talk to junkies about copping heroin and also about avoiding a bust. Are there common patterns in the way I have learned to give accounts of those two different events? I call this process of searching for common principles that cross events and define the context in which accounts occur a *concern with themes*.

Then you can take events and themes and turn *them* into data. Why do folks interpret reality like this? What circumstances gave rise to and continue to maintain such a view? Is it a human universal, a product of group history, a response to some aspects of the physical, biological, or social environment?

---

[37] Margaret Mead (1969) makes this point.
[38] Paul (1953) outlines these three basic problems in checking out ethnographic data.

The search moves to a higher level as a context is sought for events and themes.

Now I'm getting way ahead of myself. Besides, my version of these three levels of analysis—*events, themes,* and what, for lack of a better word, I'll call *adaptation*—is clearly just one way of looking at ethnography. Besides, we are now struggling with the notion of "culture," and that will be discussed in Chapter 9. But let me at least give a brief example from my Lexington study. This isn't the best example, since I was working in a place remote from the actual events I was interested in, but it will hopefully give you the general idea. When I first arrived in Lexington, I spent time in the patient's situations—the living unit, the dining halls, therapy groups, social activities, and so on. My first observation was that although we spoke the "same" language, junkies talked about events in ways that I didn't understand. Their accounts of things were different from mine.

I narrowed the focus to some street events, and then did informal interviews about them. Since I was distant from these actual events, we invented a way to "simulate" them to get some observational data. (All of this is discussed in detail in Chapter 7, so I won't repeat it here.) By going back and forth between interviews and events, I built a theory of the nature and interrelationships of at least some of the key events in junkie street life.

Although I didn't systematically study themes, I did speculate on some. For example, I noticed that a concern with the background of social others was something that might be talked about in a variety of event-specific discussions. Whether it was buying or using heroin, or being busted or ripped off, the interpretation often included some consideration of the question, "Who are these people involved in this event?"

Next I speculated on the adaptive nature of that theme. In the junkie street environment, there are no institutions dedicated to your protection. When you encounter people, you must evaluate the likelihood that they are *informants* (that word in a new context), people who will cheat you, or people who will pull a weapon and take your money or heroin. In the social environment of street junkies, the theme is useful if you are to survive in the streets.

Although I stopped there in the Lexington study, the analysis could have continued. For example, I might have turned the environment into data, and tried to figure out where drug policy came from. In fact, there is some recent work in the history of narcotics legislation in the U.S. that addresses just that issue. Or, since junkies are not born into the group, I might have wondered more about their socialization as a personal adaptation to circumstances.

At any rate, you will see much more of the Lexington study in Chapter 7. My purpose here was to offer a sketch of my version of the ethnographic process. In this chapter the focus has been on that critical first phase of learning to give and understand accounts. I'm not sure what to tell you about looking for themes. That's a problem I'm interested in right now, and another example in Chapter 7 will deal with some of that work. But early participant observation is critical—it is the bedrock on which the rest of your research will rest. It is because so much of social-science research skips this phase that there are so many ethnographic critiques of hypothesis-testing research.

So, you're off and rolling. You are suitably cautious about the people that approach you to talk early on. In your conversations and informal talks over a tape recorder, you draw on some strategies that help you form questions to lead into new areas. The role of observations and field notes has been clarified somewhat, though you may very well take issue with the formulation given here and put together your own.

After some months of this, your language skills should be in fairly good shape. Your ability at giving accounts should be quite good at this point as well. When you hear or see something about an actual or reported event, you should be able to comment in a manner that makes sense to group members. Now it's time to take stock. The materials gathered during the informal work need to be gone over again, and you need to make some choices. In the limited amount of time left, you will probably want to fill in some important gaps informally. But you can also pick some of the key areas of what you have learned and document them more systematically. And that leads us into the next chapter.

6
Narrowing the Focus

Narrowing the focus of an ethnography can be a painful operation. By the time choices must be made, you are probably nearing that arrogant stance, partly grounded in truth, that no one understands "these folks" like you do. This is the "my people" syndrome viewed a bit more sympathetically than it was earlier in the book. There are undoubtedly dozens of things that you would like to pursue in more depth. But if you are committed to the goals of social science, you *must* narrow the focus.

One goal is the presentation of evidence to show a skeptical outsider why you have come to certain conclusions. You have learned a great deal during the informal work—some of it in a way that you can display effectively. But much of what has been learned comes from insight and intuition. You may be willing to bet a large amount of money that you are correct, but why should someone who has not shared the experiences believe you? If you are going to "do science," you must offer the outsider some way to evaluate your statements.

Sometimes the task may seem dreary because you already know how the more systematic procedure will come out. On the other hand, you may be unpleasantly surprised. If you design the systematic test correctly—so that the statements you are checking can be proven false—you may learn that your understanding was not as complete as you originally thought. Before worrying about the form taken by systematic tests, though, some thought needs to be given to the people with whom the check will be done.

Sampling People

During the informal work, the primary people worked with have been those who talk to outsiders, like deviants and stranger-handlers—and a few people in the community with whom, for a variety of reasons, a close relationship was established. These types of informants are often called *key informants,* for obvious reasons. Probably as time went on the cliques of which these key informants were members also opened up. This enlarged the world of possible informants, but it might also have closed off other parts of the community.

At any rate, as you moved through the community talking with people you met, you were gathering what one ethnographer calls an *opportunistic sample.* Your first priority in picking people to talk with had to do with the quality of the relationship and their aptitude as informants. You may also have sought out a *judgmental sample,* seeking out particular people who are specialists in an area you want to know more about. (By the way, some people use the term *key informant* only for members of judgmental samples. I use it in a broader sense than that.)[1]

For a systematic test, though, you must broaden your world of informants. If you only check what you have learned against the people who taught you, there is a good chance of success, unless you have truly misunderstood. But if you check what you have learned among that group *and* among others who have not talked to you that much, you build the credibility of your statements as representative of the entire group.

The best of all samples, they say, is random, where every member of the total population has an equally likely chance of being included. There is a philosophical argument that a random sample represents just another sort of systematic bias in choosing people, but we will not resolve that one here. At any rate, ethnographers often do not get truly random samples, in part for very good reasons.

The main reason is the problem of rapport. By now you are sensitive to the cues that tell you when a person is willing to give you information and when they are trying to give you something to get rid of you. The importance of this judgment increases with the sensitivity of the topic, something else you are now able to judge. Just because you are about to shift to more systematic ways of obtaining information, you should not abandon your concern with the quality of the relationship within which the information exchange takes place. Even though you are now taking the "one-up" social scientist position, the relationship is still negotiable.

So, if one-third of your "random" sample is giving you poor information,

[1] Honigmann (1970) discusses opportunistic and judgmental sampling.

and you know they are, do you blindly stick with the sample frame? That strikes me as a pointless ritual adherence to procedure without a concern for the intended goals. First of all, you should note the kinds of people who are not interested—perhaps you can find some pattern there. Then you should try to replace them with people who are like them. Failing any success at all, you can only note that your results do not represent some percentage of the sample, since that subsample did not respond well. The goal is to be as explicit as possible about *sample bias*—who did not respond and what might that suggest about bias in your results? You want to be able to characterize the *representativeness* of the sample, however informally.

One way to ameliorate the problem is to hire field assistants from cliques other than the ones you know well. Many ethnographers hire a field assistant early on. You might hire one to incorporate at least part of the community into the research process. This person will undoubtedly come from the circle of your key informants. But adding a field assistant throws a new personal screen between the ethnographer and the group members. For these reasons, my feeling is that a field team should not be assembled until well into the informal part of the ethnographic research. By then, you know who the groups are within the community, and you can try to represent different cliques.

Even if you get around this, there are other problems. As you design a sample, sometimes it makes sense to stratify it. Say you are working in a suburban town, and you know that most inhabitants are Anglos, with fewer Chicanos and blacks. Since you are interested in ethnic differences in how folks feel about the town, you decide to overrepresent Chicanos and blacks when compared to their number in the population.

Researchers often stratify on variables like sex, age, ethnicity, and education, depending on their interests.[2] You may want to stratify your sample as well, but your problem is that you are going to be more knowledgeable about the dimensions of social variation in the population. For example, you may lose friends among your sociological colleagues by pointing out that stratification by sex may be an oversimplification. What about homosexuals and bisexuals, and the variety of sex roles that they and "straight" people perform? And by "race," one may really mean ethnicity. What about the politically committed minority member as opposed to the person acculturated to Anglo society, whatever that is. It may not be at all clear what these

---

[2] Sechrest (1970) talks about this problem in cross-cultural work. He notes that in cross-cultural studies, random sampling confounds culture with demography. But stratification on demographic variables will have different meanings in different cultures. Does it mean the same thing to be 18 on a Pacific atoll, in an Indian village, in a town in the Rio Grande Valley, and on Nob Hill in San Francisco?

"straightforward" stratification variables represent. Yet their use guarantees that results will be interpreted in terms of them. Perhaps by cutting the sample in ways that reflect a deeper understanding of the group, the variation that resulted would make more sense.

Consider an example from the drug field again. Imagine that you want the sample to include a certain number of "dealers." The first problem is that most junkies who have been in "the life" for a while practice several different hustles, so it is a problem to draw a line between dealers and nondealers. Then, as reported in Preble and Casey's article, there are several different kinds of dealers.[3] They list seven, ranging from the high-level importer to the street junkie who occasionally sells a few bags to support his own habit. Stratifying the sample for "dealers" is going to be a complicated process, one you would not know how to do until after some ethnographic work.

Finally, as mentioned earlier, the topic you want to pursue systematically may be known by only a few specialists in the group. In this case, a broad sample does not make any sense because people will refer you to the specialists. In some work I did on the folklore of the heroin addict at Lexington, for example, there were very few individuals who could recite the lengthy narratives.[4] I had to search until I could find four or five. Among the Lambardi, a specialist was brought to the *tanda* to recite the origin myth for me. The Lambardi listened with as much interest as I did, since they did not get to hear it that often.

Because of your informal work, you are condemned to too much knowledge about your population. To return to sampling design, you can easily think of numerous variables that should be used to stratify the sample. Let me take an example from New York. Imagine that you want to do a systematic test of the use of methadone in the streets. You immediately think of the following variables: age, years in "the life," ethnicity, neighborhood, closeness of methadone clinics, history of clinic enrollment, sex, contacts in Chinatown, attitude towards the heroin-centered street life, kinds of hustles and personal attachments to them, and so on. I will stop there because any of these might make a difference in the orientation of a person towards methadone use.

As if the list were not imposing enough, you know that ethnicity, to take only one example, is going to be complicated to define. There will be Irish and Jewish, Haitian black and West Indian black, Dominican and Colombian. And within each of these categories there will be variation in what ethnic membership means. To take another example, neighborhoods cannot neces-

[3] Preble and Casey (1969).
[4] This work is reported in Agar (1971).

sarily be defined by census tracts. Rather, you must learn how people lump different parts of the city together into separate spaces, and what each of those lumpings means.

Even with just 12 variables, assume that each has only two values, for the sake of argument. They would, of course, have many more. You now have a sampling frame of 2^{12}, or 4096 cells to be filled with interviewees. If you only put 5 in each cell, your grand total would be 20,480 interviews. Impossible, and yet that is the price you pay for being sensitive to the many things that might relate to methadone use. Again we have a collision between ethnographers and hypothesis-testers.

This hypothetical example is important because it represents just the sort of bind that hypothesis-testers put ethnographers in when ethnographic grants are reviewed. On many site visits, I have seen the hypothesis-testing site visitor march to the blackboard and say, "You say this, this, and this (etc.) are important. Well, that indicates a sampling design like this. Yet you say you are only going to talk to 50 people. How can you test all the variables?"

Well, one strategy is to tell the site visitor to go and commit an obscene act. But perhaps a more reasonable answer is possible. The first answer is a pragmatic one. You are, after all, only one ethnographer, and it is hardly your fault that dozens of variables are relevant to the issue. Better to understand their interrelationship in a few cases than to misunderstand three of them in a population of 500. A second strategy is to have different ethnographers, working with similar groups, compare notes, but I am saving that one for the last chapter.

But there is a moral to this story. Occasionally in the literature people warn against the ethnographer taking over hypothesis-testing techniques without thinking through what they're doing.[5] A nod in the direction of probability sampling, instrument design, or test selection can get you in trouble, especially when those you are nodding at have done that type of work all their professional lives. I have heard many colorful summaries of the problem by hypothesis-testers after reviewing ethnographic grants.

In your ethnographic work, you are after the complex understanding that will enable you to give, and then analyze, accounts. When you decide to systematically check those accounts, be sure you know what you're after. Is it a simple test of distribution of account-giving? Or is it a comparison between the accounts given by males and females? Or is it a hypothesis that wealth has certain effects on the interpretation of some kinds of events?

---

[5] For example, Mensh and Henry (1953) argue that a survey of psychological test measurements in fieldwork suggests that they were not used appropriately in many cases, either because of the way they were administered or the way they were evaluated.

The nature of the question implies a sampling design. At minimum, you must worry about the representativeness of your sample. But even if you can't get a probability sample—such as a random or stratified one—there are other options between that and an opportunistic sample. For example, Glaser and Strauss introduced the idea of *theoretical sampling* to cover a practice long used by ethnographers. The procedure can be used in informal work, or it can be more formally documented to add credibility to a statement you want to make.

Theoretical sampling simply means that the ethnographer chooses the next people to talk with in a self-conscious way to obtain data for comparison with that that she already has. Say you've worked with four men on agriculture. You've talked with them about their interpretation of the flow of events that constitutes agricultural work, and you've made several observations working with them in the fields. Now you seek out four more men for shorter interviews/observations who live on the other side of the village. You select them for the purpose of checking similarities in the accounts given by your original sample.

Assume you find out that, for the most part, the data are the same. You are now approaching what Glaser and Strauss call *theoretical saturation,* where you are not learning anything new, so your next theoretical sample is a group of landless men. Now you are again looking for differences in interpretation. Then you perhaps go after a female sample, again looking for differences in interpretation along social lines that you either think might be important or that you have learned are important in that group. There are no firm guidelines to tell you when you have sampled "enough" similar and different groups, and there is no exact indication of when saturation occurs. But theoretical sampling is an improvement over opportunistic sampling because you can document the sampling design as it unfolds during the research.

Notice that theoretical sampling fits both informal and more systematic procedures as well. Say you have a systematic test on weddings in the *tanda.* If you have been working with members of one Lambardi lineage, for example, you take your systematic test to members of all the others. Or, if you have been working with Anglo male junkies, you go talk to some Puerto Rican female junkies in another neighborhood. No one knows how much is enough, but say you do 5 to 10 checks with several "different" members of the same group. If the pattern is the same as the clique you originally worked with, you can report your results and talk more confidently about junkies in New York or the Lambardi of Ashapur. If your results differ, then you need to back up and do some informal work with the different groups to find out what is going on. It all depends on how much time and help you have.

Another strategy to use if you're having problems with a formal sampling design is what Glaser and Strauss call *slices of data.*[6] This simply means that you look for other information on the group you are studying, or on similar groups, and see if it fits or contradicts the statements that you think are correct. For example, this is now the time to go to the literature. Hopefully, your key concerns have also been addressed by other ethnographers working with similar groups. If that is so, then you can compare your results with theirs. You may also be able to show how your ethnographic work accounts for the results of other social scientists, be they survey researchers or psychologists.

In New York I wrote a paper on the use of methadone in the streets. It was strictly based on informal ethnography. Later Dick Stephens collaborated with me to do a check of my conclusions. There will be more on that study in Chapter 7. But at the time, being somewhat compulsive about methods (obviously), I was nervous about writing a paper with such heavy political connotations without better documentation. Fortunately, while I was writing it, I received a copy of a survey that documented an increase in methadone in the streets. *The New York Times* ran a couple of articles on methadone that also fit my general conclusions. And between the acceptance of the article and my response to a commentary, another ethnographer, Irving Soloway, published an article with a very similar argument based on his research in Philadelphia.

So, even though my work was done along the lines of the informal ethnographic strategies outlined in the earlier chapters, I was able to show how it tied in to other work done independently by survey sociologists, ethnographers, and investigative reporters. Although I did not have my own systematic data to make or break the model of methadone use I had developed, I did have other material that substantiated my account. The study of pattern in a small sample, then, can be supported by reference to other studies that the pattern also interprets.[7]

Sampling Events

Sometimes events will be the focus of interest rather than people. Remember the "one drummer at the wedding" example used earlier? You may have a thing about drummers and decide to find out something about the

[6] See also Hill (1970).

[7] For discussions of the interaction between survey and ethnographic studies, see, among others, Back and Stycos (1959), Jones (1963), Myers (1977), Vidich and Shapiro (1955), Bennett and Thaiss (1970), and Sieber (1973). For some comments on the relation between ethnography and psychological approaches, see Cole and Scribner (1974), Edgerton (1970), Campbell (1961), Lindzey (1961), and Price-Williams (1974).

number of drums people have. Though the sampling problems here are similar to those discussed in the previous section, they take on something of a different twist.[8]

First, you need to decide what kinds of events to sample. There are three ways to get at them—*direct observation* of an event in process, someone's *recall* of events, or events that are *hypothetically created* for informants to react to. Notice, by the way, the improvement over the field note concept. You set out to get some specific information to test an ethnographic statement. You do not try to record everything in sight.

Direct observation can only be done if the event occurs while you are there. Some occur several times a day, some perhaps only once in 10 years. For the wedding example, assume that the Lambardi have most of their weddings around March, and by asking around you find out that about four are scheduled. Since that March is the only time you will be in the *tanda,* those four will be the only direct observations you can make. You can, of course, also ask people about weddings that occurred in the past. Since you are specifically interested in the role of the drummers, you can probably collect several event reports in a short period of time. Though sampling people will not be a problem here, you should be sure and ask three or so people who were at the same wedding to check possible faulty recall.

Finally, you may want to create some hypothetical weddings for informants to respond to. You might try something as simple as a series of "Suppose that . . ." questions to get informants' reactions to the meaning of different numbers and types of drummers. Using this technique, you *do* need to worry about people-sampling issues, for you now have shifted focus from reports of actual events to people's conceptions of them.

Ideally, if parts of a specific event are important, you should gather all three kinds of data. Whatever technique you choose, though, you must be sensitive to the time problem with events. Weddings last year might have been different from this year because last year the harvest was better. Weddings scheduled early in the season might be better attended than those scheduled later because people lose their enthusiasm after a few. Weddings in the afternoon might be different from weddings in the morning because other events are less likely to conflict in the afternoon. And so on.

Since sampling inaccessible events will be a theme of some of my own work discussed in detail later, that is all I will say for now. The main point is simply that event sampling has a few characteristics that differentiate it from people sampling.

---

[8] Whiting and Whiting (1970) discuss problems in event sampling.

Distributions

The sample, of whatever type, is checked out on the questions of interest, with the usual goal being a characterization of a distribution. Distributions are a topic treated in great detail in statistics courses, but we need to talk of them here as the underlying goal of the systematic tests that you conduct.[9] A *distribution* is simply a picture of the variation in the sample. It summarizes the differences in informants' responses and gives you an indication of how well the ideas you're checking are supported.

Let us take a simple example. After a few months of work, you notice that junkie accounts of events in the streets have changed. By comparing accounts, it is obvious that a major reason for the change is a shift from heroin to methadone. You summarize this with an ethnographic statement: "Methadone is replacing heroin in the streets." As part of the check of that statement, you ask 50 male narcotics addicts who are *not* in methadone programs the following question: "How many times in the last week did you use methadone?" Remember that this is intentionally oversimplified. In a true check, you would no doubt also ask about heroin, dosage taken, and many more questions, and you would look at whatever other data you had.

First you discuss your sample. You take all 50 from the neighborhood in which you have been working. It is a "casual sample," which is jargon for grabbing whoever comes along who will talk with you. A true random sample is impossible since you cannot enumerate the total population from which the sample is drawn. Besides, considerations of rapport are important here because you are asking about illegal behavior. You are known in this neighborhood, so there is a greater likelihood that people will talk with you. Besides, you will keep track of some basic things about the people who do respond— the old standbys of age, sex, and ethnicity, for instance—so that you can at least get an idea of what the sample was like.

Now consider some possible hypothetical results. Assume they look like this:

Times used per week	Number of people
7	48
6	2
5	0
4	0
3	0
2	0
1	0
0	0

[9] See Thomas (1976) for an anthropologically oriented introduction to statistics.

Usually a distribution is expressed in proportions, but we will leave it in raw numbers. This table brings joy to your heart, for it means that your ethnographic statement is clearly supported. Since methadone is longer acting than heroin, use seven times a week probably means use of methadone once a day as the only narcotic. You will check that, of course, with other questions.

With this kind of result, the casual nature of the sample loses its problematic nature. The nature of the sample should be discussed to show you did not just talk to one kind of person, but as long as there is a reasonable amount of variation in the sample you can be confident that you have hit the proverbial nail. If you have done the informal work well, many of your tests will come out this well on the key general statements you have made about the group. This test adds credibility to your eventual ethnographic report.

The test might, however, have falsified your statement if you had gotten results like this:

Times used per week	Number of people
7	0
6	0
5	0
4	2
3	1
2	7
1	11
0	29

These results do not support your conclusions. Perhaps the folk theory of methadone use emphasizes that use for other reasons. Perhaps the small amount of use reflected in the table is striking in comparison with junkies of the 1960s. Or perhaps in your informal work you tended to stumble into a few key informants who, according to this distribution, were atypical. At any rate, you now clearly have more work to do.

Sometimes results may be less crisp but interesting nonetheless. For example:

Times used per week	Number of people
7	11
6	8
5	5
4	1
3	2
2	2
1	7
0	14

This table presents a more complicated picture. However, it looks like informants cluster at both ends, leaving the middle sparsely populated. One idea you might get here is that your statement is correct for one subgroup, incorrect for another. Some junkies may be replacing heroin with methadone use, and those are the ones you talked to during your informal work. However, there is another subgroup you missed that does not use methadone, and you now know you had better go talk with some of them.

In a case like this, you might also look at different parts of the sample. Let us say you talked with some people who had been junkies since the 1960s, and others who entered the street life in the 1970s. There were 25 of the old-timers and 25 of the new kids. So you break the table down accordingly:

Times used per week	Old-timers	New kids
7	0	11
6	1	7
5	0	5
4	1	0
3	1	1
2	2	0
1	6	1
0	14	0

Now you have a clue. It looks like the old-timers, who were active in the days of abundant heroin, are less frequent users of methadone, while the new kids tend to be the heavier users. Again, it is time to go back and talk to some people. You might also have done similar breakdowns by age, sex, ethnicity, or whatever other information you have on your casual sample. Such breakdowns will not always help because sometimes the underlying pattern that helps understand the distribution will be related in some complicated way, if at all, with the sample characteristics you have collected. But try what you do have.

Finally, you might also get something like this:

Times used per week	Number of people
7	6
6	7
5	5
4	7
3	8
2	8
1	4
0	5

A distribution like this is about what you would expect by chance since 50 people distributed across 8 categories would give you 6.25 per category.

Assume that you try some breakdowns by sample characteristics, but they all come out looking about the same as the original. Well, first of all, it is interesting that what should be an indication of methadone replacing heroin neither supports nor falsifies the statement. These results may suggest that you have asked the wrong question. Perhaps the strong sense that methadone is replacing heroin has nothing to do with frequency of use, as we discussed in the earlier sample results that falsified the statement. And, of course, randomness is not necessarily bad news. Perhaps the fact that use is so evenly distributed in the sample is itself a striking indicator of its acceptance, when compared to the infrequent use in the 1960s. Again, you need to return to the field.

As you glance back over all the possible outcomes, you might wonder if there are not ways of summarizing the tables. There are indeed, though you lose some information in the process. One way is called a *measure of central tendency*. There are a variety of these—*mean, median,* and *mode*—but generally the idea is to look for the center of balance of the distribution. A second measure is one of dispersion. *Dispersion* gives you an idea of how wide a spread the distribution covers is. Consider two more short examples:

Times used per week	People in group 1	People in group 2
7	10	0
6	10	0
5	10	20
4	10	20
3	10	20
2	10	20
1	10	0
0	10	0

Each of the samples would have the same measure of central tendency (mean = 3.5), but they would have different measures of dispersion.

The problem here is that measures of central tendency and dispersion can obscure the specific pattern in the data that allowed the ethnographer to interpret them. Sometimes preparing a simple table like the examples used here is all that you will need to do. However, an ethnographer needs training in statistics. These simple examples hopefully suggest why such training is important and give you a context in which such skills are used.

For example, you should know how to estimate the characteristics of the population by the characteristics of the sample you have taken. If your data fit the assumptions of some mathematically defined distributions (like the normal curve, the binomial distribution, or the chi-square distribution), you can check whether or not what you have differs from what you might get by chance. The famous *statistical significance concept* relates to this—Do your results depart significantly from what you might expect by chance? I admit that that is not very exciting—so your results are not due to chance.

This is where the idea of *control* is so important. Remember that this notion came under fire in characterizing the relationships that ethnographers had with their informants. Suppose two groups differ on only one variable. If you compare their answers and the differences are greater than what you would expect by chance, then you assume that the single different variable is the reason. Your problem as an ethnographer is that you will see the groups as differing between themselves, as well as *within* themselves, on a whole variety of things. Again, your vision of complex pattern will hinder your acceptance of the simplifying assumptions of statistical tests.

The experimental model and statistics can represent powerful resources for you, though, even if only as metaphors. Besides, this discussion is dramatically oversimplified. For example, most of the distributions discussed here are only of one variable (univariate). There are other things you can do if you want to deal with two variables at the same time (bivariate) or several at once (multivariate). In the bivariate area, for instance, you might want to explore the various measures of correlation, such as *Pearson's R* or the *Spearman rank–order correlation.* If you want to deal with several variables at once, you might draw on techniques for getting what is called a *Multiple R,* or you might look at analysis of variance, or take a plunge into factor analysis.

But, as I said in the beginning, this is not the place to learn statistics, but that field should be studied at some point. There are at least two reasons for doing so, even if you do not use statistics in your own research. First, you need the information to operate from a position of strength rather than weakness. If you read something you do not like in a journal, you need to be statistically literate so that you can understand the role statistical procedures played in the argument.

Then even if you do not use the specific procedures much, they provide useful metaphors to guide ethnographic work. Take central tendency and dispersion again. In some ethnographies, the authors usually follow some implicit procedure for "taking an average." They reread what they have in certain topic areas, and then come up with some kind of statement that "averages" all the material they have.

But, carrying through with the metaphor, what about the idea of dispersion? Unfortunately, many ethnographic statements are given with no indication of variation, yet they easily could be. Instead of just reporting central tendency, a person could also summarize the kind of variability found around the topic. Sometimes ethnographers try to do this with words like *most, sometimes, once in a while.* But since it usually is not clear what such terms mean to the writer, readers do not get as much information as they might. Even if no systematic testing is done at all, the results of ethnographic work might be made more credible just by pursuing the metaphor of dispersion as well as that of central tendency.

A final word on my own prejudices. Anthropologists, more than many social scientists, have mathophobia. One of my favorite wisecracks is to define mathematical anthropology as what happens when anthropologists number their pages. The problem is that such distancing from mathematics is not without reason. The very simplicity and clarity of the mathematical formulation may miss the complexity and ambiguity that interests the ethnographers. As I have mentioned several times, an ethnographer's appreciation of the complexity of pattern often makes procedures focusing on the relationship of a few variables look superficial at best, delusional at worst.

So in some ways, the prejudice is a healthy one. One should focus on the question of interest, not on the procedures available that will make him look more sophisticated. In my own work, as you will see shortly, most of the points I need to make are made with simple frequency distributions. If that is all you need, stop there. But while the position is healthy, it becomes pathological with an a priori rejection of anything mathematical. For one thing, mathematics is much more than statistics. For another thing, if you choose not to use statistical procedures in your systematic testing, it should be because you know enough about them to know they are inappropriate, not because the very thought causes you to break out in a rash.

The Systematic Test

Now you know what your sample will be and what kind of distribution you are after. Unfortunately, you still do not have a systematic test. This is the great moment I have been avoiding and, by and large, I am going to continue to avoid it. There are books full of psychological tests, sociological questionnaires, codes for observing events, and forms for recording census information. It is depressing to think one should know about them all.

As if that were not bad enough, many of them may be inappropriate for the group you are working with. Michael Cole and Sylvia Scribner, for example, have done a great deal of work showing that psychological tests for cognitive abilities developed in one group will often make another group to whom it is given look less intelligent. The tests subtly draw on the experiences of the group in which they were developed. If the new group has not had those experiences, tough luck.

The ethnographer's problem, then, is not only which procedure to steal, but how to adapt it. On the other hand, she may decide to start from scratch and create her own test. But to do this, one needs some understanding of the process of developing psychological tests or survey questionnaires, processes that can be learned in the appropriate research design courses of different disciplines. It may sound like I am advocating a curriculum heavily weighted towards methodology, but then what would you expect from someone who would write a book like this?

Rather than listing all methods, which would be impossible at any rate, let's worry for a minute about what "systematic" testing is all about. Many of its characteristics were described in Chapter 4, only then we were criticizing it. The reason for the criticism, if you recall, was because that was *all* that most social science research did. At that time, I mentioned that it should be used as a part of ethnographic fieldwork when the time is appropriate. Now that you have a substantial understanding of the group in which you are working, the time has arrived.

Systematic means that each informant's behavior is fit into the same framework. The assumption is that if the framework is the same, then any differences among informants will be due to their response, not to changes in the framework. Long ago we surrendered that fiction. Even in the most carefully controlled situation, the ethnographer–informant relationship is too complicated to support that assumption.

On the other hand, there are degrees of standardization. In informal fieldwork, one strength is the ability to adapt questions to the personal and situational demands of the moment. While this can result in better information, it is difficult to record and report in all its variety. Now, later in the fieldwork, the assumption is that you know enough to design a standard framework that will cover the topic in a manner that makes sense to the informants you plan to sample. Besides, part of your relationship guarantees that you can ask for and receive comments from informants on whether or not the framework makes sense in the first place.

So, although you are not seduced by the idea that each informant perceives the task in an identical fashion, the standardized framework does eliminate some of the differences that were important in informal interviews or observations. Besides, you now have something that you can display to the skeptical outsider, so that he can see the questions or tasks that you used to check your ethnographic statements. You get some credibility points for that.

The second important feature of the systematic test is the idea of falsifiability. There must be a possible set of responses that informants can give that prove you wrong. This is a key point. A frequent criticism of ethnographic work goes roughly like this: "Well, all I see are some conclusions and a few supporting anecdotes. How do I know the ethnographer didn't just see those things that supported a conclusion that had already been reached." Our critic is right; she cannot know from the text. Good ethnographers, of course, always try to falsify their conclusions, but they often do so in informal ways that are not reported in their published works. One of the key roles for the systematic test in ethnography is to provide a focal point for public display of a critical issue.

By systematic, then, I mean a test that will fulfill the goals of standardization, public display, and potential falsification of conclusions. Standardization seldom occurs in informal fieldwork, and it should not. It contradicts the whole idea and destroys the very strength of ethnography. Public display might occur more often than it does, but it is difficult and requires much space to display and interrelate transcripts of informal interviews or notes of specific observations. And finally, falsifiability is possible during informal work, but again it occurs improvisationally in conversations, interviews, and observations, and it is a difficult, lengthy process to pull all the material together. Once you learn the appropriate research skills, and know the group from your informal work, you will find that it takes very little time to systematically check key statements on which your ethnographic conclusions rest.

Putting the test together is another area where your creativity gets a workout. You know the group better than any outsider at the point in time when you begin checking your statements. After picking your topical interest, you must draw from a breadth of knowledge about the group to assemble a framework that will make sense. At the same time, the framework must fit the notion of systematicity, including the all-important ability to prove you wrong. It is one of the more creative moments of ethnographic research.

The Formal–Informal Mix

Traversing the methods literature, I was impressed with the variety of interactions between systematic or formal and informal approaches to ethnographic work. In most cases, the approaches are kept distinct, though they may occur in any order. In one research text, Brim and Spain argue for an experimental design as the core method with informal ethnography preceding and following to set up sensible procedures and interpret the results.[10] Bennett and Thaiss suggest using surveys to check "typicality" or "representativeness" of informal results. Powdermaker used a survey as a jumping-off point for her ethnographic work in South Africa.

[10] See Brim and Spain (1974), Bennett and Thaiss (1970), and Powdermaker (1966).

Although this book is written in the direction of informal to formal, these and other examples suggest that there is no hard-and-fast rule on the grammar of formal and informal. Nor is there any limit, in principle, on the length of the string. A particular research project might combine several approaches in any number of possible ways, limited only by the number of researchers and the length of time available.

Then there is the interesting possibility of losing the distinction between formal and informal altogether. Myers, for example, reported on a "synthesis" of ethnographic and survey methods.[11] Confronted with the problem of studying drug use in a job-training program, he noted that traditional survey approaches were ineffective. He then incorporated group members into the research team in "collegial" roles. They participated in study conceptualization, instrument development, coding, and data interpretation. Another interesting modification, in view of examples earlier in the book, is that "stimulus standardization" was abandoned as an interviewing goal.

The possibility of such "methodological convergence" is an exciting one. It suggests that there may be new ways of thinking about ethnographic methodology that are just emerging. In the examples of my own research in Chapter 7, you'll see the same kind of variety that is in the literature. In some cases, the relationship between formal and informal work is straightforward and linear—the one is a check against the other. But in other cases, it's not always clear where one orientation ends and the other begins. There will be more on that when the examples are presented.

The possibilities of synthesis are intriguing, but I don't feel clear enough to define them. Perhaps one way of looking at it would be as the problem of providing an explicit documentation of the ethnographer's learning during informal work. Or perhaps another way would be to return to the problem of "de-indexicalizing" an ethnographic statement, as mentioned in Chapter 1, complete with personal equations, social relations, and the various sources of information drawn from.

For now, I'll rely on the rhetoric of formal and informal. The distinction is useful, at least today, for such pragmatic tasks as article and proposal writing. It is also useful for explaining ethnography to hypothesis-testers and other nonethnographers. Formal approaches make for better ethnography, but if you strip away the procedures discussed in this book as informal, ethnography is no longer being done.

---

[11] See Myers (1977). A sample of an equivalent argument for experiments can be found in Goodman (1970).

The Narrowing Funnel

So far the informal and formal approaches to research have been presented as two phases of ethnography—informal first, followed by formal.[12] Yet throughout Chapters 5 and 6 there are hints of bouncing back and forth between the two approaches to data collection. The second view is the more realistic one. The division in chapters here is more a rhetorical device, with a view towards later discussions of ethnographic research design.

Perhaps a better model of fieldwork would be a funnel. You begin wide-open to whatever you can learn, but within such a broad boundary, you are already bouncing between learning and checking what you have learned. In Chapter 5, for example, we discussed the critical role of observation as a check on what you learned in an interview, and vice versa.

As you begin to focus your interest on certain topics, the funnel narrows. You may focus because of an a priori interest you brought to the field, because of what you learned in the first period of fieldwork, or because of both. But still you are alternating learning with tests of what you have learned.

Finally, as you approach the narrow end of the funnel, you begin some systematic testing. Even here, though, the results of the tests will often pose further questions, so you return to your learning role to get a better understanding of why the tests worked as they did, or why they did not work at all. As the funnel narrows, your questions may get more and more specific, but you never stop learning.

Now for some examples from my own work. Not surprisingly, they will illustrate many of the strategies advocated here. After that, we can try to pull out the implications of all this for the design of ethnographic research proposals.

[12] Levine (1970) and Brim and Spain (1974), among others, also advocate an early informal phase and a later hypothesis-testing phase.

7
Informal to Formal: Some Examples

The problem for the ethnographer as scientist is much the same as for the ethnographer as fieldworker. During informal fieldwork, improvised questions are put together based on what he has learned. For systematic testing, procedures are also improvised, drawn from the ethnographer's background in research design and his knowledge of the group. That is why, throughout this book, frequent nods have been made in the direction of being trained in the research procedures of many disciplines. These procedures will be your resources for the rest of your professional life when you put together systematic tests of your informal work. As mentioned earlier, I have no intention here of putting together a list of formal methods. There are hundreds that are scattered throughout the social science literature. What I would like to do is illustrate the development of formal methods by using three examples from my own work.

The first example is taken from the Lexington hospital.[1] I was really doing two studies at Lexington—one of the patient in the institution and the other of the junkie in the street, though the two were not mutually exclusive. I would spend time hanging around in the patients' areas of the institution, listening and trying to learn how they viewed the world by attending to how they talked about it. I also went to patient social events, and eventually lived in a residence area for a couple of weeks, at their invitation, to get a feeling for life in the joint.

After doing this for several months, and after conducting several

---

[1] Much of the material in this section is adapted from Agar (1973) with the permission of Academic Press.

informal interviews and assembling a dictionary of slang, I began to worry about being more systematic. So I worked up three interlinked methods to help me display my understanding of the junkie world view. The first method was called the *simulated situation*. As a method, it was informal because it defined a situation that was typical for the group members and they, then, enacted it. But it did give a public, transcribed record of at least some segments of junkie talk. The other two methods were frame elicitation and hypothetical situations. *Frame elicitation* was an intermediate method on the formal-informal continuum—it tested my conclusions from the informal data, but also allowed new information to appear. The *hypothetical situation* method was the most formal. It was a restricted framework into which junkie responses were forced, with clear outcomes that either supported or refuted my ethnographic conclusions.

Simulated Situation

First, I approached a Lexington patient with whom I had some rapport. I explained that I was interested in learning about life on the streets and asked if he and a friend or two would act out parts of that life so that it would be taped. The response was usually enthusiastic. A frequently heard patient complaint is that the staff at Lexington consists entirely of squares ('nondrug users'), and the patients seemed to perceive the simulated situation as a means of getting the squares to understand the street life. For the situations used here, the simulations proceeded in the following way:

The patient organized a group of his friends and set a time for the taping. The groups varied from three to five male members, and all groups were racially homogeneous. The group was taken into a conference room with a large one-way mirror on one wall. Since the first group expressed discomfort with the mirror, a movie screen was pulled down to cover it. Chairs were arranged in a semicircle in one corner of the room, with a floor microphone placed several feet away from the group. I sat at the other end of the room, partially hidden by the recording equipment.

The group was asked to simulate "copping" and "getting-off." They were told that they could hear some previous simulations as an example. If requested, two or three 1-minute excerpts were played. The group then set the initial conditions. The members were from different communities, so they selected the home city of at least one of them as the location. They then outlined the circumstances of being together or meeting each other in the selected city, and they were then ready to begin. Just prior to taping, I told the group that the tape would be played immediately after the session, and any material that a patient felt to be potentially harmful would be erased. (No request for erasure occurred in the tapes used in this study.) At this point, the taping began.

The "realness" of the behavior in the situation was checked in at least three ways. A type-1 check was indicated, for example, when one or more members of the group referred to the observer and the taping equipment, gestured or whispered during the taping in order to control the others' behaviors, or stopped the taping to redefine the situation. Behavior that did not fit the situational context suggested that the situation broke down in some way and the group tried to redefine it.

At the end of the simulation, the tape was replayed and the group's reactions to various behaviors in the tape segments were noted. These type-2 checks took several forms: A participant might say something like, "Isn't that the way it is?" and receive nods and murmurs of assent from the rest, or he might accuse another of not being "real," with the others agreeing or disagreeing. On the other hand, the group as a whole might laugh and point out a particular mistake or an artificial statement and comment on it.

In the type-3 check, the tape was played to a different group for comment. Reactions varied as in the second check. For example, an earlier tape on the relapse of an ex-addict elicited sympathetic groans and expletives from the listening group. At the end of the tape, one listener explained that addicts had very similar life experiences. He, too, had encouraged a friend who was on heroin, and had also begun using again. It was, he explained, the same kind of situation as that portrayed on the tape. On the other hand, another listening group severely criticized a tape of an individual telephoning a prescription to a pharmacist. They pointed out his mistakes and explained why his method would never work in the streets.

Using these methods, four tapes were collected. Since rapport with whites was achieved somewhat more easily than with blacks, three tapes were done by white groups. One other tape by a black group was collected to check against the white tapes. While the four performances are not the same as real street events, they are probably quite good approximations.

Frame Elicitation

A second method used in the study is related to decision making. Although numerous decisions on different levels can occur as the junkie engages in the simulated events, the focus here is on the selection of event prerequisites and the estimation of an undesired event's occurrence. To study this, a method for the systematic elicitation of alternative attributes or outcomes would be useful.

One such methodological tool used here is that of frame elicitation. As noted by Metzger and Williams:

The establishment and employment of specifiable eliciting frames, formulated in the informants' language and in terms "entertainable" by informants, constrains their response in some great degree to a focus or foci which are in turn defined in the informants' terms, rather than by the categories of the investigator.[2]

Thus, a linguistic frame is an utterance(s) with some empty slot that may be filled by more than one item.

Most frame elicitation in cognitive anthropology has contained slots that were filled with monolexemic utterances. This is quite consistent with the primary interest in naming behavior since many names take a monolexemic form. There is, of course, no reason why slots requiring longer utterances could not be used.

First, frames were each typed on index cards. For each respondent, a sample frame was first shown. I asked him to read through the sample, filling in the blank with anything he might say if he were in the streets. If the informant was confused, I read through the sample once and filled in the blank. When the informant understood the task, he was told that he should repeat the task up to five times before moving to the next card. However, he was told that he need only read the last line (the one with the frame slot) after the first time.

The cards were then handed to the informant. A tape recorder was turned on, and he was told to proceed. When the informant shifted to the next card, if less than five responses were given, I asked if he could think of anything else that he might say. Aside from this, I did not interfere.

Frames came from two major sources. In some cases, they were lifted directly from a transcript; in others, they were created with the help of assistants. The initial sets were assembled using tapes from white informants and white assistants. Later, when the first black informant was interviewed, he said that although he understood the situation perfectly well, the "script" did not feel quite right. Together we made minor changes in some of the wording, and no further complaints were heard from subsequent black respondents. Only after I left Lexington, unfortunately, did I learn that he was teaching me sociolinguistics—certain speech forms did not fit certain situations.

The frames were administered to a sample split evenly along white-black racial lines. Sample size varied for different frames. As an example of a frame, consider the following:

"You can always go somewhere else and get better stuff, too. But look at the changes ['difficulties']—taking a chance of _____ ."

This frame was administered to 14 respondents, 7 white and 7 black. The responses were elicited as shown in Table 1.

[2] See Metzger and Williams (1963, 1966).

TABLE 1
Responses to Sample Frame

Card Number	Response	Frequency
1	Being taken off	1
2	Getting busted	9
3	OD'ing	1
4	Not getting back in time	1
5	Getting ripped off somewhere else	1
6	Getting busted by the man in a place you don't know	1
7	Getting robbed	1
8	Getting bad stuff	1
9	Getting burned	3
10	Getting beat	5
11	Getting ripped off	2
12	Getting taken off	1
12a	The man not having nothing	1
13	Getting garbage	1
14	Fooling with the wrong people	1
15	Getting cracked	1
16	Getting a bogue blow	1
17	Like, you don't know who you're dealing with	1
18	Getting some bad stuff	1
19	Blowing the scratch	1
20	Maybe O.D.'ing	1
	Total responses	36

Each response, together with the sentence in which the slot occurred, was typed on an index card and numbered. When identical responses were given by different respondents, only one card was typed, and the frequency of the response given was noted. Both the card numbers and the frequency are also shown in Table 1.

The stack of numbered cards was given to a sorter who was asked to sort the cards into piles. To place two cards into the same pile, they had to "be different ways of saying the same thing." For the example, three individuals performed the sorting task—one black, two white. The results of the task are presented in Table 2. The numbers are the card numbers.

Clearly, there is some "sharedness" in the sorting, some agreement between the three independent sorts. For example, the First Sorter's number 2, the Second Sorter's number 1, and the Third Sorter's number 3 piles are almost identical. These sortings can be said to contain equivalent responses. On the other hand, the First Sorter's number 1, the Second Sorter's number 5, and the Third Sorter's number 4 piles obviously share some items, al-

TABLE 2
Results of Sorting Task

First Sorter
1. 1, 5, 7, 8, 9, 10, 11, 12, 13, 16, 18, 19
2. 2, 6, 15
3. 14, 17
4. 3, 20
5. 4
6. 12a

Second Sorter
1. 2, 6, 15, 16
2. 4
3. 3, 20
4. 8, 9, 10, 12a, 13, 14, 17, 18, 19
5. 1, 5, 7, 11, 12

Third Sorter
1. 3, 20
2. 8, 13, 16, 18
3. 2, 6, 15
4. 1, 5, 7, 9, 10, 11, 12, 14
5. 4, 12a, 19
6. 17

though membership in this sort is hardly as clear-cut. The problem then, is how best to deal with these ambiguities.

One possible solution would be to confront the three sorters with the differences. This was rejected for two reasons, one practical, the other methodological. The practical reason was the short stay at the Lexington facility. Since patients stay a maximum of 6 months, it was sometimes the case that a sorter would leave before such a confrontation could be arranged. This was a minor problem. More important was the close relationship between the sorters and me. Because of the close relationship, and the probable natural bias toward consistency, I felt uneasy with the possible distortion introduced by asking sorters to resolve inconsistencies.

A second solution was developed. A "sort table" was constructed for each frame. The following rules were used to construct the table:

1. Disregard sorts where all items in the sort were elicited from only one respondent.

The assumption here is simply that any sort containing the elicited utterance of only 1 of the 14 respondents is not shared enough to be considered. Anything that is culturally significant is assumed to be culturally salient;

anything that is salient should be elicited from more than one respondent. This rule eliminates the First Sorter's number 5 and 6, the Second Sorter's number 2, and the Third Sorter's number 6 (see Table 2).

2. By inspection, locate sorts for the three sorters that share more than one item.

This rule follows immediately from rule 1. If a set of shared responses can be constructed on the basis of one shared response, we have a condition covered by rule 1, since it would be based on the response of only one respondent. Therefore, the sorts must share more than one response.

3. List the sorts on the sort table, where the nth column lists responses sorted by the nth sorter.

If we find that each of the sorters has a sort that shared more than one item of each of the other sorters, then we list these sorts on the table. The First Sorter's number 1, the Second Sorter's number 5, and the Third Sorter's number 4 shared more than one response. In this case, the shared responses are numbers 1, 5, 7, 11, and 12. The three sorts are listed on the sort table, as shown in Table 3. The notation at the top simply refers to the original sort data in Table 2. Thus, "1.1" indicates that column 1 includes those responses in the First Sorter's number 1; "2.5," the Second Sorter's number 5; "3.4," the Third Sorter's number 4.

4. Indicate those responses that are shared in all the sorts.

In Table 3, the shared responses—1, 5, 7, 11, 12—are underlined.

TABLE 3
Example of Sort Table

1.1	2.5	3.4
<u>1</u>	<u>1</u>	<u>1</u>
<u>5</u>	<u>5</u>	<u>5</u>
<u>7</u>	<u>7</u>	<u>7</u>
8	<u>11</u>	9
9	<u>12</u>	10
10		<u>11</u>
<u>11</u>		<u>12</u>
<u>12</u>		14
13		
16		
18		
19		

All responses not underlined are called *residuals.* Residuals are dealt with in one of two ways. The first way is *partitioning* the sort. Sometimes, one sort includes responses that are listed as two sorts by another. That is, one sorter makes a finer discrimination than another when he is sorting the responses. To partition the sort, then, all residuals are taken together as a new sort; that is, the original sort is partitioned into two subsets of that sort. The first subset includes those responses that are underlined; the second subset includes all residuals. The subset of residuals is treated as another sort, and rules 1 through 4 are applied again.

Again, to give an example, refer to Table 3. Under "1.1," 1, 5, 7, 11, and 12 are underlined. Responses 8, 9, 10, 13, 16, 18, and 19 are not; they constitute the residuals. This subset is now treated as a separate new sort of the First Sorter. Inspecting the original data in Table 2, we see that this residual subset shares three responses (8, 13, 18) with the Second Sorter's number 4 and the Third Sorter's number 2. We can now add these three sorts to the sort table, as illustrated in Table 4. We now have two sets of equivalent responses, the first consisting of 1.1, 2.5, and 3.4; the second consisting of 1.1, 2.4, and 3.2. A P is placed over sort 1.1 every time it occurs (see Table 4) to indicate that a partitioning occurs. The sets of equivalent responses are labeled with roman numerals. In the example in Table 4, the first set is labeled "I"; the second set, "II."

This procedure for deriving sets of equivalent responses does not, of

TABLE 4
Example of Sort Table

I				II		
P				P		
1.1	2.5	3.4		1.1	2.4	3.2
1	1	1		8	8	8
5	5	5		9	9	13
7	7	7		10	10	16
8	11	9		13	12a	18
9	12	10		16	13	
10		11		18	14	
11		12		19	17	
12		14			18	
13					19	
16						
18						
19						

course, stop at this point. There are several more sorts to deal with; furthermore, there are still residual sets in Table 4 that can be extracted and possibly used later. The final results of the application of this procedure for the example frame are indicated in Table 5.

Note that the residuals that did not fit into the sets of equivalent responses are prefaced by a minus sign ($-$) each time they occur. Response number 16, for example, could not be used as a shared response, thus, a minus sign appears each time it occurs; that is, in all three partitions of 1.1, as well as 2.1 and 3.2. These residuals are called *error residuals*.

The final results are shown in Table 6. The roman numerals refer to the labels used in Table 5. Similarly, the numbers of the utterances are the same as the underlined numbers in Table 5. Using this procedure, the original sort data are reduced to sets of equivalent responses. For this frame slot, then, the "changes" include the possibility of being robbed (I), getting low-quality heroin (II), losing money in a sale of fake heroin (III), being arrested (IV), or taking an overdose (V).

What about the error residuals? First of all, it would be useful to know the proportion of cards that did not fit in one sort or another. This would essentially be a measure of the usability of the responses. Thus, we define a simple function U (usability) as:

$$U = \frac{n_u}{n_t}$$

where n_u is the number of responses used in the final table of equivalent responses and n_t is the total number of original responses. For the example frame, the value of n_u is 30 (see Table 6), and the value of n_t is 36 (see Table 1). Thus:

$$U = \frac{30}{36} = .83$$

The six members of the error residual set are:

4. Not getting back in time
12a. The man not having nothing
14. Fooling with the wrong people
16. Getting a bogue blow
17. Like, you don't know who you're dealing with
19. Blowing the scratch

It is clear to assistants consulted independently that the last four could be in more than one equivalence set because of the response ambiguity. For example, 14, 16, and 17 could refer to any of the five sets of equivalent

TABLE 5
Sort Table for the Sample Frame

I			II			III			IV			V		
P 1.1	2.5	P 3.4	P 1.1	P 2.4	3.2	P 1.1	P 2.4	P 3.4	1.2	2.1	3.3	1.4	2.3	3.1
1	1	1	8	8	8	9	9	9	2	2	2	3	3	3
5	5	5	9	9	13	10	10	10	6	6	6	20	20	20
7	7	7	10	10	-16	-16	-12a	-14	15	15	15			
8	11	9	13	-12a	18	-19	-14			-16				
9	12	10	-16	13			-17							
10		11	18	-14			-19							
11		12	-19	-17										
12		-14		18										
13				-19										
-16														
18														
-19														

146

TABLE 6
Equivalent Response Sets

I.	1.	Being taken off
	5.	Getting ripped off somewhere else
	7.	Getting robbed
	11.	Getting ripped off (2)
	12.	Getting taken off
II.	8.	Getting bad stuff
	13.	Getting garbage
	18.	Getting some bad stuff
III.	9.	Getting burned (3)
	10.	Getting beat (5)
IV.	2.	Getting busted (9)
	6.	Getting busted by the man in a place you don't know
	13.	Getting cracked
V.	3.	O.D.'ing
	20.	Maybe O.D.'ing

Total responses used = 30

responses. The "wrong people" or people you "don't know" could rob you, give you bad heroin, fake a sale, arrest you, or give you an overdose; and all of these are a "bogue blow." Similarly with 19, since you could lose your money through robbery or a fake sale. Thus, a final rule is defined:

5. Error residuals that are ambiguous enough to be placed in more than one set of equivalent responses are dropped from the total response inventory for the frame.

Using the new value of n_t, U is recalculated. The new value is called "U corrected for ambiguous residuals," or U_c. For this frame, 14, 16, 17, and 19 are dropped, reducing n_t to 32. The value of U_c, then, is:

$$U_c = \frac{30}{32} = .94$$

For this frame, the values of U and U_c are quite high. One interpretation of this is as follows: Most of the responses elicited from a heterogeneous group of addicts fit into a cognitive structure held by three other addicts, as indicated by their independent performance in sorting tasks. Since the existence of an addict culture is really an empirical question rather than an established fact, such high values can be interpreted as a measure of agreement for the addict sample. This is interesting in and of itself, independent of the substantive content of the frame.

It would also be useful to have a measure for each equivalence set, since U is a measure defined over the entire response inventory. We thus define a second function, A (agreement):

$$A = 1 - \frac{n_e}{n_t}$$

where n_e is the number of errors and n_t is the total number of responses in the equivalence set. The value of n_e is obtained by counting the minimal number of changes in the sorts necessary to eliminate the error. In the case of three sorters, if one sorter included an error residual and the other two did not, we need to drop the error residual to eliminate the error. By making one change, then, the error is eliminated, so the value of n_e increases by 1. If two sorters included an error residual and the third did not, then by adding the error to the third sorter, the error would be eliminated. Again, the value of n_e would increase by 1, since one change was made. In the case of three sorters, then, the value of n_e will increase by 1 in both cases.

The value of n_t is simply the total number of responses included in the set. This includes both the underlined members of the set and the error residuals, although it does not include the responses that are partitioned out and used in another set (n_t is the maximum value of n_e). In the limiting case, if every response in a sorter's sort was shared in no other sort, the value of n_e would equal n_t. In this case, the value of the expression would be:

$$A = 1 - \frac{n_e}{n_t} = 1 - 1 = 0$$

At the other extreme, the value of n_e would equal 0, that is, all responses in a sorter's sort are shared in all the other sorters' sorts. Here the value of n_e would equal 0, and the value of the expression would be:

$$A = 1 - \left(\frac{0}{n_t}\right) = 1 - 0 = 1$$

Thus, the value of A ranges from 0 to 1, with 0 indicating no agreement and 1 indicating total agreement. For the sample frame, the values of A are as follows:

$$
\begin{aligned}
\text{I. } A &= .83 \\
\text{II. } A &= .67 \\
\text{III. } A &= .62 \\
\text{IV. } A &= .90 \\
\text{V. } A &= 1.00
\end{aligned}
$$

As with the function U, we can drop the ambiguous error residuals and recalculate the value of A_c, or A corrected for ambiguous residuals. This produces the following values:

I. $A_c = 1.00$
II. $A_c = .93$
III. $A_c = .92$
IV. $A_c = 1.00$
V. $A_c = 1.00$

As with U and U_c, A and A_c give a measure of "sharedness" for the individual sets of equivalent responses.

Hypothetical Situation

In the study, some of the items of information on decision making were examined by postulating interactions between them. To empirically examine some of those interactions, constructed hypothetical situations were used.[3] A *hypothetical situation* is simply a stated set of conditions. In the study of decision making, alternative sets of conditions were specified, and the respondent was asked to choose the one he preferred. By varying conditions, the interactions of the variables were tested in a systematic way.

Let me give an example. Suppose we wanted to find out whether a junkie would rather get money alone or with someone else. In the first case, it is safer to be alone in terms of arrest possibility, although in the second case an addict can make more money working with someone else. We could construct a straightforward hypothetical situation to test the preference. For example:

You're just going out to make some bread. Joe, a dude you've known for some time, comes up and asks if you want a partner for the day. What would you tell him?

The ethnographer can vary factors such as amount of police pressure, financial need, and so forth to see how these variations effect the preferences in the hypothetical situation.

In this study, the situations were administered in the following way. The Lexington hospital employs three interviewers who administer a comprehensive interview to every patient admitted to the institution. When I had a series of situations ready, I asked the interviewers to administer them to the next 30

---

[3] See Herskovits (1950). See also Wager and Miller (1969) for a critique of the method.

consecutive admissions who were urban male heroin addicts. Although these data help us understand some of the decision-making processes, I should note that they are the data with which I was least confident. In all other cases, work was done with trusted friends, an important consideration in interviews with deviant groups. This was not the case with the hypothetical situations. On the other hand, the interviewers were all experienced, working-class people representing a variety of races, so results may not have been too distorted. At any rate, the hypothetical situations, as we shall see, were helpful in understanding decision making.

The Three Methods in Use

Now that you have wandered through sort tables and other things in the abstract, let me show you a specific example. In the analysis of the tapes, one of the things that junkies had to do was pick a place to "get off" in. The following discussion shows how the tapes, the frames, and the hypothetical situations were used to get both a better understanding and a better documentation of how junkies pick a place.

SELECTING A PLACE

In three of the simulated situations, the junkies "got off" at the dealer's; in the fourth, they got off in one of the group's "crib." In no case was there any verbal decision making. This is partially an artifact of the method. Since the group was simulating two consecutive events, and since the simulations were restricted to one room, the natural mapping of street behavior into the experimental situation would be a street situation where the two events occurred in the same place.

To probe for relevant decision assessments, two frames were used. The second (B) is simply the negative of the first (A). The text of the frames is as follows:

A. "Yeah man, let's fix over there, 'cause _____ ."
B. "Naw man, can't go getting off over there, 'cause _____ ."

The frames were separated by five other frames, and the wording was changed, again to minimize any cognitive carry-over.

The results are listed in Tables 7 and 8, along with corrected and uncorrected values of U (usability) and A (agreement). The frame responses focus on a series of continuous decision assessments. The most predominant of these is the possible occurrence of a bust (Frames A.I and A.V; Frames B.I,

TABLE 7
Frame A—Selecting a Place $(U = .74)$

$A = .94$	I.	1. It's cool (5)
		2. There's a good lock
		3. There's no heat on the spot
		4. It's safe (2)
		5. It's away from the window
		6. It's a cool place to do it
$A = .82$	II.	1. The broad is good and cool
		2. The broad'll let you lay and nod
		3. That's a groovy spot
		4. That's a hip place
		5. It's out of sight
		6. You can always hang out after you get high
		7. I can be comfortable
		8. It's groovy
		9. It's a hip spot
		10. The place is nice
$A = .67$	III.	1. There's more light
		2. It's warm
		3. It's close (2)
$A = 1.00$	IV.	1. There's not much traffic
		2. There's no one home
		3. There's not that many people there
$A = .60$	V.	1. The police don't bother around here
		2. We can do our thing without getting ripped, you know
$A = .61$	VI.	1. Nobody won't be begging
		2. There's nobody around (2)

B.II, and B.III). A second group focuses on possible requests for dope by others at the place (Frames A.VI and B.VI). The third group has to do with the general characteristics of the place (Frames A.II, A.III, A.IV, B.IV, and B.V). Whereas this last group is somewhat ambiguous, the generality is indicated by the content of the items in the equivalence sets. Items refer to, for example, specific people who are there, physical characteristics of the place, or general statements about it being groovy or bad. In these last equivalence sets, Frames A.II and B.V could also refer either to the possibility of a bust or to others asking for dope.

Now, there is another item interacting with the probability of a bust. Getting off can vary. If a junkie were busy hustling, he would fix rapidly and leave whatever place he had chosen. If he had time, he would lay and nod for a

TABLE 8
Frame B—Selecting a Place ($U = .86$, $U_c = .88$)

$A = .96$
$A_c = .98$
	I. 1. It's hot (3)
	    2. The place's too hot (2)
	    3. It's a hot spot, you know
	    4. The place has been spotted
	    5. They're hip to us (2)
	    6. There's too much heat
	    7. The place is hot
	    8. The gas station man's hip to it
	    9. We got a new superintendant and he prowls the halls
	  10. The police was just there
	  11. It's too hot (2)
	  12. It's a hot spot
	  13. Cops are watching that place

$A = .78$ $A_c = .89$	II. 1. The spot's been busted two or three times 2. The joint's been ripped two, three times, you know

$A = .95$
$A_c = 1.00$
	III. 1. The lock is broke
	    2. It's not cool
	    3. Too many people coming in and out
	    4. We might be seen
	    5. Too many people around
	    6. There's too many people

$A = .90$
$A_c = 1.00$
	IV. 1. The dude's wife ain't cool
	    2. That broad's gonna scream
	    3. My mother's home

$A = .75$ $A_c = .88$	V. 1. It's a bad spot 2. I don't dig that spot

$A = .86$	VI. 1. Too many guys are over there. We'll have to give them some dope
	    2. We might have to give some of it away, man
	    3. They'll want some

while. Thus, the factor of how much time he wanted to remain in the place would be an influence on his decision of where to get off.

In short, the probability of a bust increases in importance if the junkie is going to spend a great deal of time in the place. A second item is expected to interact with the probability of a bust. If a junkie is sick, then the probability diminishes in importance since he is more willing to take chances in order to get off quickly. The probability of a bust is expected to be the most frequent determinant for decision making. If there is a lot of heat on a place, the junkie will not go there.

TABLE 9

Summary of Questions to Ask in Place Selection with Effect on Value of Individual Place[a]

Question	Answer	Effect of value
1. How much heat is there on X?	More	Lower
	Less	Higher
2. How much can you expect people to hassle you for dope at X?	More	Lower
	Less	Higher
3. How hip a spot is X?	More	Higher
	Less	Lower
4. How far away is X?	Farther	Lower
	Closer	Higher
M1. How sick are you?	More	
	Less	
M2. How much time are you going to spend at X?	More	
	Less	

[a] Where: X is any place.

The next consideration is that of cost in terms of others at the place asking for dope. In this case, the higher the expected cost, the less the value of the place. Similarly with the characteristics of the place, as the characteristics are estimated to be better, the value of the place will increase. Finally, we expect distance to be a factor (see Frame A.III.3). As distance increases, we expect the value to decrease. Again, the sicker the junkie becomes, the more important the distance factor becomes.

The attributes of a place can be listed as a series of questions that a junkie would ask to determine the value of a particular place. Referring to Table 9, note that the question that is expected to be most important is listed as number 1, with the two questions that are expected to shift the weights of the other items indicated by an *M*. To check our hypothesis about the weights given to each question, the hypothetical situations were used. The situations are listed in Table 10. In all three, the probability of a bust, expected to be the most important, is matched against characteristics, cost, and distance, respectively. To check the effect of the questions related to sickness and time, the three hypothetical situations were asked under four sets of conditions:

1. The junkie has to leave right after he fixes, and he is not sick at all (low time, low sickness).
2. As above, only he is very sick (low time, high sickness).

TABLE 10
Hypothetical Situations for Selecting a Place

1. There's a lot of heat on Joe's place, but there's no heat on Red's. Joe's place is a hip spot, but Red's place is bogue. Everything else about the two places is the same.

2. Some dudes at Mac's will hassle you for some dope, but no one will ask you at Pete's. But there's a lot more heat on Pete's place. Everything else about the two places is the same.

3. Bob's place is a lot closer than Jack's. There's a lot of heat on Bob's, but none at Jack's. Everything else about the two places is the same.

3. The junkie wants to lay and nod for a while and he is not sick at all (high time, low sickness).
4. As above, only he is very sick (high time, high sickness).

The results are listed in Tables 11, 12, and 13. First of all, note that in the usual street situation (low time, low sickness), the probability of a bust does indeed dominate. Note also that the metaquestions change the responses, although the sickness question as related to distance seems most powerful. To review the changes briefly, when compared to place characteristics (Table 11), the bust probability is decreased in importance by an increase in sickness, and increased in importance by an increase in time to be spent in the place. The same relationship holds between bust probability and the other two factors, cost (Table 12) and distance (Table 13). With the exception of distance as affected by sickness, the changes are not dramatic, although they always occur and are always in the predicted direction.

This example shows how the Lexington work blended formal and informal in a variety of ways. For the first few months, I did participant observation in the hospital. My records at that point consisted of some working notes, a lexicon of junkie argot, and some transcribed informal interviews. As the work

TABLE 11
Preferences Where Place A Is a "Hip Spot" and Place B Has "No Heat"[a]

	Low time		High time	
	Low sickness	High sickness	Low sickness	High sickness
A (Good characteristics)	7	11	5	7
B (Low bust probability)	23	19	25	23

[a] N = 30.

TABLE 12
Preferences Where Place A Has People Who Will "Hassle You for Some Dope"
and Place B Has "No Heat"[a]

	Low time		High time	
	Low sickness	High sickness	Low sickness	High sickness
A (High cost)	9	16	6	9
B (Low bust probability)	21	14	24	21

[a] N = 30.

began to take focus, the first method used was the simulated situation—
formal in the sense that all groups were guided by the same events and the
verbal behavior was recorded and checked, but informal because content and
interpretation were left to group members.

The next method—frame elicitation—was more formal yet. Standardized
frames were presented, and there was more of a concern with an even sample
along white-black lines. An informal hypothesis was operating, in that I
wanted to see if the responses checked out with what I thought would be
important. But at the same time, there was room for new responses to appear.
The sorting was also guided by an implicit hypothesis—namely, that although
different sorters would differ, there would also be a shared structure implicit in
the results.

The hypothetical situations were more of a hypothesis test of the classic
sort. In this example, the variables used in picking a place were isolated and
certain relations among them were specified. The hypothetical situations were
a specific way of checking out at least some of those hypotheses. Notice that
statistics were not used in the tables. I remember sitting down with Paul Kay,

TABLE 13
Preferences Where Place A Is "Much Better" and Place B Has "No Heat"[a]

	Low time		High time	
	Low sickness	High sickness	Low sickness	High sickness
A (Low distance)	5	27	1	19
B (Low bust probability)	23	3	29	11

[a] N = 30.

my thesis adviser, and experimenting with a few possible techniques. We decided that there weren't any that seemed to add any information not obvious in the distribution of cases in the tables.

At the same time, mathematics did play a useful role in the measures of usability and agreement. Although the measures were simple, with the meanings of different values uninterpretable because the underlying distribution was unknown, they were useful in giving a rough idea of "sharedness" in the sorting. The moral here is simply that if you need to formally measure something, but there aren't available procedures in your mathematical background, it might be possible to invent a simple one.

Now let me give another example of a formal study based on ethnography, this time from my work in New York. When I began that work, I was struck by the amount of methadone being used in the streets. I conducted informal interviews in the streets and in treatment settings, and also spent some time in different neighborhoods in the Lower East Side of Manhattan. Eventually, I took my notes and transcripts and did the sort of analysis described earlier in Chapter 5. For me, the interesting part of the analysis was that the pattern of talk and behavior fit with the earlier junkie world view described in my Lexington work.

For now, I want to emphasize the systematic test. In collaboration with my colleague, Dick Stephens, I designed a study to check some of my ethnographic conclusions. Unlike the previous example, where methods were taken primarily from linguistic anthropology, this study took the form of a small sociological survey. Let me now turn to the original work to show the methodology and results of the study.[4]

Systematic-Test Methodology

The test sample was composed of 41 persons interviewed in June 1974. All subjects were males currently enrolled in treatment programs for their narcotic addictions; 21 were enrolled in a methadone maintenance treatment program, and 20 were in an abstinence-oriented modality. Prior to their current program involvement, 13 of the total 41 were involved in a methadone program, 6 of these more than once. The sample is composed of 19 blacks, 14 Puerto Ricans, 7 whites, and 1 American Indian. The ages of the subjects ranged from 20 to 44 years, with a median age of 24 years. The median age

---

[4] This section is taken from "The Methadone Street Scene." *Psychiatry* 38 (1975): 381–387, and is used with the permission of the publishers. Copyright © 1975 by the William Alanson White Psychiatric Foundation, Inc.

of first addiction to heroin was 17. Most subjects reported semiskilled occupations.

The methadone program sample was interviewed on a clinic pick-up day. The interviewing team sampled from a six-hour time period, thus obtaining both working and nonworking patients. The abstinence sample was drawn from either the orientation unit or the recent-violators unit of the program. In this way, virtually all of the sample was either on the streets or had only recently arrived from the streets. The interviewers introduced themselves and informed the subjects of the purposes of the study. Initially, a few minutes were devoted to establishing rapport, primarily by indicating that the interviewer was "streetwise." Confidentiality and anonymity were assured (no names were taken), although such considerations were not as pressing as usual in this study because the focus of the interview was on the subject's perception of the street scene rather than on what his behavior was.

Although most of the reported findings in subsequent sections were clearly indicated by a large percentage of respondents, the nature and size of the sample do call for some caution in generalizations. First of all, the sample consists entirely of addicts in treatment with the New York State Drug Abuse Control Commission. As others have indicated, the path from the court to the clinic leaves behind a large percentage of those addicts arrested, and, of course, those arrested constitute a biased population as well.

Second, opinions expressed by the sample are, like any opinions, subject to bias. However, it is difficult to speculate on the nature of the bias. On the one hand, an addict respondent might bias his statements toward an overinflation of illicit methadone use, to take one example, to minimize his own sense of deviance. On the other hand, he might reduce his estimates in order to minimize illicit use, as a protective strategy. Although these and other sources of bias should be held in mind, the respondents do represent a variety of neighborhoods, age groups, and ethnic backgrounds. Further, the reported patterns, as noted previously, usually are strongly supported by a large percentage of the sample.

Third, all respondents are lumped together for the purposes of this study. With an N of 41, a sample breakdown into methadone-program versus abstinence-program respondents would not be worthwhile. However, an informal overview of the data indicates that differences between the two subsamples are not striking. The only major variation is in subsample characteristics since the methadone program had more Hispanic members and fewer blacks.

The subjects were interviewed by three trained interviewers, all of whom are knowledgeable about the New York street scene. A structured interview schedule was developed after informal consultations with the interviewers and addicts and two formal pretests. In the text and tables that follow, the total N sometimes does not equal 41 because some respondents gave no answers to some of the questions, some of the questions were not applicable, and some of the respondents gave more than one response.

THE STATUS OF STREET METHADONE

One of the first areas explored with the respondents was the current status of street methadone. An attempt was made to define the frequency of methadone use on the streets. Thirty-four persons indicated that they knew people who had gotten strung out on the streets, and 19 of these respondents estimated the pattern of street methadone addiction to be a frequent one. In further support of methadone's emergent role as an important drug, 30 of the respondents reported that they knew of persons whose principal drug of abuse was methadone. Of the 22 respondents who felt that they could give an estimate, one-half reported that they knew of "many" persons whose "main thing" was methadone; 26 respondents also noted that they knew of users whose experimentation with narcotics first began with methadone, and about one-third of those respondents estimated that the frequency of the pattern of methadone as the first narcotic was "high." Finally, 32 respondents noted that they knew of persons who used methadone recreationally; that is, for sprees on weekends or at parties. Of the 28 who felt that they could give an estimate, 16 said that recreational use of methadone was widely prevalent among their acquaintances.

Consistent with this picture of methadone as an important drug of both addiction and recreation is its use in connection with other drugs. When asked what drugs people usually use methadone with, the respondents answered as follows:

Wine	38
Pills (principally barbiturates)	20
Cocaine	12
Marijuana	12
Valium	3
Other alcohol	3
Heroin	2
LSD	2

Several respondents distinguished between the initial or occasional user and the addicted user, whether on a program or in the streets. The early user, it was asserted, is more likely to use only methadone. With increased addiction, wine or pills are increasingly likely to be used to boost the methadone high. The use of methadone, as a narcotic, with both cocaine and marijuana is, in all likelihood, a continuation of a pattern previously established with heroin.

Thus, the pattern that seems to emerge from these data is one of a widespread use of methadone. Apparently, not only are there many persons addicted to street methadone, but also it plays a role as a drug of entry into the narcotic street scene. Its use as a recreational drug appears to be significant, and the evidence indicates that it has been integrated into the recent polydrug scene.

REASONS FOR METHADONE USE

Obviously, the preceding data support the view that methadone is an important drug on the street scene. It might even be conjectured that these findings and those of other studies indicate that methadone may be beginning to rival heroin as the preferred narcotic on the streets. Two questions that naturally emerge from these data are: "Why would a person want to score methadone instead of heroin?" and "How does a methadone high compare with heroin?"

In answer to the first question, the respondents reported the following reasons for methadone use:

Is inexpensive	13
Gives a good high	12
Is not diluted like other drugs	10
The high is long-lasting	10
More readily available	5
Easy to use	5
Lower likelihood of arrest when methadone is used	2
More powerful than other drugs	2

Several findings emerge from the above data. First, it is interesting to note that two of the four top reasons for methadone use lie in the pharmacological properties of the drug—namely that methadone gives a good and long-lasting high. The other two reasons relate more to the conditions of the street scene; that is, methadone, unlike other narcotics, is relatively inexpensive and its quality is more assured than the highly "cut" drugs such as heroin. Cited less frequently were methadone's widespread availability and its ease of administration. Conspicuous by its absence was methadone's more traditional use as a substitute drug when no other narcotic is available or as a withdrawal drug when the habit becomes unmanageable.

These data are consistent with those studies that have documented the increased use of methadone. These data support the viewpoint that methadone is valued both for its own euphoria-producing pharmacological properties and for its quality and low cost when compared with heroin.

Because heroin has been "king" for so long, several questions were devoted to comparing it with methadone. Respondents were first asked, "Do most people who use methadone on the streets still prefer heroin if they can get it?" Surprisingly, methadone emerged as the preferred drug: 17 of the respondents said that they felt methadone would be preferred over heroin; 14 felt that heroin was still the drug of choice; 3 felt both drugs were equally favored. The reasons for these choices were not consistently and completely assessed. However, those who said that methadone was preferred apparently felt so because of the higher quality and greater availability of methadone as compared with the poorer quality and lessened availability of heroin. Respondents who still felt heroin was favored cited heroin's better high as the most important reason for its choice as preferred drug. Other reasons included heroin's traditional role as the preferred drug, the ease of kicking it vis-a-vis methadone, and the negative effects of methadone.

Because heroin still appears to be the yardstick against which other narcotics are measured, all of the respondents were asked to compare the heroin high with the methadone high. All of the comparisons noted by two or more respondents are listed below.

Highs are similar	12
No rush with methadone	9
Methadone high longer-lasting	5
Methadone high comes in slower	4
Methadone sleepier high	3
Methadone more relaxing high	2
Methadone more active high	2

While the most frequent response is that the two highs are similar, there is an interesting pattern in the responses provided by those who saw a difference in the highs. With only a couple of exceptions, the heroin high is seen more as an intense, active high while the methadone high is pictured as a more subdued kind of experience. To some extent, this difference is an artifact of the usual route of administration. Heroin is usually injected intravenously, resulting in a "rush" as the chemical enters the system. Methadone, usually taken orally, is absorbed into the system much more slowly.

These data may be related to the rapidly changing street market. Perhaps a return to higher quality, lower cost heroin would mean that heroin would again rival the emergent methadone market. However, according to 25 of 36 who answered a question in this area, the heroin situation is not improving in the streets.

In short, then, this section shows that methadone is used for reasons related both to its euphorigenic properties and its availability. In the light of heroin's current low quality and reduced availability, the widespread use of methadone is not difficult to understand.

COPPING METHADONE

Another major area of exploration focused on where methadone was obtained, in what forms, at what price, and from whom. All respondents were asked, "If you wanted to find methadone on the streets right now, where would you go?" While various answers were provided, only two responses were given by more than two persons: 19 persons said they would go to a specific neighborhood in order to cop methadone, either their own or a known drug-copping area. More significantly, another 19 said they would go to the area surrounding a methadone maintenance treatment center if they wanted to cop some methadone. The latter response points to the importance of programs as a major source of illicit methadone, an issue to be discussed more completely in a later part of this section.

When asked how difficult it was to cop methadone, 38 of the respondents said there was little or no difficulty involved. Some respondents noted that there were certain time periods or certain days when methadone was easier to obtain than at other times. However, the clear implication was that methadone was plentiful and easy to cop.

The price of methadone was relatively constant. A price of $10 or less for 80–100 mg of liquid methadone was given by 16 respondents, while 14 pegged the price at more than $10 but less than $15. Only 5 respondents estimated the average cost to be more than $15. Price variations were attributed to a number of factors. Generally, the price was less if the seller knew the purchaser. A few respondents mentioned that street methadone could be more costly on days when clients did not "pick up" their methadone. And in the more middle-class and suburban neighborhoods, the price was higher.

With regard to the tablet or disquette forms of methadone, 23 respondents said that they were currently impossible to purchase, another 10 said tablets were available but very difficult to obtain, and only 5 respondents felt that tablets were still obtainable without too much difficulty. Those few who did give price estimates gave wild fluctuations in cost for the 40-mg disquette, ranging from $5 to $25. Because of the liquid's constant availability, its prices are apparently more stable.

Apparently, the oral route is the predominant route of administration for methadone: 19 of the respondents said they had never heard of anyone shooting methadone; 16 said they had heard of it but virtually all of them indicated that it did not happen often; only 4 respondents indicated that they themselves shot methadone, and for them it was more for the sake of experimentation.

The major finding that emerged from the data on copping methadone was its source. Virtually all the respondents reported that the chief source of illicit methadone was methadone maintenance program patients. Although 19 respondents did say that there were dealers who sold methadone, only 2 felt dealers handled methadone extensively. Thus, the distribution pattern of methadone is unlike that of other illicit drugs, undoubtedly because street methadone, for the most part, is diverted from programs by individual patients.

Diversion is accomplished in two basic ways. First, 11 respondents stated that methadone is often obtained at the time of administration in the clinic. This can be accomplished in several different ways: holding the methadone in the mouth until departure from the clinic, immediately spitting methadone into cups, bottles or sponges, and so on. The more frequent method of diversion, mentioned by 27 respondents, is through the sale of take-home doses.

The respondents were asked to report what proportion of a patient's dose they felt was ordinarily sold, whatever the method of diversion. These proportions are:

1/4	1
1/3	1
2/5	1
1/2	21
2/3	5
3/4	2
All	2

As one can see, the proportion of the dose that can be sold is surprisingly high. In fact, of the 33 respondents who answered this question, 30 estimated that half or more of the maintenance dose was sold by the patient.

The immediate question that comes to mind is how the patient can so drastically reduce his intake of methadone without suffering what one would suppose to be the inevitable withdrawal syndrome. Three answers were provided to this question by the respondents. First, some patients who have take-home doses have put themselves on what amounts to their own self-maintenance programs. In other words, they have reduced the amount of methadone they take in a consistent manner, and they sell the remainder. Other patients supplement their lowered methadone doses with other drugs purchased on the streets. These techniques of staving off withdrawal were relatively minor, however; neither was mentioned by more than 7 respondents. For the others, as 24 respondents mentioned, no special technique of coping with withdrawal was necessary because withdrawal did not occur, or occurred only minimally. Respondents noted that methadone was potent enough so that the proportion of the dose retained by the patient was usually sufficient to "hold" him for a day or two. Thus, he could regularly sell part of his maintenance dose with little fear that he would become sick.

In short, methadone is apparently easy to cop in a variety of settings, with the liquid form being the most available at a fairly stable price. Though there are some indications of a continuation of the shooting and dealing of the old heroin scene, the data indicate that methadone, for the most part, is obtained from program patients and is taken orally. Finally, it appears that the very potency and long-lasting effect that make methadone desirable from a clinical point of view also facilitate the process of diversion, whatever the method used by a program patient.

At the end of the research article, we talked a great deal about the equivocal policy implications of the study—methadone use in the streets had both its favorable and unfavorable aspects. But for the present, the study does show how a sociological survey allowed us to check some of my ethnographic conclusions.

For the most part, this example represents the strategy of checking the distribution of a pattern, as suggested in Chapter 6. After doing extensive informal work in both treatment and street settings, I had a sense of the use of methadone from the street perspective. The survey was a way to check another group independently, in a more systematic way, to learn if the pattern was also suggested by their responses.

This work was guided by an implicit hypothesis that the pattern would be widely distributed. Most of the questions in the survey—which came from my own work plus extensive consultations with interviewers (I was one of the three) and junkies—were designed to indicate if the distribution was in fact wider than just the original groups with whom I had worked. Again, statistics were seldom used, but the pattern of responses, in most cases, clearly showed that the pattern I had learned in my informal work was supported by the survey.

An Example from Houston

To give a final example, let me take some recent work that I have been involved with in Houston. Under a small grant from NIDA, I have been doing some theoretical and methodological exploring of the idea of "life-style." The strategy was to take an intentionally limited data base and try to come to some characterization of life-style for a small number of individuals. Let me now shift to the original article to give you some idea of the interaction of informal and formal data in this particular study.

In the Houston study, a number of interviewers collected three interviews from a small sample of informants. The first interview was biographical, while the second covered the informant's daily routine. In both of these, the interviewers were trained only to start things rolling. Their participation after that was limited to expressions of interest, or probes that requested more detail in areas already selected as significant by respondents. The third interview requested comprehensive self-evaluations of life-style by asking things about future plans, advice that would be given to someone younger, heroes that the informant might have, and so on. Also, a drug history and a current pattern of drug use was obtained.

The interview discussed in detail here was collected by Noreen Kincaid, a graduate student in anthropology at the University of Houston. The informant is a mid 20's white male, married with one child, his wife's by a previous marriage. The interviews were collected in the informant's home and were taped on a cassette recorder. The goal of the research is to identify themes[5] that summarize the key concerns of the informant that recur throughout the interview material.

When confronted by the pages of transcribed material, the abstract problem of methodology takes on an intimidating physical presence. How to begin a systematic search for themes? Because of the creativity of language, no mechanistic solution seems immediately apparent. A logical first step would be to code the material in some way.

One preliminary source for coding categories lies in the traditional world-view literature. Many have suggested lists of general categories that are dealt with by themes: categories such as self, others, space, time, and the supernatural. For openers, then, one could take such a list of categories and abstract from the transcripts all statements that, in the judgement of the coder, relate to each category. In the example used here, the category "other" is used. The methodological strategy is simply to pull out all statements that the informant makes about social others.

First of all, the boundary around "statements about others" is far from unambiguous. (This will be discussed more when some data are presented.) Second, once a set of statements has been lifted from the text, how does one begin to look for themes? Again, there is no immediate apparent substitute for the scanning of a qualitative eye.

---

[5] The term is adapted from Opler's work. See, for example, Opler (1959). This material is taken from "Getting Better Quality Stuff: Methodological Competition in an Interdisciplinary Niche." *Urban Life*, forthcoming, and is used with permission of the publishers.

One pattern in the data is clear after a few readings. A series of statements is listed in Table 14. The statements all deal with a relationship between the informant and a social other, where the relationship is asymmetrical and the informant is in the subordinate position. Affect is uniformly negative towards the dominant member. This authority theme appears early in life in the family setting, and recurs through a variety of contexts in the interview. Whatever it is, it acts as a theme should. It might be stated as: "People in authority are concerned only with control."

Before continuing, note the variety in the statements in Table 14. Some are specific descriptions of specific people. Others are more centered on social institutions rather than social others. Some are ego-centered statements involving social others peripherally or by implication in a passive-voice construction. Coding, as mentioned earlier, is not a simple task.

It is apparent, though, that this authority theme is important to this informant. To test the theme further, one might ask how the informant feels about himself when he is in the authority position. If the theme is consistently

TABLE 14
Asymmetrical Social Relationships

Childhood

He (father) can't talk to a kid; he just lectures.
Boys are always looking for approval from their fathers.
He (father) doesn't know how to talk. Well, he doesn't know how to listen.
My folks tried to pour it (religion) down my throat from the fucking first day.
I was so frustrated by it (religion). Somebody please give me a real answer.
I may have a lot of hostility. I was picked on as a kid. I was never big at the time. I was small.

School

I was on the swim team, but quit because I hated the coach.
They (teachers) were more worried about whether you were in your seat, if you were chewing gum, if you had to pee.
It (school) was where are you?, how long is your hair?, how well can we regiment you?, crap, authoritarian.
I became a nervous person. King Kong and pounding your chest was it. It was all fucked.

Job

They (job interviewers) ask you questions that they have no right to ask you.
We are all good workers, and the director is such a dipshit; such a jerk, we can't do it.
There is no reason for it (inefficiency and stupidity) other than it is just the way things have always been, and the wrong people are in the wrong positions.

Miscellany

He (elder br) gets carried away trying to shove it down your throat.
There is nothing more boring than a man's man.

TABLE 15
Informant Dominant

I went out (with girls in high school) but I always waited for them to ask me out.
I think that I was trying to conquer the female sex.
It is very difficult being a father.
We (wife) can tell the other person to get fucked. We talk in our cat voices and that way we can blame it on the cats and the other person doesn't get mad.
It is right that he (child) learns to live in the system, to learn how to be punched and not have a bad attitude.

---

applied, he should be uncomfortable. Now glance at Table 15. First of all, there is not much discussion at all to draw from, as we might expect. However, the statements do show his avoidance or unease with situations where he is to be dominant. The last statement, referring to the child, shows that he is trying to train him not to have the same theme, and it ties in with a discussion elsewhere where he says if he had it to do over again, he wouldn't be such a "rebel."

There are two statements that do not fit the theme, though. These are listed in Table 16. In the first case, the informant is positively characterizing college students in terms of "leadership qualities." In the second case, mother, dominant in her role as parent, is characterized positively. In considering why these two counterexamples exist, one is led to another series of statements (Table 17) that cluster around the idea of knowledge or awareness.

First of all, note that mother is characterized as aware, intelligent. Meanwhile, note that many of the social others characterized negatively in Table 14 are noted here for their lack of knowledge, others like father, elder brother, teachers, and boss. Further, in response to a question about heroes, the informant's two choices (Da Vinci and Fuller) are partly admired for their knowledge. No wonder college students are characterized as potential leaders in a positive way.

The last statement in Table 17, linking stupidity with conventionalism, also leads to another set of statements, listed in Table 18. This short list contains statements in praise of variety or lack of rigidity. While one counterexample exists, also noted in Table 18, it is immediately qualified by comparison to self.

TABLE 16
Counterexamples to Authority Theme

I was with college people so I figured that everybody had leadership qualities.
My mother is pretty neat, pretty liberal.

TABLE 17
Knowledge, Awareness

She (mother) is not highly educated, but she has a lot of road smarts. She knows what is going on in the streets.

He (father) is limited in lots of ways even though he makes a small fortune. He has no outside hobbies.

My folks were uneducated and didn't stress it or feed my fervor to know.

He (elder br) knows key words, but he doesn't know the depth of ideas.

They (teachers) couldn't take deep questions.

Looks are important, but after you talk to them, it doesn't matter how good looking they are.

But graduate school was a collection of all your literary midgets.

You know he (boss) doesn't know his ass from a bucket of nails about statistics. He is picking up my key words.

Yeah, he (Da Vinci) is a very inventive guy, very original, very ingenious.

He wasn't just good in art, he was good in astronomy, he was good in math, anatomy, everything.

He (B. Fuller) can back his optimism up with facts.

By "stupid," I mean conventional, conservative.

At this point in the preliminary analysis, it becomes difficult to find sets of statements united by a theme. As a crude measure, of the 64 excerpts originally abstracted from the interviews, roughly 75% were drawn from to conduct this analysis. In other words, most of the statements about others were grouped around the three major themes of *dominance, knowledge*, and *change*, which in themselves are interrelated.

How can we talk about these interrelationships? While some clear patterns emerge from the data, it is difficult to decide how to formally articulate the themes and their interrelations. Perhaps it is best to say, "People in control are only interested in remaining in control, *unless* they have knowledge." Then we could make *change* fit the picture by saying, "Knowledge occurs through openness to a variety of experiences. A preoccupation with control

TABLE 18
Change

You have to change and move around, see different things. You have to have dreams.

We (elder br) have kind of grown apart because he hasn't changed much.

Business is the only thing that I have never tried, so I might as well do it.

What are your plans for the future? Absurd questions—how the fuck should I know?

Counterexamples to Change

My little sister is growing up real fast, too fast. (Qualified by next statement.)

Maybe her and I had the same problem, and I didn't turn out so bad, so who knows.

---

precludes openness; therefore, people in control usually do not have knowledge."

The consistency is appealing, and the relationship to the data is still maintained. But I nervously wonder what another analyst might come up with. At this point, I feel a bit like the magicians who name factors after the factor analysis has been done. Clearly, this analysis does not easily allow the replicability that many methodologies do. The selection of categories, the coding of content into those categories, the analysis for pattern, the interpretation of those patterns, and the linking of the different themes all involved subjective judgements on my part. However, at least the steps are explicit and the data are displayed so that readers can argue with the conclusions if they wish.

The results obtained in the sample case analyzed here can now be converted to hypotheses for further testing. The problem is that one must either shop around for an appropriate procedure, or design one that fits the unique requirements of the fieldwork. In this case I designed one, although psychological tests may be available that would do the job.

For this informant, the test went as follows. First of all, eight "role terms" were selected. Four of them—father, mother, employer, and teacher—represented dominant social roles. The other four—friend, wife, coworker, and teammate—encoded roles of a symmetrical nature. The role terms were selected for their relevance to the transcripted material. They all represented roles that the informant talked about.

Next, a list of things that could be said of the roles was compiled. Since the analysis yielded the themes of control, knowledge, and change, four items each were created that would indicate the orientation of a given role to one of the three themes. The items are listed in Table 19. Although some of the items were based on statements made by the informant, others were created either by myself or by Ms. Kincaid, the interviewer who obtained the material.

The problem with such ad hoc tests, of course, is that nothing can be said about reliability or validity, as those terms are formally measured. In fact, in retrospect, there are some items that may be ambiguous in their relationship to the theme they supposedly represent. Nonetheless, the test will offer some independent data, another perspective on the themal structure of the informant.

In the test itself, the informant was asked to match a statement with a role term, and then say whether the statement was true or false of that term, or whether it was irrelevant. The test was presented in matrix form, with role terms in the columns and statements in the rows. Both role terms and statements were randomly arranged. The informant simply had to move

TABLE 19
Items for Deductive Test

Items	Dominance score	Symmetrical score
Control		
Easily threatened by others	T	F
Cooperates well with others	F	T
Breaks the rules a lot	F	T
Worries about losing control	T	F
Knowledge		
Not aware of what's going on	T	F
Converses over a wide range of topics	F	T
Has narrow interests	T	F
Is a quick thinker, fast on his/her feet	F	T
Change		
Prefers to socialize with people just like him/her	T	F
Would dislike moving to a new town	T	F
Always into something new	F	T
Doesn't know what he/she will be doing in a few years	F	T

down each row and insert "T," "F," or "irrelevant" in each space. In no case did he answer "irrelevant."

Before the test was given, we predicted which answer should be given for dominant roles and which for symmetrical roles. This information is also listed in Table 19. The pattern of true–false responses listed under Dominance Score predicts how he should answer for the dominant roles. Dominant roles should be concerned with control, lacking in knowledge, and resistant to change. The pattern of answers listed under Symmetrical Score is the mirror image. Symmetrical roles should not be concerned with control, should have knowledge, and should be open to change.

A simple procedure was used to show where each pattern of responses fell between these two possibilities. The number of correct responses was scored using the dominance end of the scale as the reference point. This number was then converted to a proportion of dominance responses when compared to total responses. The final results are listed in Table 20.

The results contained some good news and some bad news. The good news lay especially at the lower end, where "friend" and "wife" are located right where they should be, given the themal analysis. "Employer" is also in the right area, with a high dominance score. Further, "mother" is located at the nondominant end of the scale. Recall that she was the one

TABLE 20
Role Terms Ranked by Dominance Score

Employer	.75
Coworker	.58
Father	.42
Teacher	.42
Teammate	.42
Mother	.33
Wife	.17
Friend	.08

exception singled out earlier in the themal analysis because she had knowledge.

The bad news is that four terms, two dominant and two symmetrical, cluster around the midpoint. "Father" should be higher, though it is relevant to note that the informant talked about how his relationship with his father had changed. He had recently decided that family ties were important, and noted that they all get along well now. "Teacher's" low position is partly explained by the four knowledge items. In all four, teacher, not surprisingly, was scored as knowledgeable. If teacher's score is refigured without the knowledge items, it becomes .63, putting the term a bit closer to where it should be. The only post-hoc explanation I can think of for "teammate" and "coworker" is that they did not carry as strong an implication of symmetry as the role terms "friend" and "wife."

Finally, I should mention that the informant performed the task twice. The first time he was asked to respond in terms of his specific life experiences. These are the data used in Table 20. In the second round, he was asked to respond "in general." Interestingly enough, almost none of the scores changed in going from the specific to the general, varying by one item or remaining the same. Two terms did change, the only two that were explicitly female. Wife became more dominant, moving from .17 to .58. Mother also changed in the same direction, going from .33 to .58. Recalling the negative affect displayed toward dominant roles, then, one can tentatively conclude that the informant's specific relationships with wife and mother have been more favorable than his general image of them. This suggests another theme to examine, one that has not been treated in this analysis.

In view of the general arguments in this book, this study should look peculiar to you. Among other things, I had no direct involvement with the informant and the data collected were of a limited kind. There is a question of whether or not this study is "ethnographic"—it is certainly more limited than any of the previous ones I have done. At the same time, the informant had a good deal of control, so it is not a standardized interview either. In Chapter 9, some discussion will be devoted to this question of "When is an ethnography not an ethnography?"

This work is also different in that there is an explicit focus on documenting how the ethnographer learns something about themes by systematically lifting and arranging statements from informal material. That is followed by a test of the results as a hypothesis—Does the informant's behavior in an independent structured task suggest the same themes as that derived from the interviews? The results were equivocal; in retrospect, I am not too happy with the test I used. Notice again that simple proportions seemed adequate for the kind of analysis I was interested in.

Hypothesis-Testing Revisited

At this point, some confusion in the notion of hypothesis-testing should be straightened out. Earlier I attacked this idea, but now, in these examples, I have tried to comment along the way on whether and in what ways the formal checks constituted tests of hypotheses. There are several reasons why I have both attacked and supported the idea.

First of all, *hypothesis* is one of those words in social science that gets used in a variety of ways. It belongs to a club that includes members like "culture," "function," "stimulus," and "-emic/etic"—terms that, though they may have a precise definition in some research contexts, become metaphorically extended to the point where they represent several loosely defined, disjunctive meanings. There's nothing wrong with metaphorical extension—it's one form of model-building.

But *hypothesis* carries a heavy load in the development and evaluation of research, so it is worth trying to clear up its different uses. In its classic form, a *hypothesis* is a statement of the covariation between two variables. This notion of hypothesis is a poor fit indeed with the kinds of things an ethnographer tries to learn in her informal work. She is not sure what the variables are, and she is interested in more relationships than simple covariation. And with a holistic view, she may find account-giving better characterized by a series of patterned states rather than a change of value in variables. To discuss this aspect of ethnography in the classic sense of hypotheses is like trying to talk about energy in square feet.

On the other hand, *hypothesis* has a broader sense as "an idea to check out." At this broader level, ethnography is full of hypotheses at all stages of the research. Something learned in a conversation becomes a hypothesis to check in further conversations or observations. Or an entire ethnography may be a test of a hypothesis in this sense. Much of Margaret Mead's early work, for example, checked out the idea that adolescence was always a time of turmoil, or that sex roles were everywhere the same. Some of the research in the drug field, including my own, tests the prevalent hypothesis that heroin addicts are social-psychological failures.

In my experience, though, when hypothesis testers react to ethnographic research, they do so more in the classic sense of the term. They want a precise theoretical and operational definition of variables and a clear statement of the hypothesized covariation before the research begins. If it does nothing else, I hope this book shows why that is an inappropriate way to talk about ethnographic research.

On the other hand, a hypothesis of the classic sort may serve very well in a formal check of informal work. That brings me to the second reason for criticizing hypothesis testers. Usually the hypotheses are not grounded in the experiential world of the group. Rather, they are derived from some social science theory. Even if there is tremendous literature on the group, one should learn something about the cuts he is making in the flow of life of group members when a questionnaire or test is administered, and return to that flow to see what kind of sense the results make. Hypothesis-testing of the classic sort is loaded with implicit assumptions about what "those people" are like and what "that interview" means to them. The best way to ferret out these assumptions and see if they hold is to jump in and learn from group members.

So I criticize hypothesis testers because often that's all they do, and because they often use the classic notion as a yardstick to talk about ethnography. As the dominant paradigm in the research establishment, they often control research resources and the current version of the "accurate" view of various human groups. Based on my experience as an ethnographer in the drug field, I don't think that's a particularly healthy state of affairs.

But after all this, I advocate hypothesis-testing in the classic sense as a potentially strong way to check out informal ethnographic conclusions. In the Lexington study, the use of hypothetical situations was a clear test of hypotheses, as was the social attribution test used in the analysis of the interview from Houston. However, hypothesis-testing is not the only way to do systematic checks.

In the Lexington study, the simulated-situation and frame-elicitation techniques were tests of hypotheses only in the metaphorical sense, and the use of the term in those contexts, in my opinion, doesn't add anything to one's understanding of the method. Likewise for the survey in New York. Its purpose was to take some pieces of an ethnographically described pattern and explore their distribution more quickly in a separate group of people.

Here again, I'm not sure what a metaphorical discussion of hypotheses would add.

Coda

So there you have three examples of my attempts to formally document informal ethnographic work. They were all different, depending on the kinds of questions asked. The work from Lexington drew from formal methods in linguistics, plus a situation-based preference test. The New York study was a small sociological survey. The Houston work was more of a test in psychological attribution for a small number of social types.

All of them had problems from the point of view of the disciplines involved. The sociological survey, for example, drew a small, biased sample. The psychological test developed in the Houston study was specific to one person, so it did not have the developmental history of most established psychological tests. In no case was the analysis sophisticated from a quantitative point of view—frequencies and proportions were the main measures used.

More often than not, if you ask the right questions, this is all the quantification you will need to support or falsify your ethnographic statements. I do not mean to belittle more sophisticated quantitative techniques. They should be used if you understand them and if they are appropriate. But, in the words of my former boss in New York, they often seem to be used to "measure a sponge with a micrometer."

Another limitation of the examples is their focus on the data of talk. As is apparent throughout this book, my bias is to place talk data at the center of ethnography and use observation as supplementary. Other ethnographers who do not share this bias might emphasize the same strategy as I, but develop a systematic observational test of their ethnographic statements. There is no reason why that cannot be done, following the same general strategy.

At any rate, this sort of formal test of key ethnographic statements should be encouraged. In Chapter 1 the importance of this development was discussed, so it will not be repeated here. Sometimes these tests are drudgery because they involve the careful documentation of something the ethnographer already has learned to the point of being 99% confident that it is true. On the other hand, one might be surprised. But in any case, if you do not make a public attempt to falsify key ethnographic statements, the skeptical outsider will forever dismiss your statements as "untested."

8
The Ethnographic
Research Proposal

Now that different aspects of ethnographic research have been discussed, you are ready to write a grant application. First of all, the discussion of grant reviews in Chapter 2 should be reread. To repeat, that discussion describes only one review process for one federal agency. Other agencies or funding institutions will be somewhat the same and somewhat different. It is your job to find out the differences before you submit a proposal, and modify the application accordingly.

In this chapter I want to focus on the written application itself. Again, I will draw on my own experience as a review committee member, but I think many of the judgements will be reflected in other review panels as well. There are two key things to keep in mind. The first is that it is not likely that many of the reviewers will be ethnographers. If some are, you are luckier than most. The second thing to remember is that the research design itself is important, but many other things are evaluated as well. However, let us talk about the core of the proposal first—the research design.

As a former Jesuit student of mine put it, the trick in designing a research proposal for a review panel of hypothesis-testers is "to render the audience benevolent." They will have questions generated by their particular biases to ask of any proposal. They will want to see some hypotheses, some operationally defined variables, a sampling design, and a specification of questionnaires and/or experimental procedures. It would be foolish of an ethnographer not to expect such questions. Since the panel has the power to award or refuse your proposal, this means that whatever your personal feelings on the matter, you must take them seriously.

At this point a little tact is in order. A few years ago a friend of mine, a survey sociologist, went to his first anthropology meeting. After a few days I asked him over a beer what he thought of anthropology. It is always interesting to ask newcomers to anthropology meetings what they think—experience often produces blind spots. After aggressively tossing down some beer and slamming the glass on the bar, he said, "You know, if one more person calls me a logical positivist I'm going to punch them in the nose."

I have seen more than one ethnographic proposal come onto the table written in the tone experienced by my friend. I can only hope that the gratification felt by the author compensated for the hostile reaction that the proposal elicited. The thing to do is explain, without being patronizing, why the research is different. I know one should not have to, but right now, at least in my experience, hypothesis-testers cover the power spot. You should be able to give a reasonable argument, and reviewers, whatever their disciplinary biases, are usually reasonable people.

Another thing you can do is be more explicit about the informal fieldwork you plan to do. Some ethnographic proposals come in with a half-page of "methodology," the standard litany of participant observation, informal interviews, and field notes. But most of the nonethnographic reviewers do not have the background knowledge to understand how ethnography gets done. A testing-oriented psychologist shared the review panel with me for three years. We had numerous arguments, but over the years gradually acquired some understanding and appreciation of the other's point of view. Not too long ago he called me in as an ethnographic consultant on a follow-up study. He wanted to include an "ethnographic component" to get some information on the changes people saw as significant in their lives since the original study. The ethnographic component, he told me, was represented by a one-hour open-ended interview.

An appropriate reaction by an ethnographer would be, "My God, I just say hello the first time I meet somebody new," but that was the amount of time and money he was willing to invest. That was his conception of ethnography, and, in fairness, from his perspective it was a major "loosening up" of the research design. His view of ethnography is not that unusual, so when you write a proposal, you need to discuss the process of doing ethnography *in detail*. What do you do during all that time that the grant is paying your salary and those of your assistants? Why do you need transcribers? Why do you have such small samples? Do you not worry about sampling bias? How do you know what questions to ask? If you ask different people different questions, how can you compare the responses? You need to answer those questions by explaining what you are trying to accomplish by using an ethnographic perspective, and how a strict hypothesis-testing approach would be difficult or simply could not accomplish the same goals.

A second way to reassure such reviewers, if you agree with the "funnel" concept of ethnography, is to talk about the narrow end somewhat. The specific details of the more formal parts of the ethnography may not be specifiable because its form will partly depend on what you learn during the informal part. Yet, there are several things that can be discussed. First of all, you can give an idea of the general strategy you will use. Are you going to try and set up some kind of experimental design? Will you conduct a survey? Do you intend to systematically sample a number of events? These and other possible strategies raise questions that your informal work must address, so you can talk about the questions and how you plan to answer them. In other words, you can show how part of the informal ethnography will fill in some blanks to enable you to formally check some of the results.

Best of all, you might offer an idea of what the more formal work will look like, qualified by changes required by what you learn in the informal work. Then if you can go on to give one or two specific examples of how the formal design might change if you learned X or Y, you have done about all you can.

In the four years I reviewed grants for NIDA, perhaps three or four ethnographic proposals came through that followed this format in the research design. Without exception, these were grants the committee responded to favorably. Applications that just discussed informal ethnography were also sometimes approved, though usually there was more controversy and a higher likelihood of a low priority score. There is no guarantee that this format will get you funded—there are a variety of other things to be discussed shortly—but based on my experience on one interdisciplinary review committee, your chances would be improved.[1]

Besides, this discussion is not intended solely as a pragmatic guide to grant-getting. As discussed in Chapter 4, ethnography's interaction with other disciplines is, I think, a good thing. It is forcing us to articulate our implicit premises and better document our experiences to address the skeptical

---

[1] Pelto (1970) discusses several types of proposals that an anthropologist might submit, including straightforward tests of hypotheses based on earlier work. My argument for research design only applies to proposals emphasizing ethnography, as do most of Pelto's types. My suggested format also allows for a common problem in ethnographic proposals: Because of proposal demands, the applicant commits himself to a model that he must later reject, in whole or in part, because of what he learns in informal ethnography. Moore (1973) discusses this problem, and Barrett (1976) is one good example of how commitment to an a priori model got in the way of ethnographic research. Freilich (1970a) also has a discussion of anthropological research proposals.

outsider. Too much inbreeding, after all, increases the chances of lethal recessives.

Budget

As I was socialized into the world of grant reviews, I learned to read the budget pages like a short story. From the pages, you get a sense of the applicant's ability to conceptualize and organize the overall project. By comparing the budget with the design, you learn how carefully the proposal was prepared. And if the applicant is a ripoff artist, the numbers on the page will tell the story.

First of all, the overall cost obviously is important. In this current time of shrinking research funding, an application costing $250,000 a year gives cause for thought. If there are four equally good applications on the table, one for $250,000 ("$250K" in reviewese), and three for $80K, what would your vote be—especially if the money available for that round is, say $400K?

If you want to do a project, and it is necessarily expensive, by all means apply for it. Some of the applications for the study of drug use in non-U.S. settings had high budgets, for example, because the applicant requested 100% support, and since the travel costs were high, so were the budgets. Nothing anyone could do about that.

On the other hand, I will never forget the reaction of an ethnographer at his first conference. The first day he listened quietly to the discussions of funding to the tune of "K's" in three digits. Later, over a beer, he said, "You know, I did my study with an NIMH small grant." A "small grant" then had an upper limit of one year at $5000. His "study" is one of the best life histories around, and is one of the few social science works to be given a major review in *The New York Times*. I would love to see his next grant application. Knowing him, it will not be a ripoff, but it will, and should be, more generous in its support of his work.

In case you are curious about ripoffs, let me give you a hypothetical example. A grant comes in for a study with a high "indirect cost" rate (see Chapter 2). At the same time, the applicant requests rental space in a new building in a major city to the tune of more than $1000 a month. What is wrong with this picture? First, a high indirect cost is not justified because the institution is not going to provide support such as office space. Then, if you are doing a study of heroin addicts, a downtown prestigious high-rise is not exactly the best place to locate. Finally, the rest of the budget, from salaries to travel, reflects the same ripoff orientation. In the golden days of the 1960s this was annoying and unethical at best; in a time of shortage, it is downright unfair to other applicants.

Another area of the budget to worry about is the staffing. In most grants, some of the staff are not supported full-time. One classic case of this is the "nominal PI" routine. Someone is listed on the grant as PI (principal investigator), but when you turn to the budget page she is only listed as available for working 10% of her time, for example, often at no cost.

The "nominal PI" might be the faculty supervisor of a graduate student's application. Or she might be a senior researcher lending her name and overall guidance to a project being conducted by new researchers. Or she might be the director of an agency who insists on getting some credit for the grant application even though she had little to do with it.

Using nominal PI's is a perfectly acceptable, and in many cases, helpful way to add some weight to an application. But other staffing patterns can suggest problems. Sometimes grants come in with three "heavies" listed for support at less than 25% time each. Then there might be a 50% time junior supervisor. Finally, you find some 100% positions among the interviewers. What you get, then, is a list of people who are spending a little time on the project, but no sense of someone who is spending most of their time supervising the project and insuring that things get done as promised. Such a staffing pattern doesn't inspire much confidence among reviewers.

Another budget problem sometimes occurs when the project goes for 2 or 3 years. Occasionally, applications mindlessly extend the budget into years two and three without noticing that the research plan doesn't require the same people every year. Say the grant is a survey research proposal, with the first year spent collecting data and the second analyzing it. But the detailed first-year budget requests four interviewers, and then extends that amount into the second year. Unfortunately, no one is scheduled to interview that year. The result is a chink in the armor of competence on the part of the applicant.

The same thing happens with ethnographic grants. Suppose the applicant schedules 3 months for library work in another country where the research will be done, and then 1 month to select a site for the research. However, he also budgets a field assistant for the first year. The immediate review question that this generates is, "So what is the assistant doing during the first 4 months?" He may, in fact, have something important to do, but unless the applicant explains this, it looks careless.

A final word on the budget. Be sure and include everything you need, including a few hundred dollars for "miscellaneous" expenditures. Little things like postage and a telephone can add up. Then what about your informants? Include something to compensate them for their time, either as an interview fee or perhaps as "gifts." If you are going to need some specialized help from someone for a couple of days, budget that as consulting. At a minimum, you can ask for $100 per day plus expenses for a consultant. If you request this, though, be sure you justify why you need the help of that particular person, and include their curriculum vita.

To sum all this up, a budget is not something you put together just before you send in the application. It should reflect a coherent plan for doing the research, and it should blend harmoniously with the research design. When the reviewer reads the budget page, he is going to make a mental note of the staff organization. Then when he reads the research design, he will look to see if the people budgeted for are reflected in the actual research activities. It is not unusual for grants—including grants submitted by experienced researchers—to fail this test.

Staff

In every project there should be a person, or perhaps two, who is the core of the project. Reviewers will evaluate the appropriateness of that person to conduct the project. This is no time to be shy or humble. Let the reviewers know what your qualifications are. In most applications, you will include a curriculum vitae that will give your "official" credentials, but there are other things you can talk about as well.

If the proposal represents a continuation of some work you have done, show how the current application grows out of your past experience. If you have done a pilot study, be sure and discuss it in some detail. Pilot studies show that the applicant's research interests have at least a short history, and the pilot also shows enough interest to have gone out and done some preliminary exploring. For an ethnographic grant, it also demonstrates that contact with the group has been made. By the time you have trained the reviewers in the importance of the diffuse, symmetrical relationships you need with informants, it will reassure them to see that you are capable of establishing relationships with group members in the pilot study—or, perhaps, in previous work.

As much information as possible should be included about staff members. Again, a grant application is an attempt to convince a skeptical audience that something interesting will be produced at the end of time and money spent. A major part of that general argument is a convincing display of people who can do the work. As many positions as possible should be specified with the actual people who will be hired, including a curriculum vitae for each one and a discussion of what skills they bring to the project. If you do not yet have specific people in mind, then at least describe the kind of people you will look for, and where they might be located.

The Research Context

The reviewers will look for the research support available to you because of your position in the institution through which you are applying. For example, you might talk here about colleagues who will be available to you as unofficial consultants to the project. Or perhaps equipment for your work—like tape recorders—is already available from the institution. If you are an academic, you may intend to incorporate some graduate students into the research, blending their support on the grant with their training role as advanced students.

For ethnographers, the research is often done outside the institution. In such cases, it is always good to have letters of support available from people connected with the group you intend to work with. If local support is going to be provided, like a connection with a university near the field site, this is also the place to talk about that.

In addition to the institutional contexts, you also need to specify the scholarly context in which you are working. To some extent, you do this when you talk about how the current application fits into your own research experience and personal interests. But it is also crucial to contextualize your research in the scholarly traditions represented in the literature.

The literature review can be a touchy thing. First of all, there will be the literature that represents your own training, and you, of course, discuss that to show how your proposed work represents a continuation and growth of that tradition. But you can safely bet that there will be other relevant literatures scattered throughout different academic disciplines, and in other sources as well. How, and when, do you draw the line? When have you done "enough" reviewing?

A colleague of mine at Houston and I were talking one day about the problem. He had just come from a meeting where a decision was being made about the computer abstracting services the library should subscribe to. It was not that long ago when a literature review involved using a few abstracts, checking a few journals and review volumes, and then sitting down at the typewriter with your note cards.

But now, with the explosion in fields and subfields, journals and volumes, the researcher needs more services that help organize all that information. As a result, there is now what appears to be an exponential growth in computer abstracting services. Our discussion concerned how the future training of researchers will not be like the training we received. Instead of teaching students about journals, we will need to teach them about different abstracting services and how to choose among them.

So, after you organize your "home base" literature, go to the abstracting services, learn how they work, and use them. This will give you a map of the new territory you need to explore. Then by checking a couple of key items in each new bundle of literature, you will get some idea of which ones in particular have something to offer you. Finally, you can invest your energy in those areas and learn something in the process.

Before leaving this discussion, I should mention something about the egos of some review committee members. First of all, it is embarrassing, after you have been on the committee for a while, to note that your work is cited more frequently. Word gets out and some applicants feel that it cannot hurt to cite as many of the potential reviewers as possible. For almost all of the reviewers I have known, this makes no difference in their judgement. If it does, it is usually because an entire area was left out of the discussion that should have been there—an area in which they have also done work. There have been a couple of occasions when a reviewer got downright nasty toward an applicant when the reviewer's own work was not cited. I do not think applicants should find out about such people and cater to them, but you should know that a few of them are around. Fortunately, their impact on the overall committee is minimal since it's usually obvious what is going on.

More important is the problem of the different interests represented on an interdisciplinary review panel. Suppose that a social psychologist is on the panel. Almost all ethnographic research proposals deal with small groups, and there is a host of research in social psychology that deals with structure and process in small groups. If the ethnographer makes little or no reference to social psychology, as is often the case, what is the social psychologist to say?

Or take another example. A survey research proposal comes in intending to ask people about sensitive areas, or perhaps something like behavior that is illegal but has never been publicly reported before. One line in the research design talks of spending a few minutes to establish rapport. (See my own example of a survey, page 157, for what is, unfortunately, an excellent example of this kind of rhetoric.) What is an ethnographic reviewer to do with that? Scream? Bite his tongue?

In my own experience, sometimes such problems have generated arguments among the reviewers that hurt the applicant. At other times, the result was an interesting argument that resulted in a "communication" to the applicant to check out other literatures, with some specific suggestions. With the information explosion and the increase in subdisciplines, the problem will not disappear anytime soon. The obvious answer is for applicants to acquire as broad a perspective as possible on the human species, so that they can at least note other relevant areas that are beyond their competence to discuss in detail. Unfortunately, such breadth is difficult to obtain and probably not as well rewarded professionally as depth in a particular subfield.

Human Subjects

Some time was spent in Chapter 3 discussing the ethical issues of the protection of human subjects. Many funding agencies—all of the federal ones—now require human subjects' clearance from the applying institution, and then they give the application their own human subjects review just to be sure. During my experience on the review panel, these procedures changed over the 4 years, generally in the direction of being more thorough.

For example, the last time I participated, reviewers received a grant application with a required section discussing the protection of human subjects, plus a form filled out by the applicant detailing procedures to be used. Material from the applicant's institution certifying that a local review had been conducted was also included, together with a report on that review.

If this sounds like it is developing into a bureaucratic feeding frenzy, I agree with you. The intent behind all this is a good one, but the procedures are becoming an annoyance that may or may not have anything to do with insuring that the intent is realized. But whatever your personal feelings, if you apply for a grant, you need to have human subjects clearance.

The key concepts underlying this protection seem to be informed consent and confidentiality. When you approach people to participate in the study, you must tell them what they are being asked to do and have them freely consent to do it. Then you must also insure that individual identities are protected, by using code names, erasing tapes, and so on. One of the things that review committees always look for is a written statement of informed consent. This is given to the informant for signature. The form is usually then cosigned and dated by the interviewer, or whoever gave the person the form.

Now, there are hundreds of problems here for ethnographers. Many were discussed in Chapter 3, so they will not be repeated here. There are other problems that any social scientist would have to deal with as well. For example, if minors are involved, how do you get parental consent, especially if the study is of some behavior of the minor that he or she does not want the parents to know about? Or what if it is an experiment in which you cannot tell the subject exactly what is going on because it would bias the results? Or what if the sample is drawn from an institution where it is questionable that the subject has any "choice"?

The end decision of a human subject's protection committee is a risk-benefit judgement, as discussed in Chapter 3. For most ethnographic studies, the problem will not be one of exposing informants to unnecessary risk—though this could happen—but rather, the problem is how to honestly deal with the human subjects review committee to satisfy them while not promising to do things that are absurd in the context of an ethnographic study.

Take the written informed consent form. Again, in Chapter 3, some situations were mentioned within which the use of such a form would be disruptive of the very relationship the ethnographer was trying to establish. "Here, before we can talk any further, sign this." That is like trying to do origami in a hurricane. And, of course, it assumes that informants are literate, which they sometimes are not.

On the other hand, an ethnographer would not object to the spirit of protecting human subjects—it is just that the *written* form can be a problem. In my experience on the review panel, some ethnographic proposals were approved on the basis of *oral* informed consent. Sometimes the ethnographer says she will tape record the oral consent and save that part of the tape. Sometimes no such promise is made. In all cases, a sample statement is requested to see just what it is that she is going to say. This conjures up an image of the ethnographer whipping out a plastic card and reading the informant his rights, but never mind.

Other ethnographers devote some time to discussing how they are going to let people in the group know who they are and what they intend to do. I think this is a promising strategy, one that fits the general flow of ethnography, and one that has always been used anyway. You talk about how you explain yourself to group members, and then note that they talk about you to each other. You can mention that you will do this each time you meet someone new, until people begin saying things like, "Yeah, we know about you."

The problem with this strategy is that there is nothing in writing—a bureaucratic void exists. In my opinion, the best you can do is say that when you sit down to do an interview with somebody "officially," you will get written or oral tape-recorded informed consent. By the time you get around to sitting down over a tape recorder with somebody, the relationship is probably solid enough so that it can withstand the assault of formal informed consent. Besides, you can present it in ways that deformalize it, like, "Here's some shit you need to sign to prove I told you you don't have to talk to me."

Do not take any of this as a comment on the spirit of field ethics. The comment is on some of the procedures, or more generally on those to whom procedures are sacred, while the goals those procedures were intended to accomplish become irrelevant. As another ethnographer said, the only true test of ethics is if the ethnographer suffers when the informants suffer as a consequence of something he has done. What committee is going to guarantee that?

In addition, there is another human subject to worry about—yourself. What kind of situation are you putting yourself into, both in terms of the group studied and in terms of the people you're taking money from? There are several cases of hostile reactions on the part of group members to the reports produced by ethnographers after a study was completed. William F. Whyte, for example, shows how his key informant tried to discourage community discussion of his book because of potential embarrassment. He gives several examples of the reactions of individuals in the study after it was published. Jennifer James argues that research now must be more carefully done, since mistakes in an information-consuming complex society can have devastating consequences.

On the other hand, there are some cases of positive reactions as well. Anthony Paredes, for example, talks of how his oral history work was favorably received by members of an Indian tribe. They used it in political ways, and even developed with him some material for distribution in the wider non-Indian community. His article was followed by several commentaries, including a few from community members. One community member said, "He has opened the eyes of people not only around Atmore, but in other towns that the Indians are not as backward as some people thought them to be."[2]

Your problem as one who achieves insider status is to judge the extent to which reports from that privileged position to outsiders in fact represents a betrayal. I have had both good and bad experiences in this regard. Up to a point, I feel that group members should retain control of the information—but where is that point? In all my work with junkies, I never had problems. I would show them things I wrote, both to use their comments as additional data and also to insure that I wasn't reporting things better left unsaid. As far as the responses I got went, junkies were generally pleased that someone besides an undercover cop was interested in what their life was like from their point of view. The undercover cop was the one person (who also happened to be the prime enemy) to whom I couldn't tell anything new anyway. He had to be a good ethnographer. He wasn't just concerned with publication and promotion; he wanted to stay alive.

[2] See Whyte (1955), James (1972), and Paredes (1976). Gallaher (1964), Becker (1964), and Vidich *et al.* (1964) discuss cases of group reactions to published ethnographies. Barnes (1967) offers some reasons why modern fieldwork presents new ethical problems that weren't as difficult in the old days of studying comparatively primitive isolated societies.

On the other hand, compare this with a disastrous experience I had at a rural commune. The directors allowed me to do a pilot study if they could control the final product. I agreed. When I sent them the final report, they cut it in half, changed technical terms, and altered the analysis. Since I had agreed to this procedure, I submitted their version together with a letter outlining what had happened. In my opinion, the final version I had written carefully protected them, and their editing produced a product that I was embarrassed to be associated with. At some point the accountability for the final product is the ethnographer's alone. I won't ever make such an agreement again.

So you see the problem. Under what conditions do you distort, lie, or leave out information to protect group members, and at whose insistence? What if the mayor of a town hates the report and the people think it's great? When are you justified in reporting something that you know group members will dislike in the interests of some higher goal, like a personal commitment to your idea of social justice, or science, or whatever it might be that personally inspires you? Fortunately, I don't think the problem occurs that frequently. But it is one you should consider when discussing human subjects.

Another consideration, related to this first one, is to think about the uses to which your ethnography will be put. Earlier in the book I suggested you consider changing your research interests to respond to funding fashions, if you could integrate it into your interests, and if it was ethical. But remember the famous cases of Camelot and Thailand, where anthropologists were criticized for not carefully considering the contributions of their ethnographies to efforts to harm the very people studied.

Some years ago I went to a conference of ethnographers who worked with deviant U.S. groups. I arrived at what turned out to be a fancy resort hotel and went to my high-priced prepaid room. After walking into our elegant reception, I (and most of my colleagues) were wondering who was paying the extravagant bills and what they wanted. An ordinary academic conference this obviously wasn't. But since no one had asked us to do anything but give papers—yet—we drank and talked and patiently waited for the pitch.

The first hint came the next day, when a previously unannounced "observer" from a federal law enforcement agency was introduced. No problem. We all welcomed the opportunity to be heard by representatives of such agencies. But then the second day he announced the deal. His agency would provide research money and, in return, all we had to do was to answer questions that came down the pipeline every month or so.

The sound of dropping jaws rivaled the waves breaking on the nearby beach. He left, angry, a few hours later, muttering something about how he could see why ethnographers didn't influence policy. Later in the evening several of the ethnographic participants were discussing the day. A few of the participants argued that as long as they could define the research and control the product, why not take money from any source. Another argument was that if the researcher was in control, it could be important to do research in connection with an enforcement agency to try to influence policy.

I think those are reasonable arguments, but I would be uncomfortable taking money from an agency whose goal is the elimination of my informants. Others would define that as self-indulgent ideology and point out that in taking money from treatment programs I was doing the same thing. At any rate, in this case the argument was academic because no one was about to consider the offer as presented, with an unknown number of informational strings attached.

The dilemma is similar to that found in some of the arguments over the Thailand case. Say an anthropologist participated in a meeting in Washington, D.C., knowing that "counterinsurgency" research was being considered in Thailand. He went hoping to influence people not to do the work. It turns out that they had already made up their mind. When the scandal broke out, the anthropologist was implicated. He was naive, the argument goes, in thinking that his association with the agency would have any effect.

Such cases are exemplars of the classic opposition between participating in an ongoing effort at some personal moral cost versus standing outside and working on alternatives that are consistent with one's personal values. Such choices are usually so complex, and so involved with the participant's personal equations, that I have difficulty thinking of absolute guidelines. When confronted with such ambiguous situations, I first try to evaluate the potential political effect of my participation and its importance to me. Then I try to estimate realistically how much I have to "sell out" to participate. Then I decide and live with the consequences. I realize that that description of the dilemma is no answer, but it will hopefully help you think through the problems.

The issues surrounding the protection of human subjects and research ethics for ethnographers are complicated and still emergent. There are sometimes problems in the discussions of these issues. They occasionally generate more heat than light, and sometimes seem to reflect a megalomaniacal concept of the ethnographer's impact on the people studied and the sponsoring agency.

But other discussions are instructive in pointing out the kinds of problems ethnographers can stumble into.[3] The grant applicant's problem is to insure that the funding source is not setting conditions on the research that are unethical. Then, when dealing with the group members as informants, the

[3] For a list of references on ethics in anthropology, see Notes 15, 16, and 17 in Chapter 3.

ethnographer must insure that they know what he intends to do with the material they give him, that he protects them from identification as best as he can, and leaves them control over the information that they personally provide. Finally, when writing research reports, he must be prepared to be held accountable for the contents, both by members of the group studied and by "outsiders" who might change their mode of dealing with the group on the basis of what he has communicated.

After 11 years in the drug field, where ethical double-binds are not an unusual event, I feel that I should have something profound and definitive to say. But all I see is a list of unresolved issues, made more confusing when I often see the value in different sides of an argument. The only definitive statement I can make is to hope that this discussion alerts you to some of the issues to worry about as you locate a funding agency, fill out the human subjects forms, and conduct your research. After that, you must make the choices.

Ethnography in Context 9

It is time now to worry about something that has been implicit throughout the discussion of methodology. Much theory lurks below the surface, and it exists at two levels. One level has to do with those mysterious procedures by which you transform what you see and hear into intelligible accounts. The second level has to do with explaining why those particular procedures exist at all. To what sort of historical, political, economic, or ecological factors do they represent a response?

Failing to keep these two theoretical problems distinct can lead to endless nonproductive arguments. In fact, the argument mentioned earlier between those who stress interviewing and those who stress direct observation sometimes occurs just because of this confusion. In addition to the theoretical contexts, ethnography also occurs in a pragmatic context that increases in complexity as time goes on. That problem also deserves some discussion.

Theory in Ethnography

Like many others, I think that linguistics is an interesting place to look for parallels to doing ethnography. First of all, the system of rules linguists develop as they account for sentences is not one that people can directly articulate. One cannot go in and say, "Tell me your grammar." Even if people have been "taught" their grammar, a linguist must cautiously view their statements as another kind of data. People's conceptions of how they should or do speak often are inexact or incorrect. The linguist needs to record what people say about their speech, but also needs to arrive at her own system of rules, and then compare the two.

Linguists are also not as compulsive about the idea of prediction as are many social scientists. While the possibility of prediction is not excluded, linguists, like ethnographers, are more concerned with accounting for things. The emphasis is more on understanding behavior rather than predicting it. Finally, linguistics has become increasingly concerned with the properties and interrelationships of the different rules used to describe their own ideas of how to account for sentences. They have noticed that there are ways to talk about many different languages using rule systems that share both formal and substantive properties.

To give a quick example of a substantive property, the categories of "noun" and "verb" seem useful in all descriptions. They organize words into groups that play different roles in the formation of sentences. Then, to give an example of formal differences, they distinguish "phrase structure" from "transformational" rules. The former takes a symbol and expands it into a string of symbols, while the latter takes a string of symbols and modifies it by deleting, adding, or rearranging it in some way.

By building the pieces and relations in the language they use, linguists are in fact developing a theory of language. The theory notes the pieces and relations that must be present to have a language at all, and also specifies optional pieces and relations that some languages may have and others may not. The suggestion for ethnography is an exciting one.

Perhaps by self-consciously focusing on the principles that ethnographers develop, we can begin to approach a similar goal. By becoming more explicit about the pieces and relations that are obligatory and optional to enable us to give accounts, perhaps we can begin building an explicit theory of culture.

From this perspective, *culture* is the name for the grammar and vocabulary of the language ethnographers use when they describe their ability to give accounts. Ethnographic methodology is the way they fit, and perhaps modify, that language to account for the specific things people in some group say or do. To describe the specific group, they draw on some part of the total language. *Culture* with a capital *C* is the name for the language; *culture* with a lower case *c* is that part of the language used to characterize a particular group of people.

I should note that this was the original purpose of the distinction in phonology between *emic* and *etic* (from phon*emic* and phon*etic*). *Phonetic* represents the set of possible distinctions that might be used in the characterization of human speech, while *phonemic* is the subset of those distinctions useful in describing the sound differences that are perceived as significant by speakers of a particular language.

In many recent anthropological discussions, *emic* and *etic* are used to characterize a different distinction, roughly translated as the "insider's" versus the "outsider's" point of view. The problem here is that it is difficult to imagine any ethnographic statement that is not a blend of these. A statement would almost always contain some assumptions about perception or intent on the part of group members, but it would also be constructed by the ethnographer in terms of his own professional context and goals. The original sense of *emic* and *etic* captures this blending and calls our attention to it. So does the use of the term *culture* that I am advocating here.

The problem is that we are not only talking about distinctions useful in characterizing the human sound stream. Rather, we are discussing a language to characterize the entire range of human experience. As a result, at least in anthropology, you can find work dealing with bits and pieces of the language, but there is no place where it has been put together in any kind of comprehensive way—a task that may be impossible anyway. Claude Levi-Strauss, for example, has excited people with his attempt, focusing on *pieces* like underlying binary attributes ("nature," "culture," "kin-emphasized," "kin-deemphasized") and *relations* like "opposition" and "mediation." Interestingly enough, he was inspired by the phonological work of Roman Jacobson, but the work is limited by the part of the rule system discussed and is weak ethnographically.

Cognitive anthropology, also rooted partially in linguistics, has made a contribution with its discussion of pieces ("lexemes" and "concepts") and relations (like "inclusion" and "part–whole"). Such work is strong ethnographically, with its explicit relationships to the things people say, and often systematic tests, such as sorting tasks, are presented as well. But again, there are limits both in the area of the rule system discussed and in the ethnographic territory covered.[1]

The limits in these and other examples derive from the comprehensive job of ethnographers. Not only must we deal with sentences, but with many other things as well. And in the area of these "other things," it is difficult to see clearly what sorts of principles apply, and how principles interrelate to form a general picture of culture. Yet the task is an important one.

In my own work, I worry about this problem a good deal. Trained in cognitive anthropology, I tried to add more pieces and relations in my work at Lexington so that I could talk about events using an explicit set of principles. Then in the more recent work in Houston, I borrowed the old anthropological idea of "theme" to begin to get explicit about other areas of my ability to account for an informant's behavior.

[1] For a sample of Levi-Strauss' work, see Levi-Strauss (1963). Some introductory treatments of cognitive anthropology are listed in Note 14, Chapter 5.

But this work, like the other examples mentioned already in this section, deals with the corners of a theory of culture rather than the whole building. What other parts of the rule system need to be developed, and when do we worry about their interrelationships? What do *events* have to do with *themes,* as I use those terms? And what do either of them have to do with the grammar of the language that group members use?

The struggle for a connection between different sets of pieces and relations underlies many of the recently emerged subfields in social science. Much of the early work in ethnomethodology in sociology, for example, developed from an interest in other principles that needed to be understood to get at what sociological surveys or analyses of records really represented. Gumperz' work in sociolinguistics attempts to locate social principles that interact with grammatical rules to better understand why people talk as they do. There are other examples as well.[2]

The struggle is an important one. The more we know about culture—the language we use to give accounts—the better our ethnographic descriptions will be. The goal is to have a language that allows us both to describe specific groups accurately and to compare the descriptions of different groups.[3] For this reason, when you set out to do your ethnographic work, you should also set out to make a contribution to culture theory. They are two faces of the same god.

A Language for Culture Theory

In the linguistics examples just discussed, logic was referred to as a source of different ways to talk about rule systems. When people link mathematics and social sciences, they usually think in terms of statistics. But statistics is most useful when testing the different parts of the procedures that you have put together to enable you to account for the things group members do. To *describe* the procedures, other forms of mathematics provide a useful resource—forms like logic, set theory, group theory, and graph theory. Once you learn set theory and logic, the others fall right into place, and you get finite probability as a bonus.

Of course, you do not have to lay out the rule system using mathematical

---

[2] An introduction to ethnomethodology can be found in Mehan and Woods (1975). An overview of Gumperz' work is in Gumperz (1971).

[3] The problem in creating a language for both description and comparison is discussed in Goodenough (1970). Honigmann (1976), on the other hand, argues that the two are such separate tasks that they require different kinds of ethnographies. I prefer Goodenough's goal as the more theoretically interesting one.

language. Most anthropologists use ordinary prose. The advantage of mathematical language is its clarity, its lack of connotations. When you use ordinary language, you need to clearly define each term before you use it. No one does, of course. The result is the sort of obscure jargon that hinders much discussion in social sciences. A. L. Kroeber and Clyde Kluckhohn wrote an entire book about definitions of *culture*, and somebody (I forget who) pointed out that Bronislaw Malinowski used the work *function* in several different ways.

When you use mathematical language, you strip away the connotations of natural language. Its use does not eliminate the ambiguities and complexities of the real world we are trying to account for, but it at least highlights the complexities so we can understand where they are. Besides, there are some new developments with something called *fuzzy set theory*, which people use to talk formally about the fuzzy areas of natural talk.[4]

You can glance at the physicists who, with the work of people like Godel, Turing, and Tarski, proved that you could never come up with a unified theory of nature using these available forms of mathematics. I do not know the arguments well enough to evaluate them for ethnography, but intuitively it would seem to me that the physicists' problems are on a different planet from those of an ethnographer trying to inject some clarity into a discussion of culture. Or perhaps an ethnographic Newton will come along and develop a mathematics better suited to our needs.

On the other hand, there is a growing movement in anthropology which considers an emphasis on formalisms the perpetuation of a long-standing cultural error with roots in Descartes and Bacon. I am not competent to represent this position. But it seems to me that doing ethnography and reporting its results assumes some sort of organization or structuring of knowledge, however implicit or disguised that structure might be. If that is true, then the growth of a more rigorous language is not only appropriate, but also crucial.

When Is an Ethnography Not an Ethnography?

As mentioned in Chapter 1, many agencies and different disciplines are currently discussing ethnography as a "new" paradigm for social science research. Now that several examples of informal and formal work have been

---

[4] For an example of the use of fuzzy set theory, see Kempton (1978). Kay (1971) has an edited volume that illustrates the use of mathematics as an ethnographic language in several of the contributions.

discussed, it is appropriate to wonder just what the minimal characteristics of an ethnographic approach in fact are. We have already seen that an ethnographic study may include paradigms from other approaches to human behavior, but what else must be present to constitute an ethnographic study?

Several themes have recurred throughout the book. One is the *student–child–apprentice learning role* of the ethnographer. The assumption here is that whatever the interests of the ethnographer, he must understand the way that group members interpret the flow of events in their lives. It is difficult to imagine any social science statement that does not make some assumptions about group members' interpretations. An ethnographer, as much as he can, tries to make such assumptions empirical questions to be checked out, while at the same time being prepared for surprises— interpretations that he had no idea existed before he began the study. At the same time, he may learn that some of the interpretations that group members make are very much like his own, or perhaps of some other group with whom he has worked, or perhaps like those that people make everywhere.

It would be ineffective to try to imagine all possible interpretations that group members might make, especially since he has no idea what some of those interpretations will look like—they might be completely outside his experience. But even if he could imagine a wide range of possibilities, and then design experiments to eliminate all but one of them, it would be an awkward way to come up with an understanding of group life. So, some of the time the ethnographer surrenders the control of situations, questions, and samples, apprentices himself to group members, and learns how they interpret their world.

A second theme in the book is the *search for pattern*. Building an ability to account for events is not currently well enough understood to represent with simple formalizations. Some recent research suggests words like *schemata* and *frame* as labels for the background knowledge that group members bring to events. These schemata are then used as guides to interpretation, and may themselves be modified as a result of that interpretation. But no one knows how to formally specify the structure of such background knowledge or the process of applying it in different situations.

What is apparent is that it involves a rich collection of different kinds of information and sentiment and relations among them. In her struggle to describe these essential aspects of account-giving, the ethnographer turns to the holistic search for pattern as a guide. The classic model of hypothesis-testing, with a small number of covarying variables, is simply too impoverished a paradigm to handle this quest. As noted throughout the book, it might be an appropriate check for the results of informal ethnography, but it is an inappropriate, distorting framework for the learning phase.

In my opinion, these are the two key features of an ethnographic perspective that derive from an interest in the interpretations of reality as seen by the group members. Because it is an unknown, or is treated as such by the ethnographer, it must be learned. And because it is a framework, a schemata, it is best modeled by a pattern that is gradually discovered and then interrelated with other patterns.

There are some further implications of this notion of ethnography that also follow. First of all, if you are going to learn a complex pattern, this implies direct, prolonged contact with group members. From this comes the concern in the ethnographic literature with the nature of the relationships between ethnographer and informants. It also explains the bias toward firsthand contact with "the data." By its very nature, an apprentice's role can't be done for you. Besides, with an ethnographer's sensitivity to the importance of the relationship in the learning process, it is difficult to allow another screen between yourself and the person from whom you are supposedly learning.

The prolonged direct contact also explains the bias toward working on the informant's turf. Besides, by establishing yourself in the group's territory, you have access to actual events. Remember that in Chapter 5, the ability to directly observe events for which you were learning to give accounts was critical to check out interview material and suggest further questions to ask. The more I think about it, the more I think I should have entitled this book *The Informant's Apprentice.*

Thinking back over my own work, some of the studies were more ethnographic than others. All of them had the characteristics of the student–child role and the search for pattern. In India I lived either in the *tanda* or in Gopalpur and did the work myself, although I had to rely on interpreters much of the time. In Lexington I was committed by my job to work in an institutional setting, but within those limits, I spent much of my time in the patients' areas of the institution, and developed the simulations of situations as a way of getting an indirect indication of what street events looked like in process.

When I worked in New York, I spent a lot of time in both institutional and street settings. I don't think I can claim to have "lived" in the field, though my own neighborhood had its share of scenes that I came to know well. Most of my work was done in other neighborhoods, though. The second time around, however, I knew that fieldwork with street junkies could be exhausting in a variety of ways, and I wanted to be sure and have a place to hide.

The Houston study was a pilot but, nevertheless, it was ethnographic only in a minimal sense. It had the characteristics of learning from informants and seeking pattern in the limited data obtained, but I had no direct involvement in the interviews, and no direct observation of the situations through which the informants moved. Although the Houston data and the work I am doing with it are suggestive of some new methodological and theoretical approaches to informal interviews, in retrospect I'm not happy with the study as an ethnography. I think it was my first and last experience with "remote control" ethnography, except for consultant jobs.

The issue of consulting raises another problem—time. Remember the example I described of a psychologist who wanted an ethnographic component that consisted of a 1-hour, open-ended interview? In a moment I'm also going to tell you about another ethnographic project that had severe time and budget limitations. As reflected in some recent discussions in applied anthropology, there is concern with "real world" agency needs for information in less time than ethnographers usually consider sufficient to gather it.

It's not clear how much time would ever be enough. Ethnographers often talk in terms of 1 to 2 years. But one of the depressing things about returning to Karnataka in 1972 as a teacher in a linguistics institute was to realize how little I had learned during my earlier fieldwork there. On the other hand, if you recall the story about working with the Haight-Ashbury clinic, I was able to learn a great deal relevant to the problem of estimating the number of untreated, unarrested junkies in just a couple of weeks.

As usual, it depends. If one wants a comprehensive understanding of several groups within a society, we are probably talking about several years of work. On the other hand, if one needs some specific information from a group, where relationships are good from the beginning, one can probably learn some things quickly, though not in much depth. It is partly because of this problem that I think that every ethnographer should have an ongoing interest in their own society as well as in an alien one. The alien society jolts you with its differences. But work in your own society teaches you how subtle differences can be, and also shows you new depths of interpretation that you bring in as a comember.

I'm not sure what amount of agreement there would be on my idea of the nature of ethnography among other ethnographers, but it's important to have the discussion. Given the current domination of hypothesis-testing paradigms, what is an ethnographer to do when she takes a position in an interdisciplinary niche? One current argument holds that one trains graduate students to fit in. Teach them the hypothesis-testing metaphors and encourage them to do research that blends into the dominant world view. To the extent that they are trained in the informal aspects of ethnography, advise them not to push it if it doesn't translate into the framework operating in the interdisciplinary research setting.

I couldn't agree more that an ethnographer needs competence in as many research paradigms as possible—that's also been a theme of this book. But in its extreme form, if you strip away all the informal ethnography, you are left with anthropologists who do the same things as sociologists and psychologists. The special features of an ethnographic approach that allow it to contribute to our understanding of human groups in its unique way are jettisoned.

The extreme form of the argument is often justified in terms of the nature of the nonacademic marketplace, in which anthropology is just beginning to develop and populate. If it's fair to characterize the nonacademic research market as oriented primarily toward hypothesis-testing—and I think it probably is—then if you want to work there, adapt to it. In these dismal days of a lack of jobs for new anthropologists, I'm not about to quarrel with that.

But this argument leaves out some important possibilities. For example, after watching the entry of ethnography in the U.S. drug field over the last 11 years, I have seen an interest in that approach grow. For the drug field, ethnography is a "new thing," and part of the reason for its growth is the effort of ethnographers to teach others about the perspective. Although one does need to adapt to the nonacademic market, one can also mix that with some aggressive work to encourage the use of ethnography. When I arrived at Lexington, I was the lone ethnographer. When I left, there were two on staff. In New York I was also the first ethnographer hired; when I left, there were three, plus some ethnographic components in the research of other types of social scientists. I don't think there is anything magical about those examples; it's just a matter of acquainting people who are unfamiliar with the perspective with how ethnography works, and showing them some of the results. You will still be harassed about instruments and hypotheses, but you can also develop some allies.

Another reason for not neglecting informal ethnography lies in the winds of change in governmental agencies and in other social science disciplines. Earlier I mentioned some examples of ethnographic movements in sociology and psychology, and the "new interest" in ethnography in a few federal agencies that I know of. Once a senior executive in a consulting firm I sometimes work with listened for the first time to a group of ethnographers talking about a proposed project. The next day, it was a delight to see him turn to a psychologist who was asking the usual questions about hypotheses, instruments, and so forth, and say, "No, you don't understand. These folks grow their own." Since that time, his firm sometimes suggests ethnographic components when they bid for contracts from federal agencies.

So by all means the move to increase the general research sophistication of ethnographers should be encouraged. But at the same time, it would be tragic to lose what some converts call "soft," "unscientific," or "fuzzy" research. Much of the world we seek to understand has just those characteristics, including our own involvements in it as researchers. If we only pick up material that can be welded, we leave a lot behind.

Accounting for the Accounts

Once you have done your ethnography, you may now wonder why things are as they are. Remember, first of all, that some things will be universal. For explanations of those aspects of why things are the way they are, human biology would be a productive place to look. But for things that differ among a range of different groups, explanations can be sought in a variety of areas. They can be sought in human biology as well, but that is a controversial new area that, fortunately, I am not competent to talk about.

One form of explanation cycles within itself—part of the ethnography is used to explain another part. You have some procedures that enable you to account for how people treat each other, and you have some others that enable you to account for how people treat their gods. Then you show that the two are partially isomorphic, and Durkheim smiles from wherever it is that old social scientists go.

Or take another example. You have some procedures that account for how people treat their kids. Then you have others that again account for how people treat each other. They are quite different, but you can explicitly show the differences. Then you can argue that it is just these transformations from one part of the "culture" to another that intuitively seem to fit the ideas of "repression" and "projection." You now have not only linked two parts of your procedures, but you have also suggested a clear definition (the necessary transformations) for two elusive concepts. Freud's grin would probably be even bigger than Durkheim's.

Such forms of explanation are important to the development of culture theory. They suggest ways to interlink different segments of the procedures that ethnographers come up with to enable them to give accounts. Such work is critical. In linguistics, tremendous discussion has been generated over how to deal with the relationship between the lexicon and the sentence, and no resolution is in sight. Imagine how much more difficult it is going to be to find the relationship, if one exists, between, say, religion and making a plow.

However, there is another kind of explanation in which the procedures are related to something outside themselves. The "something" can be a variety of things—power, for example. Perhaps all groups that are subordinate within their wider society share certain properties, as do all groups that are dominant. Or consider economy. Oscar Lewis argued for a "culture of poverty"— that all groups in states of poverty were similar in certain ways, at least in capitalist societies. Properties of the ecosystem in which the group is embedded is another source of explanations. Perhaps all societies in arctic environments, for example, are similar in certain ways. Another explanatory focus that might include any of the above possibilities and others would be the group's history, adding time depth to the ethnographer's characterization of the present system.

To continue with this discussion would be to write a book on anthropology. I do not intend to do that. The point is that it is important to relate ethnographies to outside factors, but to do so presupposes that good ethnography has been done. There is a dialectic in the history of cultural anthropology. The early evolutionists tried to account for differences in groups by their evolutionary stage. Then Franz Boas said the data were no good and returned to a concern with doing ethnography. G. P. Murdock started the Human Relations Area Files (HRAF) to begin to look for outside explanations of group differences. Then others found the comparisons difficult to make and called for a return to doing better ethnography. And so it goes, and will continue to do so.

If one does run from a theory into the field, and lifts out pieces to hang on the theory, she must be sure that the cuts have been made appropriately, that the pieces mean to group members what she assumes they mean, and that her interpretation of the results is a sensible one. The only way to be sure of that is to do some ethnography.

The Pragmatic Context

The last few sections zeroed in on the different sorts of theoretical contexts in which ethnography is done. However, there are also some changes in research context that can make a difference. In the old days, the ethnographer was usually a loner. Sometimes an ethnographer would take a student or two to the field. But, for the most part, during a specific fieldwork period one professional was running the show. But as time goes on, ethnographers will find themselves more frequently working as part of a team.

There is a history of team research in anthropology, including such well-known examples as the early Torres Straits expedition, Ralph Beals' work in Oaxaca markets, Holmberg's Vicos project, the Whitings' six-cultures studies, and a few others. And there is occasional mention in the methodological literature of the advantages of team research. More territory can be covered, for example, helping to resolve the tension between a holistic and problem oriented focus. And the results of one member of the team can be compared with others as a cross-check on results.[5]

[5] Price (1973) reviews several uses of team research in anthropology, and argues that it is a good way to maintain a holistic perspective. However, others caution against potential problems

In many cases, the team consists of other ethnographers. Let me illustrate with a project I am consulting on now. Recently (1978), there has been an increase in popular discussion of a drug called "angel dust" or PCP. Its effects are reported to be overwhelmingly negative, yet it apparently is increasing in popularity among youth. Because of the increase in concern, NIDA found itself in the embarrassing position of having little information to distribute. Some material was issued, like a TV advertisement with a well-known actor warning kids of PCP's dangers. The problem, as so often happens in U.S. policy, was that the information was not based on any firsthand knowledge of use or users.

A NIDA staff member with ethnographic tendencies (he had been a street worker in New York) decided to try an ethnographic study. He asked that a small team of ethnographers be assembled to get some preliminary feel for the situation. Because of the time rush and money constraints, four ethnographers were selected who had done good ethnography with drug users in the past. Further, because of their ongoing work, they all had rapport so that they could begin work immediately.

The group met for 2 days to work out a strategy for doing the ethnographies. Informal interviews were to be the focus. In addition, the group came up with a four-page guide to specific items of information that would be easy to get from each informant. In this way, bits of comparable information would be available without harming the sensitivity of the informal interview to the uniqueness of the person and the local situation. Flexibility was also maintained as a guide since an ethnographic "coordinator" was to keep in touch with the four working ethnographers and visit them all midway through the project.

A few months later, the group met again to discuss the results. Even with the limited time and sample, the work suggested several interesting possibilities. First of all, it showed that some in the sample used PCP in occasional or controlled patterns. Second, the effects of the drug were variable, as might have been expected, depending on such well-known influences as dosage, psychological set, and setting. Third, many had used for a year or two and then stopped. Fourth, some had histories of use long predating the current agency concern with PCP.

There are many more interesting results as well, to be presented in a forthcoming volume. But overall, they show that the assumptions about PCP users on which policy are based are, at best, oversimplifications. Since the

---

in team research. Examples of such problems include community acceptance (Herskovits, 1954), possible establishment of "enclaves" (Nash, 1963), and role conflicts with fellow professionals (Kloos, 1969).

entire project is directed and manned by experienced ethnographers who have worked with U.S. illicit drug users, there is a similarity of world view that makes discussion of how to do the study easy. This does not always happen when you populate the niche with folks of substantially different research world views, as we will see in a moment.

Notice also that in this example, the ethnographers are all working in different settings. At the beginning of the book I mentioned working in an Austrian village on an ethnographic project that included three ethnographers. Rather than having different ethnographers do the same study in different places, the strategy here was to divide up the chores in one place. I was brought in for a couple of months only to look at a question in bilingual semantics. Because of the short period of time, I was only to elicit some folk taxonomies in areas like "crops," "animals," and so on. (Recall from Chapter 5 that taxonomies are structures where concepts are linked by the "X is a kind of Y" relationship.) I would do the eliciting in both Slovenian and German, and then compare the two structures. Were they the same structures with different tags attached, or different structures?

As the specialist, I just checked what I thought I would do with the other two ethnographers who had done elaborate ethnographic work in the area. I relied on them to see if the task made sense and to introduce me to informants. One of those informants had the best opening line of an interview I have ever encountered. As I fumbled with the tape recorder, he said, "Wait a minute. Before you run a tractor, you put gas in it, right?" I nodded. "Well then," and with that he pulled out a bottle of schnapps which improved my German considerably.

The work went smoothly. In fact, even though I was trained as a cognitive anthropologist, I had never actually sat down with an informant for the sole purpose of eliciting a taxonomy. I was a bit surprised to find that it worked so well. I will not discuss the results in detail, but in the best traditions of the social sciences, they were mixed. While there were no major structural discontinuities, there were some differences in the amount of lumping and splitting. And some of the similarities were what would have been predicted by the work of Brent Berlin on the universality of the "generic" level of folk taxonomies.[6]

The combination of the three of us, then, was productive. Not only did we share the labor and thus accomplish more, but we had the benefits of each other's criticism while in the field, rather than waiting until a professional meeting after the fieldwork was done. The only problem was that since we all liked each other, we probably associated together more than we should have.

[6] For an introduction to this argument, see Berlin (1977).

A loner talks more to group members; part of an ethnographic team probably tends to seek other members of the team for company. That is a tendency that team members must be concerned with.

Both of these cases involved teams all of whom are ethnographers. As time goes on ethnographers are finding themselves more frequently associated with groups that include not only other social scientists, but also such bizarre types as doctors, administrators, and social workers. This will occur more frequently, especially with the current interest in applied anthropology and the "nonacademic" marketplace.

I have spent a lot of time in such settings, as both employee and consultant. For the most part I have found such settings stimulating. All of your ethnographic premises have to be dredged up, dusted off, and examined, so that you can present your world view to people who have little or no background in it. The experience is invaluable for teaching you to think about what you do, and for alerting you to the problems in communicating your work outside the "family."

On the other hand, such settings can also present new kinds of frustrations. Most of the people you deal with, to the extent they have any research training at all, will have been brainwashed by hypothesis-testers. Thus, you will often finish explaining ethnography, you think, only to be greeted with the question, "Yes, that's very interesting, but where's your instrument?"

Such world view differences become more frustrating when you are a powerless member of the research team. A friend of mine, a graduate student in anthropology, wanted to do a study of a medical clinic. She had to meet with people who headed two supervisory offices, as well as with several administrators of the clinic itself. While they were all sympathetic, and while she did get final approval, everyone pushed for hypothesis-testing research. Eventually she will hand them some, but they did not understand that in the kind of study she wanted to do, one does not start with hypotheses; one finishes with them, if that approach lends itself to the needs of a systematic test.

When I worked in New York I had a similar problem. By the time I got there, I had acquired some "credentials," as they were so fondly called around the office. Because of these, I could do my research with less hassle from higher-ups in the Civil Service. But when I was deciding whether or not to set up a storefront in the neighborhood I was working in, I quickly became nervous. Many of my hypothesis-testing friends began talking with interest about the possibility of "noninstitutionalized samples." With nightmarish visions of tests and questionnaires spilling out my storefront door onto the street, I decided to float from bar to coffee shop rather than to establish a permanent base.

There are other problems inherent in such settings as well. As mentioned earlier in the discussion of human subjects, as part of your position in an agency, you will concede to some extent the agency's program assumptions. The problem is that ethnographers have a nasty habit of turning agency assumptions into empirical questions, sometimes with results that may call into question the fit of those assumptions to the nature of the group dealt with by the agency.

Though I am sometimes surprised at the receptiveness to this kind of analysis, probably a more frequent response of an agency would cause you frustration at best, and perhaps loss of your job. When you add to this Delmos Jones' observations that problems and solutions are often defined before researchers are called in, and Erve Chambers' observation that ethnographers in such settings sometimes become "pieceworkers," the image of Malinowski pitching his tent among the natives recedes into the distance.[7]

This kind of setting will, I think, be occupied with increasing frequency by ethnographers. Such settings are not as simple as remaining within an ethnographic world view, but it is the type of setting in which ethnographers need experience if they ever want to talk to anyone besides themselves. The problem for an ethnographer who contemplates association with such agencies is that he must check out the assumptions and find out if he can live with them. He should also get a feeling for the consequences of calling them into question in the eyes of other agency personnel. After that, "you dance with who you brung."

Ethnography in Prospect

Ethnography, as it has been characterized in this book, is a perspective that coexists with some important contradictions—humanity and science, involvement and detachment, breadth and depth, subordination and dominance, friend and stranger. My own attempt to resolve these has been to talk of a *funnel approach,* where the first member of each opposition is emphasized in the beginning, the second member at the end.

Of course, this oversimplifies since both parts of each opposition will coexist to some extent throughout fieldwork—no doubt part of the reason that ethnography is stressful. But if your goal is to understand the world of some human group, it strikes me that the second member of each pair is easier to accomplish in the context of the first. One first takes an involved, humanitarian position, striving for breadth of understanding in a student–child–ap-

[7] See Jones (1976) and Chambers (1977).

prentice position. As the fieldwork progresses, one in part takes a detached scientific view, focuses on some specific issues, and designs systematic approaches to formally document the experience from the perspective of a stranger. It is because this progression makes sense to me that the book is organized in the informal-to-formal funnel sequence.

In the classic days, ethnographers worked with fairly isolated groups, often a tribe or village with stable traditions and few social links outside the community. Now compare this with the study of a contemporary urban group. Where are its edges? What do you do when one of your key informants changes from a street junkie into a devotee of a guru? How do you deal with the multiple-group membership of a single individual? The difference from the traditional field setting is striking. As more and more of the world becomes urbanized and exposed to the deluge of information, traditional settings are going to disappear.

The new settings require some methodological flexibility. No doubt the resurgence of interest in the life history, the development of network theory, and other areas, such as the study of voluntary associations, are responses to this new kind of fieldwork. In fact, I sometimes think that the new "area specialties" will be institutional rather than geographical. Notice the recently growing specialties in medical, educational, and industrial anthropology, to name three examples.

At the same time, it amazes me how similar doing ethnography has been in the different settings I have worked in. Whether in a small Indian village, a closed institution, or the streets, the basic idea remains the same. An ethnographer must assemble different strategies for informal and formal systematic work with each group, but then that has always been true. I think that a good ethnographer who has worked in one type of situation can begin working in another type tomorrow. That kind of creative response to a new field situation is what good ethnography has always been about.

At the same time, as ethnography moves from an academic exercise to a coparticipant in the many niches of complex modern societies, we must continue to be more explicit about its underlying theory and the procedures by which it is done. Ethnography is, I think, potentially the strongest social science metaphor within which members of some group can display the complexity and variability of their lives. Earlier I spoke of ethnography as "humanizing stereotypes," but unless this is done in a credible way, we lose whatever political value there is in operating within "social science." I think that would be tragic. To the extent that ethnography can complicate the simplified and often incorrect notions that one group has of another, it can play an important role in present and future worlds.

References

Ablon, Joan. Field Method in Working with Middle Class Americans. *Human Organization* 36(1977): 69–72.

Adams, Richard N., and Jack J. Preiss (eds.). *Human Organization Research.* Homewood, Il.: Dorsey Press, 1960.

Agar, Michael. Folklore of the Heroin Addict: Two Examples. *Journal of American Folklore* 33(1971): 175–85.

Agar, Michael. *Ripping and Running.* New York: Academic Press, 1973.

Agar, Michael. *Cognition and Ethnography.* Minneapolis, Mn.: Burgess, 1974.

Agar, Michael. One–up, One–down, Even up: Some Features of an Ethnographic Approach. *Addictive Diseases* 2(1976): 619–626.

Agar, Michael. The Junk Novel. *Drug Forum* 5(4)(1977). a

Agar, Michael. Going Through the Changes: Methadone in New York. *Human Organization* 36(1977): 291–295. b

Agar, Michael. Getting Better Quality Stuff: Methodological Competition in an Interdisciplinary Niche. *Urban Life, forthcoming,* 1980.

Agar, Michael, and Richard C. Stephens. The Methadone Street Scene. *Psychiatry* 38(1975): 381–387.

Allport, Gordon. *The Use of Personal Documents in Psychological Science.* New York: SSRC, 1942.

Andersen, Barbara Gallatin. Adaptive Aspects of Culture Shock. *American Anthropologist* 73(1971): 1121–1125.

Angrosino, Michael V. The Use of Autobiography as "Life History." *Ethos* 4(1976): 133–154.

Arensberg, Conrad M. The Community Study Method. *American Journal of Sociology* 60(1954): 109–124.

Arensberg, Conrad M. The Community as Object and as Sample. *American Anthropologist* 63(1961): 241–265.

Axinn, George H., and Nancy W. Axinn. The Indigenous Diary-Keeper: A Methodological Note. *Human Organization* 28(1969): 78–86.

Back, Kurt W. The Well-Informed Informant. *Human Organization* 14(1956): 30–33.

Back, Kurt W., and J. M. Stycos. *The Survey under Unusual Conditions.* Society for

Applied Anthropology Monograph no. 1, 1959.

Barnes, J. A. The Collection of Genealogies. *Rhodes-Livingston Journal* 5(1947): 48–55.

Barnes, J. A. Some Ethical Problems in Modern Field Work. In *Anthropologists in the Field,* edited by D. G. Jongmans and P. C. W. Gutkind. New York: Humanities Press, 1967.

Barret, Stanley R. The Use of Models in Anthropological Fieldwork. *Journal of Anthropological Research* 32(1976): 161–181.

Beals, Ralph L. *Politics of Social Research.* Chicago, Ill.: Aldine, 1969.

Beattie, John. *Understanding an African Kingdom.* New York: Holt Rinehart and Winston, 1965.

Becker, Howard S. *Sociological Work.* Chicago, Ill.: Aldine, 1970.

Becker, Howard S. Problems in the Publication of Field Studies. In *Reflections on Community Studies,* edited by Arthur J. Vidich *et al.* New York: Harper and Row, 1964.

Becker, Howard S., and Blanche Geer. Participant Observation and Interviewing: A Comparison. *Human Organization* 16(1957): 28–32.

Bell, J. H. Observation in Anthropology. *Mankind* 5(1955): 55–68.

Bennett, John. The Interpretation of Pueblo Culture: A Question of Values. *Southwestern Journal of Anthropology* 2(1946): 361–74.

Bennett, John. The Study of Cultures: A Survey of Technique and Methodology in Field Work. *American Sociological Review* 13(1948): 672–89.

Bennett, John W., and Gustav Thaiss. Survey Research in Anthropological Fieldwork. In *A Handbook of Method in Cultural Anthropology,* edited by Raoul Naroll and Ronald Cohen. New York: Columbia University Press, 1970.

Berlin, Brent. Speculations of the Growth of Ethnobotanical Nomenclature. In *Sociocultural Dimensions of Language Change,* edited by Ben Blount and Mary Sanches. New York: Academic Press, 1977.

Berreman, Gerald D. *Behind Many Masks.* The Society for Applied Anthropology Monograph no. 4, 1962.

Beteille, Andre, and T. N. Madan. *Encounter and Experience.* Honolulu, Hi.: University of Hawaii Press, 1975.

Blanchard, Kendall. The Expanded Responsibilities of Long Term Informant Relationships. *Human Organization* 36(1977): 66–69.

Blau, Peter M. The Research Process in *The Study of the Dynamics of Bureaucracy.* In *Sociologists at Work,* edited by Phillip E. Hammond. New York: Basic Books, 1964.

Boas, Franz. The Method of Ethnology. *American Anthropologist* 22(1920): 311–321.

Bogdan, Robert, and Steven J. Taylor. *Introduction to Qualitative Research Methods.* New York: John Wiley, 1975.

Braroe, Niels W., and George L. Hicks. Observations on the Mystique of Anthropology. *Sociological Quarterly* 8(1967): 173–186.

Brim, John A., and David H. Spain. *Research Design in Anthropology.* New York: Holt, Rinehart and Winston, 1974.

Bruyn, Severyn T. *The Human Perspective in Sociology.* Englewood Cliffs, N.J.: Prentice–Hall, 1966.

Burnett, J. H. On the Analog between Culture Acquisition and Ethnographic Method. *Council on Anthropology and Education Quarterly* 5(1974): 25–29.

Campbell, Donald T. The Mutual Methodological Relevance of Anthropology and Psychology. In *Psychological Anthropology,* edited by Francis Hsu. Homewood, Ill.: Dorsey Press, 1961.

Campbell, Donald T., and Julian C. Stanley. *Experimental and Quasi-Experimental Designs for Research.* Chicago, Ill.: Rand-McNally, 1966.

Cancian, Frank. Informant Error and Native Prestige Ranking in Zinacantan. *American Anthropologist* 65(1963): 1068–1075.

Casagrande, Joseph B. (ed.). *In the Company of Man.* New York: Harper & Row, 1960.

Cassell, Joan. The Relationship of Observer to Observed in Peer Group Research. *Human Organization* 36(1977): 412–416.

Chambers, Erve C. Working for the Man. *Human Organization* 36(1977): 258–267.

Cicourel, Aaron V. *Method and Measurement in Sociology.* New York: The Free Press, 1964.

Cohen, Ronald, L. L. Langness, John Middleton, Victor C. Uchendu, and James W. VanStone. Entree into the Field. In *A Handbook of Method in Cultural Anthropology,* edited by Raoul Naroll and Ronald Cohen. New York: Columbia University Press, 1970.

Colby, B. N. A Partial Grammar of Eskimo Folktales. *American Anthropologist* 75(1973): 645–662.

Cole, Michael, and Sylvia Scribner. *Culture and Thought.* New York: John Wiley, 1974.

Colfax, J. David. Pressure Toward Distortion and Involvement in Studying a Civil Rights Organization. *Human Organization* 25(1966): 140–149.

Collier, John, Jr. *Visual Anthropology: Photography as a Research Method.* New York: Holt, Rinehart and Winston, 1967.

Conklin, Harold C. Ethnogenealogical Method. In *Explorations in Cultural Anthropology,* edited by Ward H. Goodenough. New York: McGraw–Hill, 1964.

Crane, Julia G., and Michael V. Angrosino. *Field Projects in Anthropology.* Morristown, N.J.: General Learning Press, 1974.

D'Andrade, Roy G. Cultural Constructions of Reality. In *Cultural Illness and Health,* edited by Laura Nader, and Thomas W. Maretzki. *Anthropological Studies No. 9,* American Anthropological Association, Washington, D.C., 1973.

Dean, John P., and William F. Whyte. How Do You Know If the Informant Is Telling the Truth. *Human Organization* 17(1958): 34–38.

Deitchman, Seymour J. *The Best Laid Schemes.* Cambridge, Ma.: M.I.T. Press, 1976.

Den Hollander, A. N. J. Social Description: The Problem of Reliability and Validity. In *Anthropologists in the Field,* edited by D. G. Jongmans and P. C. W. Gutkind. New York: Humanities Press, 1967.

Denzin, Norman. *The Research Act.* Chicago, Il.: Aldine, 1970.

Devereux, George. *From Anxiety to Method in the Behavioral Sciences.* The Hague: Mouton, 1967.

Diamond, Stanley. Nigerian Discovery: The Politics of Field Work. In *Reflections on Community Studies,* edited by Arthur J. Vidich *et al.* New York: Harper & Row, 1964.

Dohrenwend, Barbara S., and Stephen A. Richardson. A Use for Leading Questions in Research Interviewing. *Human Organization* 23(1964): 76–77.

Dollard, John. *Criteria for the Life History.* New York: Peter Smith, 1949.

Douglas, Jack D. *Investigative Social Research.* Beverly Hills, Ca.: Sage, 1976.

Dumont, Jean-Paul. *The Headman and I.* Austin, Tx.: University of Texas Press, 1978.

Edgerton, Robert B. Method in Psychological Anthropology. In *A Handbook of Method in Cultural Anthropology,* edited by Raoul Naroll and Ronald Cohen. New York: Columbia University Press, 1970.

Edgerton, Robert B., and L. L. Langness. *Methods and Styles in the Study of Culture.* San Francisco, Ca.: Chandler and Sharp, 1974.

Evans-Pritchard, E. E. *The Nuer.* New York: Oxford University Press, 1940.

Fillmore, C. J. The Case for Case. In *Universals of Linguistic Theory,* edited by E. Bach and R. T. Harms. New York: Holt, Rinehart and Winston, 1968.

Freilich, Morris. Toward a Formalization of Field Work. In *Anthropologists at Work,* edited by Morris Freilich. New York: Harper & Row, 1970. a

Freilich, Morris. Marginal Natives: *Anthropologists at Work.* New York: Harper & Row, 1970. b

Furk, Ruth. Techniques of Observation and their Social Cultural Limitations. *Mankind* 5(1955): 60–68.

Gallaher, Art. Plainville: The Twice-Studied Town. In *Reflections on Community Studies,* edited by Arthur J. Vidich *et al.* New York: Harper & Row, 1964.

Geer, Blanche. First Days in the Field. In *Sociologists at Work,* edited by P. E. Hammond. New York: Basic Books. 1964. Reprinted in McCall and Simmons 1969.

Geertz, Clifford. Under the Mosquito Net. *New York Review of Books* IX(4)(1967): 12–13.

Geertz, Clifford. From the Native's Point of View: On the Nature of Anthropological Understanding. In *Meaning in Anthropology,* edited by Keith Basso and Henry Selby. Albuquerque, N.M.: University of New Mexico Press, 1976.

Glaser, Barney, and Anselm Strauss. *The Discovery of Grounded Theory.* Chicago, Il.: Aldine, 1967.

Gold, Raymond L. Roles in Social Field Observation. *Social Forces* 36(1958): 217–233.

Golde, Peggy (ed.). *Women in the Field: Anthropological Experiences.* Chicago, Il.: Aldine, 1970.

Goodenough, Ward H. Residence Rules. *Southwestern Journal of Anthropology* 12(1956): 22–37.

Goodenough, Ward H. *Cultural Anthropology and Linguistics.* Washington, Georgetown University Series on Language and Linguistics no. 9(1957): 167–173.

Goodenough, Ward H. *Description and Comparison in Cultural Anthropology.* Chicago, Il.: Aldine, 1970.

Goodman, Paul C. The Natural Controlled Experiment in Organizational Research. *Human Organization* 29(1970): 197–203.

Gottschalk, L. A., and G. C. Gleser. *The Measurement of Psychological States Through the Content Analysis of Verbal Behavior.* Berkeley, Ca.: University of California Press, 1969.

Gottschalk, Louis, Clyde Kluckhohn, and Robert Angell. *The Use of Personal Documents in History, Anthropology and Sociology.* New York: SSRC, 1945.

Gudschinsky, Sarah C. *How to Learn an Unwritten Language.* New York: Holt, Rinehart and Winston, 1967.

Guest, Robert H. Categories of Events in Field Observations. In *Human Organization Research,* edited by Richard N. Adams and Jack J. Preiss. Homewood, Il.: Dorsey Press, 1960.

Gumperz, John J. *Language in Social Groups.* Stanford, Ca.: Stanford University Press, 1971.

Gutkind, P. C. W. Orientation and Research Methods in African Urban Studies. In *Anthropologists in the Field,* edited by D. G. Jongmans and P. C. W. Gutkind. New York: Humanities Press, 1967.

Gutkind, P. C. W., and G. Sankoff. Annotated Bibliography on Anthropological Field Work Methods. In *Anthropologists in the Field,* edited by D. G. Jongmans and P. C. W. Gutkind. New York: Humanities Press, 1967.

Hall, Edward T. A System for the Notation of Proxemic Behavior. *American Anthropologist* 65(1963): 1003–1026.

Harre, R. and P. S. Secord. *The Explanation of Social Behavior.* Oxford: Basil Blackwell, 1972.

Harris, Marvin. *The Nature of Cultural Things.* New York: Random House, 1964.

Harris, Marvin. Why a Perfect Knowledge of All the Rules One Must Know to Act Like a Native Cannot Lead to the Knowledge of How Natives Act. *Journal of Anthropological Research* 30(1974): 242–251.

Hatfield, Colby R., Jr. Fieldwork: Toward a Model of Mutual Exploitation. *Anthropological Quarterly* 46(1973): 15–29.

Heider, Karl G. *Ethnographic Film.* Austin, Tx.: University of Texas Press, 1976.

Henry, F., and S. Saberwal (eds.). *Stress and Response in Fieldwork*. New York: Holt, Rinehart and Winston, 1969.

Herskovits, Melville. The Hypothetical Situation: A Technique of Field Research. *Southwestern Journal of Anthropology* 6(1950): 32–40.

Herskovits, Melville. Some Problems of Method in Ethnography. In *Method and Perspective in Anthropology*, edited by Robert F. Spencer. Minneapolis: University of Minnesota Press, 1954.

Hockings, Paul (ed.). *Principles of Visual Anthropology*. Chicago, Il.: Aldine, 1975.

Hoffman, Nicholas, Irving Horowitz, and Lee Rainwater. Sociological Snoopers and Journalistic Moralizers. *Trans-Action* 7(7)(1970): 4–10.

Honigmann, John J. Sampling in Ethnographic Fieldwork. In *Handbook of Method in Cultural Anthropology*, edited by Raoul Naroll and Ronald Cohen. New York: Columbia University Press, 1970.

Honigmann, John J. The Personal Approach in Cultural Anthropological Research. *Current Anthropology* 17(1976): 243–261.

Horowitz, Irving L. (ed.). *The Rise and Fall of Project Camelot*. Cambridge, Ma.: M.I.T. Press, 1967.

Hymes, Dell. Models of the Interaction of Language and Social Life. In *Directions in Sociolinguistics*, edited by John J. Gumperz and Dell Hymes. New York: Holt, Rinehart and Winston, 1972.

James, Jennifer. "On the Block": Urban Research Perspectives. *Urban Anthropology* 1(1972): 125–140.

Johnson, Allen W. *Quantification in Cultural Anthropology*. Stanford, Ca.: Stanford University Press, 1978.

Johnson, John M. *Doing Field Research*. New York: The Free Press, 1975.

Jones, Delmos, J. Culture Fatigue: The Results of Role-playing in Anthropological Research. *Anthropological Quarterly* 46(1973): 30–37.

Jones, Delmos J. Applied Anthropology and the Application of Anthropological Knowledge. *Human Organization* 35(1976): 221–229.

Jones, E. L. The Courtesy Bias in South–East Asian Surveys. *International Social Science Journal* 15(1963): 76.

Jones, Robert W. A Note on the Phase of the Community Role of the Participant Observer. *American Sociological Review* 26(1961): 446–450.

Junker, B. H. *Field Work*. Chicago, Il.: University of Chicago Press, 1960.

Kaplan, David, and Robert A. Manners. Anthropology: Some Old Themes and New Directions. *Southwestern Journal of Anthropology* 27(1971): 19–40.

Kay, Paul (ed.). *Explorations in Mathematical Anthropology*. Cambridge, Ma.: M.I.T. Press, 1971.

Kempson, Ruth M. *Semantic Theory*. Cambridge, Cambridge University Press, 1977.

Kempton, Willett. Category Grading and Taxonomic Relations. *American Ethnologist* 5(1978): 44–65.

Killworth, Peter D., and H. Russell Bernard. Informant Accuracy in Social Network Data. *Human Organization* 35(1976): 269–286.

Kloos, Peter. Role Conflicts in Social Fieldwork. *Current Anthropology* 10(1969): 509–511.

Kluckhohn, Florence R. The Participant–Observation Technique in Small Communities. *American Journal of Sociology* 46(1940): 331–343.

Kobben, A. J. F. Participation and Quantification in Field Work Among the Djuka. In *Anthropologists in the Field*, edited by D. G. Jongmans and P. C. W. Gutkind. New York: Humanities Press, 1967.

210

References

Langness, L. L. *The Life History in Anthropological Science*. New York: Holt Rinehart and Winston, 1965.

Lave, Charles A. and James G. March. *An Introduction to Models in the Social Sciences*. New York: Harper & Row, 1975.

Leach, E. R. An Anthropologist's Reflection on a Social Survey. In *Anthropologists in the Field*, edited by D. G. Jongmans and P. C. W. Gutkind. New York: Humanities Press, 1967.

Levine, Robert A. Research Design in Anthropological Fieldwork. In *A Handbook of Method in Cultural Anthropology*, edited by Raoul Naroll and Ronald Cohen. New York: Columbia University Press, 1970.

Levi–Strauss, Claude. *Tristes Tropiques*. New York: Atheneum, 1961.

Levi–Strauss, Claude. *Structural Anthropology*. New York: Basic Books, 1963.

Lewis, Oscar. Controls and Experiments in Field Work. In *Anthropology Today*, edited by A. L. Kroeber. Chicago, Il.: University of Chicago Press, 1953.

Li–An–Che. Zuni: Some Observations. *American Anthropologist* 39(1937): 62–76.

Lindzey, Gardner. *Projective Techniques and Cross-Cultural Research*. New York: Appleton–Century–Crofts, 1961.

Labov, William. The Logic of Non–Standard English. In *Report on the Twentieth Annual Round Table Meeting on Linguistics and Language Studies*. Washington: Georgetown, 1969.

Labov, William. The Social Stratification of English in New York City. Washington: Center for Applied Linguistics. 1966.

Lounsbury, Floyd G. Field Methods and Techniques in Linguistics. In *Anthropology Today*, edited by A. L. Kroeber. Chicago, Il.: University of Chicago Press, 1953.

Lundberg, Craig C. A Transactional Conception of Fieldwork. *Human Organization* 27(1968): 45–49.

Malinowski, Bronislaw. *Argonauts of the Western Pacific*. New York: E. P. Dutton, 1961.

Malinowski, Bronislaw. *A Diary in the Strict Sense of the Term*. New York: Harcourt, Brace and World, 1967.

Mandelbaum, David G. The Study of Life History: Gandhi. *Current Anthropology* 14(1973): 177–196.

Maybury-Lewis, David. *The Savage and the Innocent*. New York: World, 1965.

McCall, George J., and J. L. Simmons. *Issues in Participant Observation*. Reading, Ma.: Addison–Wesley, 1969.

Mead, Margaret. More Comprehensive Field Methods. *American Anthropologist* 35(1933): 1–15.

Mead, Margaret. From Intuition to Analysis in Communication Research. *Semiotica* 1(1969): 13–25.

Mehan, Hugh, and Hugh Woods. *The Reality of Ethnomethodology*. New York: John Wiley, 1975.

Meintel, Deidre A. Strangers, Homecomers, and Ordinary Men. *Anthropological Quarterly* 46(1973): 47–58.

Mensh, Ivan N., and Jules Henry. Direct Observation and Psychological Tests in Anthropological Field Work. *American Anthropologist* 55(1953): 461–480.

Metzger, Duane, and Gerald E. Williams. A Formal Ethnographic Analysis of Tenejappa Ladino Weddings. *American Anthropologist* 65(1963): 1076–1101.

Metzger, Duane, and Gerald E. Williams. Procedures and Results in the Study of Native Categories. *American Anthropologist* 68(1966): 389–407.

Middleton, John. *The Study of the Lugbara*. New York: Holt, Rinehart and Winston, 1970.

Miller, S. M. The Participant Observer and Over Rapport. *American Sociological Review* 60(1955): 354–360.

Moore, Janet R. The Best-Laid Plans—Research Pre-design and Field Revision. *Anthropological Quarterly* 46(1973): 7–14.

Morris, Patrick G. Problems of Research in a Stratified Little Community. *Anthropological Quarterly* 46(1973): 38–46.

Murdock, George P. *Outline of Cultural Materials.* New Haven, Ct.: Yale University Press, 1950.

Myers, Vincent. Toward a Synthesis of Ethnographic and Survey Methods. *Human Organization* 36(1977): 244–251.

Nadel, S. F. *The Foundations of Social Anthropology.* Glencoe, Il.: The Free Press, 1953.

Nadel, S. F. The Interview Technique in Social Anthropology. In *The Study of Society,* edited by F. C. Bartlett *et al.* London: Routledge and Kegan Paul, 1939.

Naroll, Raoul. Data Quality Control in Cross-Cultural Surveys. In *A Handbook of Method in Cultural Anthropology,* edited by Raoul Naroll and Ronald Cohen. New York: Columbia University Press, 1970.

Naroll, Raoul, and Ronald Cohen (eds.). *A Handbook of Method in Cultural Anthropology.* New York: Columbia University Press, 1970.

Nash, Dennison. The Ethnologist as Stranger. *Southwestern Journal of Anthropology* 19(1963): 149–167.

Neisser, Ulric. *Cognition and Reality.* San Francisco, Ca.: W. H. Freeman, 1976.

Nelson, Richard K. *Hunters of the Northern Ice.* Chicago, Il.: University of Chicago Press, 1969.

Olesen, Virginia, and Elvi W. Whittaker. Role-Making in Participant Observation. *Human Organization* 26(1967): 273–281.

Opler, Morris. Component, Assemblage and Theme in Cultural Integration and Differentiation. *American Anthropologist* 61(1959): 955–964.

Owusu, Maxwell. Ethnography of Africa: The Usefulness of the Useless. *American Anthropologist* 80(1978): 310–334.

Paredes, Anthony J. New Uses for Old Ethnography. *Human Organization* 35(1976): 315–320.

Passin, H. Tarahumara Prevarication: A Problem in Field Method. *American Anthropologist* 44(1942): 235–247.

Paul, Ben. Interview Techniques and Field Relationships. In *Anthropology Today,* edited by A. L. Kroeber. Chicago, Il.: University of Chicago Press, 1953.

Pelto, Pertti J. *Anthropological Research: The Structure of Inquiry.* New York: Harper & Row, 1970.

Pelto, Pertti J., and Gretel H. Pelto. Ethnography: The Fieldwork Enterprise. In *Handbook of Social and Cultural Anthropology,* edited by John J. Honigman. Chicago, Il.: Rand-McNally, 1973.

Phillips, D. C. *Holistic Thought in Social Science,* Stanford, Ca.: Stanford University Press, 1976.

Phillips, Herbert P. Problems of Translation and Meaning in Field Work. In *Human Organization Research,* edited by Richard N. Adams and Jack J. Preiss. Homewood, Il.: Dorsey Press, 1960.

Plotnicov, Leonard. Anthropological Fieldwork in Modern and Local Urban Contexts. *Urban Anthropology* 2(1973): 248–264.

Poggie, John J., Jr. Toward Quality Control in Key Informant Data. *Human Organization* 31(1972): 23–30.

Powdermaker, Hortense. *Stranger and Friend.* New York: W. W. Norton, 1966.

Powdermaker, Hortense. An Agreeable Man. *New York Review of Books* IX(8)(1967): 36–37.

Preble, Edward, and John J. Casey, Jr. Taking Care of Business—The Heroin User's Life in the Street. *International Journal of the Addictions* 4(1969): 1–24.

Price, John A. A Holism through Team Ethnography. *Human Relations* 26(1973): 155–170.

Price-Williams, Douglass. Psychological Experiment and Anthropology: The Problem of Categories. *Ethos* 2(1974): 95–114.

212

References

Radin, Paul. *The Method and Theory of Ethnology.* New York: McGraw-Hill, 1933.

Redfield, Robert. The Art of Social Science. *American Journal of Sociology* 54(1948): 181–190.

Rivers, W. H. R. Report on Anthropological Research Outside America. In *The Present Condition and Future Needs of the Science of Anthropology*, edited by W. H. R. Rivers, A. E. Jenks, and S. G. Morley. Washington, 1913.

Roe, A. A Psychological Study of Eminent Psychologists and Anthropologists and a Comparison with Biologists and Physical Scientists. *Psychological Monographs* 67(1952): 1–55. a

Roe, A. Analysis of Group Rorschachs of Psychologists and Anthropologists. *Journal of Projective Techniques* 16(1952): 212–224. b

Romanucci-Ross, Lola. With Margaret Mead in the Field: Observations on the Logic of Discovery. *Ethos* 4(1976): 439–448.

Romney, A. Kimball, and Roy G. D'Andrade. Transcultural Studies in Cognition. *American Anthropologist* 66(3)(1964): Part 2.

Royal Anthropological Institute of Great Britain and Ireland. *Notes and Queries in Anthropology.* London: Routledge and Kegan Paul, 1951.

Salamone, Frank A. The Methodological Significance of the Lying Informant. *Anthropological Quarterly* 50(1977): 117–124.

Sanjek, Roger. A Network Method and Its Uses in Urban Ethnography. *Human Organization* 37(1978): 257–268.

Schatzman, L., and A. Strauss. *Field Research.* Englewood Cliffs, N.J.: Prentice-Hall, 1973.

Scheflen, Albert E. *Communicational Structure: Analysis of a Psycho-therapy Transaction.* Bloomington, In.: Indiana Press, 1973.

Schusky, E. *Manual for Kinship Analysis.* New York: Holt Rinehart and Winston, 1965.

Schutz, Alfred. The Stranger. In *Collected Papers*, Volume II, edited by Arvid Brodersen. The Hague: Martinus Nijhoff, 1964.

Sechrest, Lee. Experiments in the Field. In *A Handbook of Method in Cultural Anthropology*, edited by Raoul Naroll and Ronald Cohen. New York: Columbia University Press, 1970.

Sieber, Sam D. The Integration of Fieldwork and Survey Methods. *American Journal of Sociology* 78(1973): 1335–1359.

Simmel, George. The Stranger. In *The Sociology of George Simmel*, edited by Kurt Wolff. Glencoe, Il.: The Free Press, 1950.

Speier, Matthew. *How to Observe Face-to-Face Communication.* Pacific Palisades, Ca.: Goodyear, 1973.

Spindler, George (ed.). *Being an Anthropologist: Fieldwork in Eleven Cultures.* New York: Holt Rinehart and Winston, 1970.

Spradley, James P. *Rules, Maps and Plans.* San Francisco, Ca.: Chandler, 1972.

Spradley, James P., and George P. McDonough. *Anthropology Through Literature.* Boston, Ma.: Little Brown, 1973.

Sullivan, Harry Stack. A Note on the Implications of Psychiatry, the Study of Interpersonal Relations, for Investigations in the Social Sciences. *American Journal of Sociology* 42(1937): 848–861.

Thomas, David Hurst. *Figuring Anthropology: First Principles of Probability and Statistics.* New York: Holt, Rinehart and Winston, 1976.

Tyler, Stephen A. *Cognitive Anthropology.* New York: Holt, Rinehart and Winston, 1969.

Vidich, Arthur J. Participant Observation and the Collection and Interpretation of Data. *American Journal of Sociology* 60(1955): 354–360.

Vidich, Arthur J. The Springdale Case: Academic Bureaucrats and Sensitive Towns People. In *Reflections on Community Studies*, edited by Arthur J. Vidich *et al.* New York: Harper & Row, 1974.

Vidich, Arthur J., Joseph Bensman, and Maurice R. Stein (eds.). *Reflections on Community Studies.* New York: Harper & Row, 1964.

Vidich, Arthur J., and Gilbert Shapiro. A Comparison of Participant Observation and Survey Data. *American Sociological Review* 20(1955): 28–33.

Wager, L. Wesley, and George A. Miller. Hypothetical Situations and Particularistic Requests. *Human Organization* 28(1969): 119–127.

Watson, Lawrence C. Understanding a Life History as a Subjective Document. *Ethos* 4(1976): 95–131.

Wax, Murray L. On Fieldworkers and Those Exposed to Fieldwork. *Human Organization* 36(1977): 321–328.

Wax, Murray L. Review of S. J. Deitchman's *The Best Laid Schemes. Human Organization* 37(1978): 400–407.

Wax, Rosalie. *Doing Fieldwork: Warnings and Advice.* Chicago, Il.: University of Chicago Press, 1971.

Weakland, J. H. Method in Cultural Anthropology. *Philosophy of Science* 18(1951): 55–69.

Webb, Eugene J. et al. *Unobtrusive Measures.* Chicago, Il.: Rand McNally, 1966.

Werner, Oswald, and Donald T. Campbell. Translating, Working Through Interpreters, and the Problem of Decentering. In *A Handbook of Method in Cultural Anthropology,* edited by Raoul Naroll and Ronald Cohen. New York: Columbia University Press, 1970.

Whitten, Norman E., and Alvin W. Wolfe. Network Analysis. In *Handbook of Social and Cultural Anthropology,* edited by John J. Honigmann. Chicago, Il.: Rand McNally, 1973.

Whiting, Beatrice and John Whiting. Methods for Observing and Recording Behavior. In *A Handbook of Method in Cultural Anthropology,* edited by Raoul Naroll and Ronald Cohen. New York: Columbia University Press, 1970.

Whyte, William F. *Street Corner Society: The Structure of an Italian Slum* (second ed.). Chicago, Il.: University of Chicago Press, 1955.

Whyte, William F. Interviewing in Field Research. In *Human Organization Research,* edited by Richard N. Adams and Jack J. Preiss. Homewood, Il.: Dorsey Press, 1960.

Williams, Thomas R. *Field Methods in the Study of Culture.* New York: Holt Rinehart and Winston, 1967.

Wintrob, Ronald M. An Inward Focus: A Consideration of Psychological Stress in Fieldwork. In *Stress and Response in Fieldwork,* edited by F. Henry, and S. Saberwal. New York: Holt Rinehart and Winston, 1969.

Wolff, Kurt H. A Methodological Note on the Empirical Establishment of Culture Patterns. *American Sociological Review* 10(1945): 176–184.

Wolff, Kurt H. The Collection and Organization of Field Materials: A Research Report. In *Human Organization Research,* edited by Richard N. Adams and Jack J. Preiss. Homewood, Il.: Dorsey Press, 1960.

Young, Frank W., and Ruth C. Young. Key Informant Reliability in Rural Mexican Villages. *Human Organization* 20(1961): 141–148.

Zimmerman, Don H., and D. Lawrence Wieder. The Diary: Diary-Interview Method. *Urban Life* 5(1977): 479–498.

Index